MW00623786

Navigating Community Development

Robert O. Zdenek · Dee Walsh

Navigating Community Development

Harnessing Comparative Advantages to Create Strategic Partnerships

Robert O. Zdenek
San Francisco, CA
USA

Dee Walsh
Portland, OR
USA

ISBN 978-1-137-47700-2 (hardcover)   ISBN 978-1-137-47701-9 (Ebook)
ISBN 978-1-349-69321-4 (Softcover 2018)
DOI 10.1057/978-1-137-47701-9

Library of Congress Control Number: 2017939313

Cover image © Caiaimage/Martin Barraud/OJO+/Getty
Cover design by Henry Petrides

Printed on acid-free paper

This Palgrave Macmillan imprint is published by Springer Nature
The registered company is Nature America Inc.
The registered company address is: 1 New York Plaza, New York, NY 10004, U.S.A.

PRAISE FOR *NAVIGATING COMMUNITY DEVELOPMENT*

"In this important and timely book Bob and Dee use case studies and their considerable experience to lead us through the complex evolution of CDCs and describe how organizations can further transform themselves and adapt to a new environment that will demand further change. The work is vital, and this book will advance how community development practice can rise to the challenge."
—**Carol Galante**, I. Donald Terner Distinguished Professor in Affordable Housing and Urban Policy and Faculty Director, Terner Center for Housing Innovation, U.C. Berkeley

"*Navigating Community Development* offers a unique perspective on how non-profit, community-based development organizations can successfully undertake the complex and interconnected strategies that are essential to the revitalization of urban and rural areas. Through the strategic deployment of capital—financial, human, and political, these institutions offer a comparative advantage to other redevelopment approaches, which the authors skillfully document in a series of case studies."
—**Kevin McQueen**, Board Chair, Partners for the Common Good and Adjunct Instructor—Community Development Finance Lab, The Milano School of International Affairs, Management and Urban Policy, The New School.

"Zdenek and Walsh provide a 21st century roadmap of the community development field that recognizes economic constraints, regional contexts, the persistence and variation of poverty and the organizational diversity of community developers. They emphasize the need for multi-sector collaborations and for community development organizations to focus on what they do best and align, when

appropriate, with other stakeholders. The mix of theory, history, case studies and lessons makes *Navigating Community Development* invaluable."
—**Robert Giloth**, Ph.D.
Vice President, Center for Economic Opportunity
Annie E. Casey Foundation
701 St. Paul Street
Baltimore, MD 21202

"Navigating Community Development" is a timely and valuable assessment of the evolving community development industry and an insightful investigation of how to enhance the impact of these important institutions. It will be an invaluable resource for practitioners, policy makers and students of this vital field."
—**Christopher Herbert**, Managing Director, Harvard Joint Center for Housing Studies

"Navigating Community Development arrives just in time for practitioners who must navigate rapid and dramatic changes in politics, public policy and worsening income inequality. Don't just sit back and read this book. Identify your non-profit's most critical challenges—then use this as a guide for success."
—**Douglas K. Smith**, Author and Architect of NeighborWorks America's Achieving Excellence

"Bob Zdenek's and Dee Walsh's new book *Navigating Community Development* benefits from the authors vast, practical operating and policy experience over decades of the evolution of community development. Their insights into how organizations can use their comparative advantages derived from core competencies, at this critical juncture, to increase impact, efficiency, and growth is must reading for all practitioners. They not only explain the evolution of community development but how to navigate it today for success. It is full of sound, thoughtful advice and challenges to conventional thinking."
—**Bart Harvey**, former Chair and CEO, Enterprise Community Partners

"Navigating Community Development presents a powerful and comprehensive roadmap through nearly a half century of community development practice and policy, highlighting the key lessons that bring greater equity and prosperity to low- and moderate-income communities. The authors take these lessons to frame out a vision for a 21st century version of community development that is designed to succeed in expanding economic opportunity so that no communities in our nation are left behind."
—**Andrea Levere**, President, Corporation for Enterprise Development

"As a practitioner of community development for over 30 years, I believe that *Navigating Community Development* has captured the history and impact of our sector in a way that practitioners and policy makers alike would find compelling. Bob and Dee celebrate the unique role that community development has played in transforming economically challenged communities into viable places for families and individuals to thrive. At the same time that the community development sector is being celebrated, the authors provide a sobering and insightful look at the future of the field and challenge us to improve our competencies and be innovative in our techniques to address the ever changing needs of community transformation. This is a must read for anyone pursuing a community development career or desiring to bring about community change."
—**Bernie Mazyck**, President and CEO, South Carolina Association for, Community Economic Development

"As our increasingly diverse nation confronts unsustainable income and wealth gaps, Zdenek and Walsh offer timely and thoughtful insights on the evolution and significance of the community development industry. *Navigating Community Development* will undoubtedly prompt constructive dialogue as the country seeks to navigate a complex matrix of social, economic and political realities."
—**Bill Bynum**, Chief Executive Officer, Hope Enterprise Corporation

FOREWORD

Navigating Community Development is an important new book that is by turns a history, a practitioner's guide, an insightful critique, a policy agenda, a research agenda, and a road map to improving the community development field based on its "core competencies," as the authors explain. Bob Zdenek and Dee Walsh are two leaders and architects of the community development field with a combined 60 years of experience. They are particularly well suited to be both guide and guru for such an ambitious project.

This book wrestles with a central paradox that has plagued many of us who have spent a career in community development: Over the past 50 years this field has become dramatically more professional and effective and yet the problems we were founded to address remain stubbornly persistent. Zdenek and Walsh write, "Nonprofit community development organizations have done incredible work over the past 50 years. Billions of dollars have been invested in low-income communities, and hundreds of thousands of units of affordable housing have been built." Yet, "Recent studies show that the number of high poverty census tracts is increasing and the overall poverty rate is holding steady at 15% (Cortright and Mahmoudi 2014)." They acknowledge that historic disinvestment and racial and economic discriminatory practices along with larger trends in the economy (technological change and global trade) have been headwinds for this work.

Nevertheless, we have to ask ourselves are we bound to forever be tinkering on the edges—beating on as boats against the current. Or is some breakthrough possible? This book stays hopeful on this question. Zdenek and Walsh believe that new ideas, new ways of working, new technology, and new leaders will forge a much more effective community development field in the future: One that is part of a larger "ecosystem" that at root does what community development always intended—to help places by involving the people who live in those places. But the ecosystem will be far more integrated with other fields and more capable of delivering the change communities need with "blended approaches to community development" that involve "partnering with education, employment, health care and environmental justice advocacy groups." This will require "networks and collaborations" as "the best ways to achieve multi-sector integrative outcomes."

In order to go forward, Walsh and Zdenek take us back to the beginning of the community development movement. Back, in fact, when debates raged on whether community development was a "movement" or an "industry." As a field that emerged from the War on Poverty, they describe its evolution from early organizations such as the Bedford Stuyvesant Restoration Corporation (the country's first community development corporation) to field of increasing complexity that was "cross-sectoral, multidisciplinary" and involved "a plethora of people, organizations and institutions."

The growth of the community development field was captured by a series of increasingly optimistic titles of a survey of the industry conducted by Zdenek's former organization the National Congress for Community Economic Development (NCCED) and later by the National Association of Community Economic Development Associations (NACEDA). From *Against All Odds* in 1987 to *Rising Above* in 2010, these surveys showed how a movement had turned into an industry; how a handful of community development corporations grew to be many thousands across the country.

That growth, however, was uneven and resulted in a wild array of organizations under the community development umbrella. In the book, Zdenek and Walsh make a useful distinction between three types of these organizations: community development corporations (CDCs), regional housing development organizations (RHDOs), and community development finance institutions (CDFIs). They go deeper in describing the vast variety within those categories depending on history, leadership, capital structure, region, etc.

What to some may appear to be hopeless heterodoxy is a positive strength to Walsh and Zdenek. They see in this variety institutions that develop unique combinations of "core competencies." This idea was first explored in a Federal Reserve Bank of San Francisco working paper in 2013 titled "Comparative Advantage: Creating Synergy in Community Development." The book builds on that earlier work and creates a useful typology of competencies including: "organizational development and management; community engagement; planning feasibility; project development; lending; property and asset management; program management; resource development; communication; collaboration and partnering; and performance measurement and performance criteria." Breaking these competencies down into their components both allows for better management of them and suggests a strategy of who to seek out as partners. The core idea is to find partners that are stronger in areas where other organizations are weak. In other words, this book is about creating new partnerships and networks where the sum is much greater than the parts. And that sum of organizations—working in concert—should be better positioned to meet the multiple and changing needs of a low-income community.

This is an important book at an important time. We need new ideas, new partners, and new resources if we are going to serve the needs of low-income America. The challenge always, however, is to stay true to the core value community development brings: improving a place while involving the people who live in that place.

David J. Erickson, Ph.D.
Director, Community Development
Federal Reserve Bank of San Francisco

PREFACE

In this Preface, we want to share some of our thoughts about community development and communicate our goals for the book and our reasons for writing it.

Community development can be defined as a purposeful effort to improve a place while involving the people who live in that place. Community development provides a forum for all voices to create a shared vision, with a goal of strengthening the economic, social, and environmental fabric of a community. Community development recognizes and builds upon community assets, rather than focusing on deficits. Community development engages residents and connects businesses, health-care institutions, educational institutions, faith-based organizations, elected officials, and administrators.

Finding solutions in the face of sometimes overwhelming odds is part of the DNA of community development. The community development sector identifies opportunity where others see adversity, creates new markets out of disinvestment, and brings hope to individuals and communities that have been ignored and disenfranchised.

While the core values, passion, mission, and vision of community development has been fairly consistent for the past 50 years, the practice of community development has evolved significantly. It has built a strong foundation based on what has worked, and it has adapted to dynamic economic markets and changing political conditions.

The raison d'etre of this book is to provide guidance to practitioners, policy makers, and academics on how best to position community development efforts in the future. There are an inordinate number of competencies needed for community development work. We believe that if organizations focus on a few of these competencies and become adept at leveraging their comparative advantages, it will lead to improved outcomes for individuals and the community.

Why Now?

The Presidential election of 2016 dramatically underscored how disconnected and polarized our country has become. The United States is divided between the haves and the have-nots, and the inclusive and the exclusive. There are those who welcome newcomers to our country and those who would prefer to build a wall to keep people out. Concentrated poverty is on the rise and racial tensions are running high. Given these dynamics, we believe that the time for developing strong, united communities is needed now more than ever, and that community development work is the way to achieve this.

The goal of this book is to show how building strong organizational competencies leads to comparative advantages that can build sustainable community development collaborations that improve economic, social, and health outcomes for underserved residents and communities.

The Authors

We bring over 60 years of leadership, program, and policy experience in community development at the local, regional, and national levels. Here is a bit on how both of us came to writing this book.

Bob's Story

I count myself very fortunate to have landed in the community development field in my early twenties at the National Congress for Community Economic Development (NCCED), the trade association of community development corporations (CDCs). The late 1970s were an exciting time to observe and participate in the early days of the community development movement/industry. Three years later (1980), I was leading NCCED and continued to do so over a 13½-year period, just as the field was coming of age and experiencing an explosion of growth, strong networks, and intermediaries. At the time, community development was one of the few concepts and sectors that responded to the genuine aspirations, skills, and assets of diverse people and communities. NCCED felt like a mini United Nations with its core strengths being the diversity of its people and the skills they embodied, and its many resources. It was a mosaic of ideas and people. While I was at NCCED, we launched a number of partnerships with faith-based organizations, financial institutions, and funding groups.

NCCED left me with a lasting community development framework that I have utilized to work in a number of different sectors at the national, state, and local levels, including a 3 year stint at New Community Corporation in the Central Ward of Newark, New Jersey. I have been a catalyst in the asset-building world and in the human services field and have held leadership positions in the United Way system, as well as with disability economic self-sufficiency work, older adult "Age-Friendly Banking" and economic security work, and the healthy homes sector.

Through all this work, one of the key themes that I have followed and researched is how multi-sector collaborations build on strengths and competencies of diverse organizations to create lasting impact and outcomes. I have seen this type of collaboration first-hand—forging the community tax partnership model at United Way of America, and playing a lead role in Congregations as Partners in Community Development with Lilly Endowment, the Ford Foundation, Local Initiative Support Corporation (LISC), and NCCED.

The two things that excite me most about this book is that I had the opportunity to learn from some of the leading community development practitioners advancing multi-sector collaborations across diverse fields. Secondly, I was able to learn of the growing interest and skills of emerging community development leaders in broadening the impact of community development to address some of our most pressing social and economic challenges.

Dee's Story

I have worked in the community development sector my entire professional life. I was attracted to this work after I experienced my first substandard housing and "slum landlord" while attending university in a city with a severe housing shortage. I recognized that once I graduated and got a job I would have better housing choices, but that people with limited incomes and opportunities would not be so fortunate. In my junior year of college I got involved with a group of urban planning and law students who were forming a tenants' union to help improve renters' rights and housing conditions. This experience was a turning point for me and led me to work as a VISTA volunteer after college with a nonprofit housing agency, and later to a graduate degree in urban planning with a focus on housing.

My work experience includes stints with the community development departments of three cities, including a remarkable 2 years working in Seattle's Chinatown-International District. In 1988 I joined REACH Community Development in Portland, Oregon, and during a 24-year period grew the organization from a small neighborhood-based CDC into a regional housing development organization. During my tenure at REACH, I launched three separate comprehensive community development efforts, partnering with private and public sectors partners. I also oversaw the development of 1300 units of affordable housing, including the one of the first passive house apartment buildings in the USA.

While at REACH, I was active on the boards of several national organizations including NCCED, Enterprise Community Partners, and the Housing Partnership Network (HPN). I also taught affordable housing policy and finance in the Master of Real Estate Development program at Portland State University. I left REACH in 2012 and spent 3 years as Executive Vice President for Network and Corporate Affairs at HPN and in early 2016 became the COO for the Network for Oregon Affordable Housing, a statewide, federally certified community development financial institution.

The book draws from my many years of experience, including first-hand work with the REACH-ACE merger, which is one of the case studies in the book. I have two goals for the book—to raise the bar of professional practice for the community development sector, and to attract young people to the sector. It is my hope that this book not only provides helpful insights and examples for current practitioners, but also inspires the next generation to join in this very important work.

San Francisco, CA, USA   Robert O. Zdenek
Portland, OR, USA   Dee Walsh

ACKNOWLEDGEMENTS

Bob and Dee would like to thank the many people who reviewed our early drafts and provided editorial advice, including: Rachel Bratt, Steve Dubb, Bart Harvey, Ted Wysocki, Jim Ferris, Michael Whitehouse, Ethan Levine, and Matt Jonas. We'd also like to acknowledge those who shared concepts and ideas including: David Erickson, Nancy Andrews, Maggie Grieve, Douglas Smith, and Joe Kriesberg. We want to thank the organizations featured in our case studies and the staff who shared information and insights about their work. While too numerous to list here, you can find them cited in the chapter endnotes and bibliography. And finally a thank-you goes to our friends and families who for too many months have been told, "I can't now, I'm working on the book."

CONTENTS

LIST OF FIGURES

LIST OF CHARTS

CHAPTER 1

Introduction

For much of the last century, the American dream of a home, family, and job has been at the heart of our nation's psyche. It has driven our domestic policy for housing, transportation, and employment, and it has shaped much of our landscape.

But the American dream has been delivered unequally. Economic recessions, structural income inequality, and racism have prevented universal success. Historically, disinvested communities that have suffered have had to learn to do more with less. In these communities, residents have discovered that to improve conditions they must band together to gain a political voice, articulate a vision, and organize others to improve their neighborhoods. There is no single solution. Each situation must be navigated based on its specific economic, political, and social conditions. This is community development.

Community development work has been underway for as long as there have been places that need improving. The work is led by those who are indigenous to the community, responding authentically to local conditions. In the last fifty plus years, there has risen a network of organizations—primarily nonprofit and public—that are dedicated to advancing this work. Community development is at its core "American" in that it embraces the concept of self-help, where people gain strength out of weakness and strive to improve their communities when government has not effectively worked. Community development is participatory and democratic, and involves hard work in lieu of handouts (Harvey 2016).

© The Author(s) 2017
R.O. Zdenek and D. Walsh, *Navigating Community Development*,
DOI 10.1057/978-1-137-47701-9_1

Given the unique nature of this work, there is no definitive road map. The challenge is finding the right tools and approaches to be successful. This book focuses on nonprofit community development organizations that are mission based, not profit motivated. These organizations work to advance the well-being of those living in urban, suburban, and rural areas who have not yet achieved the American dream.

A New Way of Working

Nonprofit community development organizations have done incredible work over the past 50 years. Billions of dollars have been invested in low-income communities, and hundreds of thousands of units of affordable housing have been built.

However, the conditions in our country have not become appreciably better, due in large part to macro and global trends. Today we face many challenges. Recent studies show that the number of high poverty census tracts is increasing and the overall poverty rate is holding steady at 15% (Cortright and Mahmoudi 2014). Government support for affordable housing and many community development programs has been steadily declining over the past 30 years (Center on Budget and Policy Priorities 2016).

In strong market cities, populations are booming and urban neighborhoods are being rediscovered and gentrified. The cost of housing in these places has skyrocketed and the number of homeless people living on the streets has reached an all-time high. Residents with modest means are often displaced to lower cost, less desirable parts of town. Suburban poverty is on the upswing.

For cities that are not booming, residents are struggling with decades of population loss and disinvestment, and with limited opportunities for economic growth and reinvestment. But every community has assets, and the key is to recognize and build upon these assets with bold solutions.

While community development organizations have spent decades honing their craft, the problems associated with poverty are complex and demand not a single multi-layered organization, but a team of organizations working together toward a common vision (Andrews and Retsinas 2012).

To effect change, community development practitioners need to be skilled collaborators and leverage their organizations' competencies with the competencies of other complementary organizations and institutions. In today's resource-constrained environment, an organization's ability to use its comparative advantage by concentrating on those things that it can do more efficiently or effectively than others, is the most productive way forward. The goal of this book is to provide a framework and rationale for this approach.

THE FIELD HAS GROWN

In the five decades since community development emerged as a field to improve the social and economic well-being and sustainability of communities, it has grown and diversified. In the early years, holistic approaches to community development work that engaged local residents were primarily done by nonprofit organizations called community development corporations (CDCs). Today, a variety of organizations, including neighborhood associations, community development corporations, regional housing development organizations (RHDOs), community development financial institutions (CDFIs), community organizing and advocacy groups, private nonprofit anchor institutions (such as universities and hospitals), for-profit real estate companies, and local, regional, and state government, are actively doing community development work to varying degrees. With such a crowded field, it becomes essential that nonprofit community development organizations understand their unique capabilities and how to best utilize and leverage their comparative advantage.

While there are many more actors at work, nonprofit organizations play a significant role in executing community development initiatives. Not only have their numbers grown, but the quality of organizations working in the sector has greatly advanced. Of note, nonprofit community development organizations provide one third of the 4.6 million social housing units, which is affordable housing owned by public agencies and nonprofit organizations in the USA (Bratt 2012). They have lent billions of dollars to support housing and community development infrastructure (OFN 2014).

There are three types of nonprofits that do the lion's share of this work: CDCs, RHDOs, and CDFIs. While each type of organization has its own unique structure and approach, all of the organizations have similar missions: to improve the lives of low- and moderate-income individuals by creating vibrant, healthy communities.

Navigating Community Development describes how nonprofit community development organizations can strategically utilize their comparative advantages to achieve their mission. Our book offers seven case studies to help illustrate how organizations can utilize this approach.

SUCCEEDING IN THE FUTURE

In writing a book about how to undertake community development work in today's complex and interconnected world, a number of questions need to be answered. For example, are there core competencies that are essential to doing the work? Are specific competencies associated with specific types of community development organizations? How can organizations best leverage their competencies? What will the next generation of a community development system look like? These questions, and more, are addressed in this book.

We believe that to successfully navigate today's environment, community development organizations will need to respond systematically and comprehensively to the economic, social, and physical conditions that impact communities. By recognizing and leading with their competencies, community development organizations can bring their specialized areas of expertise to address complex community challenges, and effectively meet their missions and objectives.

REFERENCES

Andrews, Nancy O., and Nicolas P. Retsinas. 2012. Inflection Point: New Vision. New Strategy. New Organization. *Investing in What Works in America's Communities*, 416. San Francisco, CA: Federal Reserve Bank of San Francisco and Low Income Investment Fund.

Bratt, Rachel G. 2012. *Social Housing in the United States: Overview*, 417. Medford, MA: Tufts University.

Center on Budget and Policy Priorities. Chart Book: Cuts in Federal Assistance have Exacerbated Families' Struggle to Afford Housing. 2016. http://www.cbpp.org/research/housing/chart-book-cuts-in-federal-assistance-have-exacerbated-families-struggles-to-afford. 12 Apr 2016.

Cortright, Joe and Dillon Mahmoudi. 2014. *Lost in Place: Why the Persistence and Spread of Concentrated Poverty—Not Gentrification—Is Our Biggest Urban Challenge*. Portland. OR: City Observatory.

Harvey III, Frederick B. (Bart). 2016. Email message to author.

Opportunity Finance Network. 2014. *CDFIs Provide Opportunity for All*. Opportunity Finance Network: Infographic.

CHAPTER 2

The Important Work of Community Development

THE BEGINNING OF A NEW ERA

When Senator Robert Kennedy (D-NY) toured the Bedford Stuyvesant neighborhood in New York City in 1967, he was challenged by neighborhood activists to go beyond rhetoric and help create tangible, programmatic solutions. Kennedy embraced this challenge and, with fellow US Senator Jacob Javits (R-NY), developed legislation that led to the creation of a new vehicle to attack urban decline: the community development corporation (CDC). Since then, CDCs and other participants in the community development sector have created important strategies for revitalizing the physical, social, and economic fabric of thousands of low- and moderate-income communities throughout the USA.

In the last 50 years, community development work, which is about engaging and empowering local citizens to improve and strengthen communities, has expanded and evolved to respond to changing social, political, and economic conditions. In this chapter, we provide a quick overview of the evolution of the sector to date.

COMMUNITY DEVELOPMENT IS COMPLEX

Communities are dynamic, complex systems, with an abundance of competing needs and differing views on best solutions. Frequently, the desire to make investments and improvement outstrips the available resources. Community development is complicated further by the accelerating pace of

© The Author(s) 2017
R.O. Zdenek and D. Walsh, *Navigating Community Development*,
DOI 10.1057/978-1-137-47701-9_2

economic, political, and technological change, which can drive transformations to social systems and culture. The work to improve communities is cross-sectoral and multi-disciplinary and involves a plethora of people, organizations, and institutions. Success depends on the effectiveness of the various parties and their ability to work together to define and solve complex problems (Amadei 2015).

Community development work can be carried out by a range of private and public entities. This book focuses on three types of organizations that have led and delivered the majority of the community development work by the nonprofit sector: CDCs, regional housing development organizations (RHDOs), and community development financial institutions (CDFIs). Each of these types of organizations has similar missions which typically comprises improving the lives of low- and moderate-income individuals by creating vibrant, healthy communities. However, the business models, approaches, and competencies of these organizations differ. Chapter 3 provides a detailed description of the characteristics of the three types of organizations.

Complex problems require comprehensive solutions that require considerable knowledge and resources. In a 1998 report, titled *More than Bricks and Sticks*, Glickman and Servon cautioned that community development organizations that take on a comprehensive approach to their work can face significant challenges because they may not have the financial and technical resources needed to be effective with a comprehensive agenda. A growing body of community development organizational research contends that supporting a large, diversified staff and series of programs is often too complicated and costly for organizations, which frequently operate on thin financial margins (Zdenek and Steinbach 2002). As circumstances shift, organizations may be forced to narrow their scope or specialize in areas where resources are available.

SHRINKING RESOURCES TRIGGER NEW WAYS OF WORKING

Financial support to community development organizations, which has historically included capacity building and operating support, and project support in the form of grants, low-cost loans, and project equity, has fluctuated over time.

Basic capacity building assistance typically included skills training and funds for operations. It was usually delivered by foundations, the public sector, and/or regional and national intermediary organizations.

These supporters of the community development sector, along with other community organizations, public and private institutions and businesses, formed a networked system for initiating and executing community development work. They functioned like an ecosystem, with interdependent organizations and institutions that are aligned in purpose and interact with each other and their environment.

Operating support and capacity building assistance took a big hit after the Great Recession of 2008 when there was a decrease in funding for the community development sector (Smith Hopkins 2012). The public sector tightened its spending and foundation support for community development operations and programs also suffered. As foundation investments experienced losses, grant giving was reduced. The demise of the Fannie Mae Foundation, which was a national leader in philanthropic support for community development, had a major negative impact on the sector. From its creation in 1979 to its closure in 2007, the Fannie Mae Foundation had spent more than $1 billion to support affordable housing production across the nation (Adler 2007; Sullivan 2011; Baer 2015). The federal government helped fill the gap for community development projects with some short-term stimulus programs including the American Recovery and Reinvestment Act of 2009, but many financial institutions withdrew from the affordable housing market.

The financial crisis and recession brought harsh consequences for communities that had been struggling to revitalize. In the years leading up to the crisis, unscrupulous lenders, 85% of whom were not regulated, exploited low-income home buyers and communities with sub-prime loan products that resulted in 7 million foreclosures. The communities hit by home loss and abandonment were disproportionately communities of color (Harvey 2016). Relaxed mortgage lending standards, low interest rates, and the proliferation of sub-prime mortgages, all contributed to the housing bubble. With profits and greed driving Wall Street, the baseline for loan quality was at an all-time low. Bad and tenuous mortgage loans were packaged and securitized and sold to many unsuspecting investors. The creation of a "shadow banking system," which included investment banks, hedge funds, and structured investment vehicles, became highly leveraged. When values stopped rising, the bubble burst and began a cycle of deleveraging and loss (Holt 2009). All of this meant huge setbacks for communities that were hit hard by the resulting foreclosures. The vast number of foreclosed properties resulted in lower property values and the reversal, in some cases, of years of community revitalization work (Hewings 2012).

After 2008, financial institutions, foundations, and public entities still working in community development gravitated toward the strongest organizations. As a result, these organizations did well and grew their portfolios during this period. The foreclosed home inventory and stimulus funding created opportunities for those organizations that were financially stable and able to take advantage of local and federal programs to acquire and reposition the housing.

But community development organizations with weak balance sheets found themselves with fewer operational grants and less access to capital and other flexible low-cost sources that they once had. These organizations suffered as project development opportunities and the related fee income shrank. With development no longer a feasible course of action, many had to redefine their role in the community and look to working with partners that could develop.

Community development organizations that still had access to capital found that the recession left them facing bigger challenges in their communities. This meant that they needed to find additional resources and/or expertise. These organizations recognized that to tackle the problems at hand, they had to work across silos with new partners who had resources and expertise to help solve the complex problems that lay before them.

In sum, after the Great Recession, the community development sector found itself needing to rethink its business approach and how it carried out its work in the community. To survive and thrive, it became essential for organizations to access new resources, become catalytic leaders, and work with new partners and constituencies.

MASTERING THE BASICS

Community development organizations have advanced significantly in the last two decades. Functioning as social enterprises that reinvest their profits to advance their charitable mission, community development organizations operate with multiple bottom lines in mind. Their real estate development and lending work must be financially viable, while meeting the social and economic needs of the residents, integrating well into the community, and, where applicable, being as environmentally sustainable as possible (Bratt 2012).

Organizations that are successful today have grasped essential competencies for doing community development work. They have mastered the "five components of community development capacity" as defined by

Glickman and Servon, which include resource, organizational, programmatic, network, and political capacity (Glickman and Servon 1998). Sophisticated community development organizations today have developed an array of technical and human skills that will allow them to function and thrive. Experienced organizations no longer have a need for "capacity building" assistance for basic skills and functions, but rather need advanced training and targeted assistance to advance sophisticated systems and processes.

Some community development organizations have found success in going deep in one particular area by creating a vertically integrated model that masters all of the steps in a particular business line. However, it can be difficult to transfer this expertise to other disciplines.

For example, Homewise, a nonprofit CDFI located in New Mexico, has created a company whose mission is to help create successful homeowners. They achieve this by offering homebuyer education, affordable home construction, financial products, brokerage services, and loan servicing (Homewise 2016). Since their start in 1986, they have developed expertise in all facets of the homeownership business, including financial products for home repair and refinancing. While Homewise has developed efficient systems for this work, if they moved into different business lines, such as job training or health care, they would either need to find a partner with that expertise or spend a lot of time and money to add organizational capacity in those areas.

PARTNERSHIPS AND COLLABORATIONS GAIN IMPORTANCE

At the same time that community development work has become more complex, funders, investors, public officials, and external stakeholders are placing a premium on strategic partnerships and collaboration, due in part to the wide breadth of community development needs. There have been some efforts on the part of funders to encourage partnerships between organizations, such as the LISC Sustainable Communities initiative which works with multiple organizations to improve the quality of life in low-income communities; the Living Cities Integration Initiative which strives to reshape programs, policies, and resources to achieve positive change for low-income communities; and the JP Morgan Chase PRO Neighborhoods program designed to encourage collaboration among CDFIs (LISC and JPMorgan Chase 2016). There is recognition that community development intersects with numerous fields and that the work of building communities needs to align with other systems that affect the success of that community, such as health care, education, employment, transportation, and environmental quality.

MORE PLAYERS ENTER THE FIELD

The movement of organizations not traditionally involved in community development to become more active in this arena stems from the fact that human needs are not neatly organized in silos. Addressing human needs requires a multi-sector approach to achieve results. As social service agencies, educators and health providers consider the influence of place on their clients, they have moved to provide solutions that are community development in nature.

For example, the affordable and decent housing can improve health outcomes. Thus, some agencies working with populations with special health needs have begun developing housing for their clients. As safe, affordable homes can help individuals in their recovery from mental and physical illness, mental health organizations have developed housing to fill this need for their clients. Agencies working with the elderly have developed programs to make housing more age-friendly.

In the future, to be relevant and impactful, community development organizations will need to respond to the economic, social, physical, and health determinates that negatively impact communities. They will achieve this by leveraging their comparative advantages and collaborating with diverse types of organizations that have complementary abilities and resources.

GOALS FOR THIS BOOK

The primary goal of *Navigating Community Development* is to propose a framework, guidance, and current examples of how community development organizations can maximize their core competencies in a strategic way to increase their outputs, outcomes, and impact, all of which are important. Outputs are those things that are done by the organization. Outcomes are the recognizable effects on the beneficiaries, while impact is the degree to which the activities of the organization improve upon the larger issues (Stannard-Stockton 2010). For example, homes built are outputs. People living more affordably and safely are outcomes. Reducing housing needs in a community is an impact.

The book aims to meet this goal by being pragmatic, instructional, and relevant. Here's how we define each:

Pragmatic: The emphasis of this book is on the application of comparative advantages in community development strategy, drawing from current experience and practice. Primary audiences for this book are community development leaders and practitioners. The book demonstrates that comparative advantages built on core competencies are a critical framework for increasing the impact and effectiveness of community development work. The seven case studies provide insight as to how this can be accomplished.

Instructional: Another important audience for this book is academia with a focus on emerging leaders and students with an interest in improving communities. The book provides students with an understanding of the historical context from which the current community development ecosystem evolved, the key competencies that organizations need to operate in today's environment, and successful approaches for maximizing these strengths through strategic alliances. As the current leadership of the community development sector is comprised primarily of baby boomers, many of whom are about to retire, educating and training the next generation of community development leaders is essential. This book aims to provide insight and information on how new leaders should approach their work in the coming decade. Emerging community development leaders need to understand the growing role of partnerships and collaboration in community development.

Relevant: The book is responsive to and reflective of current condition. The community development ecosystem, which is comprised of networks of organizations engaged in community development, has undergone a significant transformation in the two past decades. While CDCs are still important players, RHDOs and CDFIs have become very influential in the community development field. Furthermore, a whole host of other organizations and institutions have become engaged in varying degrees in some community development activities, including hospitals, transit authorities, public school districts and charter schools, local food sourcing networks, and some for-profit real estate companies.

The current community development landscape has changed. While today's successful community development organizations have effective capacity, in the future they will need to engage with multiple sectors in a collaborative approach. In the book, we review the results of a survey of community development leaders addressing how they envision their strategies will change in the coming years. The survey highlights leaders' understanding that the changing ecosystem in which they operate will require that they hone their competencies and collaborate with others. Emphasizing core competencies and comparative advantages is of relevance to practitioners as they navigate and succeed in the new community development ecosystem.

QUESTIONS FOR THE FIELD

In writing this book, we also have strived to define and answer what we believe to be the most important issues confronting our field. The new community development ecosystem raises a series of compelling questions and challenges:

- *Does the community development environment require increased specialization and collaboration to effectively address today's challenges?* As noted, community development work deals with complex issues and involves an array of disciplines and sectors. The community development field is also comprised of very diverse organizations in size and focus, from small, neighborhood-based organizations to large, multi-faceted regional and even national organizations. Each organization has an important role to play. It is important that organizations both specialize and collaborate as they tackle these issues and work to create a healthy community.

- *Are there existing core competencies specific to each type of community development organization?* While community development organizations may share a number of common characteristics, they are differentiated by their history, leadership, capital structure, business lines, programs, size, sophistication, and location. As such, some types of organizations are better suited to perform certain activities and develop core competencies in specific areas and in response to selected market conditions. The research underlying this book will illustrate how these competencies align with the different types of organizations and how this segmentation can be used for advantage.

- *How do organizations best maximize their comparative advantages?* To best maximize one's impact, organizations should fully understand their mission, priorities, end goals, and the competencies and resources they bring to address these goals. At the same time, they need to do an inventory of what competencies and resources are lacking, and how these competencies can be developed through forging new partnerships. Once partners are identified, a very clear scope of work and understanding of roles should be prepared and followed to achieve desired goals and results. The book will investigate some of the key factors in making these alliances successful.

- *Does the community development support system (government, philanthropy, intermediaries, and private capital) encourage or discourage collaboration?* While the community development support system advocates for collaboration and partnership among different types of organizations, it has not always rewarded these strategic alliances. American political and economic culture emphasizes individualism, entrepreneurship, and competition. This mindset can make it challenging for launching collaborative efforts. Two or more groups working together may result in more support initially, but too often the overall financial support drops once the effort is past start-up. In the book, we examine some of the institutional behaviors that support this work and those that do not, and we suggest what could be done to enhance support to build the capacity and competencies of community development organizations. We pay special attention to innovative networking strategies and models for the growing cross-sectoral work that community development organizations are performing.

- *What new strategies and support systems are needed?* In order to fully support collaboration among various organizations, the community development support system needs to facilitate the organization and funding of these types of alliances. In this book, we consider various approaches to providing support, including forums and electronic platforms where various groups can come together to identify the potential partner, financial incentives that reward collaboration, as well as other examples. Additionally, we explore different roles that community development organizations can play in launching collaborative initiatives including the quarterback model articulated in the book *Investing in What Works in America's Communities*. Our book also highlights new funding strategies and approaches, including impact investing.

- *What can we learn from the experience of community development organizations to more fully utilize and develop a comparative advantage framework?* Community development organizations have shown a strong ability to adapt and grow as their environments have changed.

Community development is an applied discipline. Learning occurs through practice, reflection, and refinement drawn from policies and some theories of change. Throughout the book, we show how community development organizations are utilizing comparative advantages to increase their resiliency, effectiveness, and impact. The seven case studies that we discuss in the book will share how organizations have attracted an array of new partners, and how they have built and maintained networks. Managing partnerships is not easy, and the challenges and lessons from these partnerships will be of value to the broader community development field and related networks.

- *What does the next generation of the community development system look like?* Through surveys, analysis, and outreach to community development practitioners, stakeholders, and thought leaders, the book captures the major trends shaping community development work. It examines the importance that comparative advantages and collaboration will have in the future for the next generation of leaders. The field will need new voices and different organizational cultures to integrate diverse capacities. As technology evolves, so too will the way we work alone and together and with the communities we serve. The community development field is experiencing a number of leadership changes as baby boomers retire. How the field attracts and trains new leaders is vital to ensure continued impact and dynamism.

THE FOCUS AND FLOW OF THE BOOK

This book is divided into eleven chapters and appendices. Following is a brief description of Chaps. 3–11 and Appendices.

CHAPTER 3. THE BACKGROUND AND HISTORY OF COMMUNITY DEVELOPMENT ORGANIZATIONS

This chapter provides a more in-depth analysis and description of the major characteristics of the three types of community development organizations discussed in this book and provides a historical overview of the community development field. For each of the organizations featured—CDCs, RHDOs, and CDFIs—we describe program mixture, geographic location, organizational size, organizational capacity, capital structure, and assets. This information is drawn from national community development census surveys, national trade associations, and community development practitioners.

This chapter also describes community development during the last five decades, from its original comprehensive vision as a key element of the War on Poverty to the present period of comprehensive, multi-sector approaches. It describes how CDCs experienced considerable growth and influence in the 1980s, due in part to the expanding community development support system at the national and local level. It will review the 1990s and the emergence of CDFIs, a term that was coined during the start of the Clinton Administration, and discuss the expansion of RHDOs, which include a number of CDCs who have grown their portfolios and geography and morphed into RHDOs.

The chapter also looks at how community development has evolved from its early days when comprehensive development was done within the confines of a large CDC, to the new approach where community development organizations partner with many other organizations that have specialized expertise, relationships, and resources.

CHAPTER 4. UNDERSTANDING THE COMMUNITY DEVELOPMENT ECOSYSTEM

This chapter introduces the theoretical roots of community development. It defines the key concepts and identifies and explores a number of internal and external factors that make strategic partnerships a critical tool for community development in the current and future environment. The chapter provides a description of the community development ecosystem. Some of the major factors that impact today's environment and the ability of organizations to perform optimally are discussed.

CHAPTER 5. COMMUNITY DEVELOPMENT CORE COMPETENCIES

Community development requires myriad competencies to revitalize low-income communities. This chapter explores a number of major community development competencies and builds on Bob Zdenek's working paper, published by the Federal Reserve Bank of San Francisco in September 2013, titled: "Comparative Advantages: Creating Synergy in Community Development," which serves as the basis of this book. The discussion of community development competencies is organized around:

organizational development and management; community engagement and public policy; planning; communication; project development (real estate); lending; property and asset management; program/business line development and management; resource development; collaboration and partnering; and performance measurement and evaluation. Each of the above-listed competency categories has a number of sub-categories that are described in this chapter.

CHAPTER 6. ADVANCING COMMUNITY DEVELOPMENT THROUGH CORE COMPETENCIES AND COMPARATIVE ADVANTAGES

This chapter provides a framework for assessing community development capacity. The chart identifies the relative strengths and weaknesses of the three community development type organizations (CDCs, RHDOs, and CDFIs) in reference to each competency. This chapter provides an overview of the evolving field of strategic partnerships and collaboration and what are the core elements for forging effective partnerships and leverage competencies for comparative advantage. The chart is meant to be suggestive and should be adapted to local circumstances.

CHAPTER 7. CASE STUDIES OF PARTNERSHIPS UTILIZING COMPARATIVE ADVANTAGES

In this chapter, we present case studies that illustrate the concepts presented in this book. They show how core competencies are utilized by organizations as comparative advantages, leading to positive outcomes for community development organizations. The strategic partnership approach demonstrates that each community development organization can bring unique value and impact to the community development process. Case studies are drawn from a variety of community development organizations and geographies.

CHAPTER 8. LESSONS FROM THE CASE STUDIES

Lessons and challenges from the case studies are presented in this chapter and common themes and patterns are identified. One of the major goals of the analysis of the case studies is to provide practical examples of how organizations can work together with multiple partners, policy makers, and funders to advance strategic partnerships built on core competencies of diverse organizations.

CHAPTER 9. THE COMMUNITY DEVELOPMENT ECOSYSTEM: THE NEXT GENERATION

This chapter focuses on how core competencies and comparative advantages will help community development organizations thrive in the community development ecosystem of tomorrow. The chapter discusses the results of a survey conducted of CEOs about their current and future strategies. A number of external factors are driving the changes in the community development ecosystem including a reduction in public subsidies, restrictive capital markets, shifts in government support, and the entrance of a wide range of new organizations to community development. To succeed in the community development ecosystem, community development organizations will need to act more as a facilitator or "quarterback" (Erickson et al. 2012); expand the target customer/client base and geographic footprint; develop new skills and expertise; and pursue new sources of capital.

CHAPTER 10. IMPLICATIONS FOR COMMUNITY DEVELOPMENT PRACTICE

This chapter revisits the questions posed in this chapter to offer a series of observations and examples of the necessity and efficacy of using a comparative advantage framework built on core competencies. It offers a series of observations for community development organizations as well as the community development support system (funders, policy makers, community leaders, and others).

CHAPTER 11. RECOMMENDATIONS AND GUIDE POSTS FOR NAVIGATING COMMUNITY DEVELOPMENT

This chapter provides a series of tactical recommendations for community development organizations and practitioners.

APPENDICES. ORGANIZATIONAL PROFILES

In the appendices 1–3, we provide profiles of several of the key actors featured in the case studies to provide the reader with more information about the size and activities of these community development organizations. We also provide a list of major national organizations active in the community development sector, and a blank Organizational Competency chart that readers can use to inventory their organization's competencies.

CONCLUSION

The functional concepts presented in *Navigating Community Development* are built on a rich field of research and practice about community development. Low-income communities have been disinvested and often impacted by discriminatory racial and economic policies. This book is focused on community development practices and the crucial work that is done to build wealth, promote equity, and improve key social determinants for all residents.

In the book, we discuss the evolution of the sector from a disparate networked system to a system where sophisticated community development organizations, be they CDCs, RHDOs, CDFIs, are stepping up to the critical role of community development quarterback. By working across traditional silos, they are tackling some of our nation's most pressing challenges (Erickson et al. 2012). Despite decades of cutbacks in federal funding, organizations are still embracing their missions, but they are changing their tactics for achieving them. Organizations are leveraging their core competencies, by working with other organizations similarly motivated, but with different expertise. This book shows how organizations can begin to think and act in this new role, thereby creating healthy and vibrant communities for all residents.

REFERENCES

Adler, Neil. 2007. Fannie Mae Foundation to Close. New Charitable Office to be Created. *Washington Business Journal*, February 23.

Amadei, Bernard. 2015. *A Systems Approach to Modeling Community Development Projects*. New York, NY: Momentum Press. Chapter 2.

Baer, Kathryn. 2015. Nonprofit Housing and Service Providers Face Funding Crisis. *Poverty and Policy Blog*, July 6.

Bratt, Rachel G. 2012. The Quadruple Bottom Line and Nonprofit Housing Organizations in the United States. *Housing Studies* 27 (4): 438–456. doi:10.1080/0267037.2012.677016.

Erickson, David, Ian Galloway, and Naomi Cytron. 2012. Routinizing the Extraordinary. *Investing in What Works for America's Communities.* Federal Reserve Bank of San Francisco and Low Income Investment Fund, 382.

Glickman, Norman J., and Lisa J. Servon. 1998. More than Bricks and Sticks: Five Components of CDC Capacity. Fannie Mae Foundation. *Housing Policy Debate.* 9 (3): 500–501, 505.

Harvey III, Frederick B. (Bart). 2016. Email Message to Author. 11 August 2016.

Hewings, Geoffrey J.D. 2012. The Hidden Cost of Foreclosures in Chicago Neighborhoods; Study Finds Distressed Properties Impact Home Prices. Illinois Realtors. http://www.illinoisrealtor.org/foreclosureimpact.

Holt, Jeff. 2009. A Summary of the Primary Causes of the Housing Bubble and the Resulting Credit Crisis: A Non-Technical Paper. *The Journal of Business Inquiry.* 8 (1): 120–129.

Homewise. 2016. About Us: How We Do What We Do, May 14. www.homewise. org/about-us/.

JPMorgan Chase & Co. Introducing PRO Neighborhoods. https://www. jpmorganchase.com/corporate/news/stories/pro-neighborhoods-main.htm. May 2016.

LISC Philadelphia. 2016. Helping Neighbors Build Communities: Sustainable Communities Initiative. http://programs.lisc.org/philly/what_we_do/sustainable_communities_initiative.php. May 2016.

Living Cities. The Integration Initiative. https://www.livingcities.org/work/the-integration-initiative. May 2016.

Smith Hopkins, Jamie. 2012. 'Huge drop' in Funding for Community Development. *The Baltimore Sun*, September 20.

Stannard-Stockton, Sean. 2010. Getting Results: Outputs, Outcomes & Impact. Tactical Philanthropy. http://www.tacticalphilanthropy.com/2010/06/outputs-outcomes-impact-oh-my/, June 29.

Sullivan, Patricia. 2011. Freddie Mac. Fannie Mae Donations Disappearing Study Predicts. *Washington Post*, October 2.

Zdenek, Robert, and Carol Steinbach. 2002. *Managing Your CDC: Leadership Strategies for Changing Times.* Washington DC: National Congress for Community Economic Development.

CHAPTER 3

The Background and History of Community Development Organizations

Overview

Historical frameworks are important for setting context, and while *Navigating Community Development* is not a definitive history on community development, this chapter does provide a decade-by-decade overview of how community development organizations have evolved since the late 1960s. There are many excellent historical articles and books on community development organizations. Authors such as Bratt, Glickman, Keyes, Rubin, Schwartz, Servon, Stoeker, Vidal, Von Hoffman, Walker, and Weinheimer have documented well the first three decades of the community development movement including the need for and impacts of capacity building, and the change and accomplishments of the sector. We have not tried to duplicate that information here.

This chapter describes in more detail the three types of community development organizations featured in this book—CDCs, RHDOs, and CDFIs. The chapter also reviews the evolution of the community development sector from a handful of CDCs in the late 1960s to a network of sophisticated community development practitioners and organizations today.

As noted previously, CDCs, RHDOs, and CDFIs are responsible for the majority of community development production and lending by the nonprofit sector. Following is a detailed description of each type of organization.

© The Author(s) 2017
R.O. Zdenek and D. Walsh, *Navigating Community Development*,
DOI 10.1057/978-1-137-47701-9_3

Community Development Corporations (CDCs)

For the purposes of this book, CDCs are those organizations that are geographically focused on a neighborhood or group of neighborhoods, or specific rural or suburban geography. They have a place-based mission focus of community revitalization, are governed by boards that have community representation, and have community revitalization as their core mission. As of 2006, it is estimated that there were 4,600 CDCs producing about 96,000 units per year (NACEDA, 2010). Since the financial crisis of 2008, it is estimated that the number of CDCs has shrunk and not grown in subsequent years due to the loss of operating and financing capital for smaller organizations; however, there have been no recent national surveys to document these numbers.

Geographic Location: Initially, CDCs were primarily located in one or a few urban neighborhoods. Over the last three decades, many have expanded to serve multiple neighborhoods, in addition to suburban or rural areas. Rural CDCs often operate in multiple counties given the lack of density in their service areas. The 2005 NCCED census, *Reaching New Heights*, was the only survey that provided data on the geographic service areas of community development organizations. The survey found that CDCs serve a variety of different types of communities. Fifty-two percent of the CDCs that responded to the census survey were urban, 26% rural, and 22% were mixed between urban–suburban and suburban–rural. CDCs that tend to serve larger geographic areas require more staff, and often have more specialized capacity. This offers the potential of strategic partnership opportunities between smaller placed based organizations and larger regional development organizations.

Staff Size: While the size of CDC professional staff varies widely, the median staff size in the 2010 *Rising Above* survey was 7.5 FTE. Per the survey, three in four CDCs have fewer than 30 full-time staff. There are some large organizations working in the field, with 10% having full-time staff of 125 or more.

Budget/Assets: There is no current data for CDCs nationally regarding budget size and assets.

Organizational Capacity: The organizational capacity of CDCs varies widely from volunteer-led/volunteer-staffed organizations to very large organizations. Since the median staff size of CDCs is 7.5, many of these organizations have moderate capacity with a mix of management, administrative, and program staff. CDCs with less than 10 staff have fewer program and development staff, which limits their programmatic capacity. One of the noticeable trends over the national community development surveys is that CDCs have increased their involvement in new initiatives that are of importance to the community. The *Rising Above* survey showed that CDCs were heavily involved in foreclosure prevention, financial literacy, and housing counseling. The last two surveys showed a growth of activity in green building design and arts and culture. The needs and opportunities in community development often outstrip the organizational capacity of a CDC. This underscores the importance of strategic partnerships with other community development organizations and sectors.

Program Mixture: The core CDC activities are affordable housing development, commercial and industrial development, enterprise development, and community engagement and advocacy. Recent years have seen growth of CDC involvement with supportive services, housing and financial counseling, asset building, youth programs, childcare, health initiatives, and job skills training. This is impressive given that many CDCs have smaller staff, and what survey data do not show are the types of organizations that CDCs are partnering with for these various programs and services.

Income Levels Served: CDCs have historically served low- and moderate-income residents in their respective communities. The data which are available through affordable housing production (Rising Above, 2010) show that 85% of CDC housing production benefits people below 80% area median income, and 23% of housing production is for people below 30% area median income, which is considered extremely low income. Interestingly, 68% of CDC housing production is rental and rental housing, notably the Low-Income Housing Tax Credit program, has requirements for serving low-income residents.

Regional Housing Development Organizations (RHDOs)

Regional Housing Development Organizations are mission-driven independent nonprofit organizations whose primary purposes are to develop, preserve, operate, manage affordable housing and community facilities, and provide related support services to low-income families, seniors, and people with special needs. While some RHDOs had their roots as CDCs, many

RHDOs were created later than the movement in the mid-1990s, with some created as a result of a program of the Ford Foundation to spawn sophisticated housing partnerships.

RHDOs share five primary characteristics. While RHDOs may be active as service providers or community organizers, they are all focused on real estate production, primarily production of affordable housing. RHDOs are also focused on scale, and strive to have a significant impact in their market by growing the volume of their work. RHDOs understand and utilize the importance of public and private partnerships, and devote a considerable amount of time to developing and maintaining key relationships. RHDOs are key players in fulfilling the public policy agenda in the communities they serve. They are often the "go to" entities that local governments seek out to implement key redevelopment work. In the context of the community development ecosystem, successful RHDOs are "keystone species" and have a significant impact on the local environment (Christman et al. 2009).

Geographic Location: RHDOs work in multiple jurisdictions that may span a metro region or multiple states. While they may have a strong geographic focus to their work, the area is typically much larger than the area of a traditional CDC, which may work in one or two neighborhoods. Typically, RHDOs have staff sizes ranging from 10 to several hundred and operating budgets in excess of $1.5 million annually, with an average of 2000 or more rental housing units under ownership.

Staff Size and Activities: Based on the most recent survey of HPN's 98 members, of which 73 are multi-family housing developers, staff sizes range average range from 5 to 3300. The size of the entities is driven largely by whether or not they do their own property management and resident services. In 2015, 10,800 affordable homes were developed, with 369,300 developed, rehabilitated, or preserved to date. The majority (77%) of the organizations serve families with children, 64% serve seniors, and 57% serve persons with special needs. Sixty-eight organizations offer resident service programs at their properties. Additionally, 36 organizations develop single-family for-sale properties.

Budget/Assets: RHDOs have significant budgets and assets, although these assets may be held by a number of affiliated entities. According to the 2014 HPN member profile and data from the IRS form 990, the operating budgets of members ranged from a low of $1 million to as high as $120 million. Net assets ranged from $5 million to $658 million. The nature of affordable housing finance in the USA is that individual development projects are frequently treated as single asset entities. While these properties consolidate up to the parent company, they are treated individually, which limits the ability of the parent company to leverage their portfolio the way a for-profit company can. It also results in extremely complex accounting, compliance, and auditing requirements.

Program Mix: In addition to housing development, RHDOs typically engage in planning, project management, development, advocacy, resident services, and asset management. Several have their own CDFIs and lend either to consumers or to their development affiliates.

Income Levels Served: The majority of housing developed by RHDOs is targeted at households earning less than 60% of area median income, with some organizations focused on households with significantly fewer resources. As public support for affordable housing wanes, some RHDOs are developing more mixed-income housing so that they can internally subsidize the lower-cost units in the property.

Community Development Financial Institutions (CDFIs)

CDFIs emerged from the community development sector more than 40 years ago to address the credit needs of low-income individuals and economically disadvantaged communities. Initially financed by the government, religious institutions, and/or individuals, early efforts to provide credit for business and housing was done by community development credit unions and banks. However, the sector grew slowly until it was aided by the creation of the CDFI Fund in 1994, and revisions to the Community Reinvestment Act (CRA) in 1995 that recognized loans and investments to CDFIs as a qualified CRA activity. CDFIs have grown more quickly in number and type over the past 20 years and operate in both urban and rural areas. As of 2015, there were 950 CDFIs certified by the CDFI Fund (CDFI Coalition).

According to the CDFI Coalition, there are six types of CDFIs: non-profit loan funds, credit unions, venture capital funds, micro-enterprise lenders, community development corporation lenders, and banks and bank holding companies. The majority of CDFIs are nonprofit, community development loan funds. Some organizations operate in more than one capacity. For example, some CDFIs have a community development loan fund and also provide micro-enterprise loans.

Community Development Loan Funds help support housing and community development projects. Loan funds obtain capital from individuals, institutions and government and re-lend to those undertaking community development real estate or business projects. Loan Funds are organized as nonprofit 501(c)3 organizations and are regulated by the laws governing these types of organizations, as well as state securities law where applicable. Borrowers are typically nonprofit service organizations, small businesses, nonprofit housing developers for-profit developers of affordable housing or public housing authorities. Funding generally is raised from individuals, foundations, banks, socially motivated investors and the government.

Community Development Credit Unions provide financial services, such as savings accounts and personal loans, to communities that are often underserved by traditional banking services. They are regulated by the federal and state government and are nonprofit cooperative institutions. Capital comes from member deposits and some non-member deposits from social investors and the government.

Community Development Venture Capital Funds provide equity and debt with equity features to stimulate job creation and advance entrepreneurial efforts that benefit low-income people and communities. They can be for-profit or nonprofit entities and typically have community representation on their boards. Funding can come from foundations, corporations, individuals or the government.

Microenterprise Development Loan Funds aim to support business development with loans and technical assistance. They are nonprofit organizations and often have a peer-lending model where members lend to each other. They are regulated under the IRS 501(c)3 regulations. Loans are typically very small and funding typically comes from foundations and/or individuals.

Community Development Banks provide capital to invest in the regeneration of lower income communities. They are federally regulated and insured institutions that lend to a variety of borrowers, including nonprofits, individuals and small businesses. Typically their capital comes from deposits or investments from individuals, institutions and sometimes the government. They are typically for profit entities with community representation on their boards.

Community Development Corporation lenders are CDCs that also have a lending function whose purpose is to improve low income communities by supporting redevelopment activity. They are nonprofit organizations run by a volunteer board of directors and regulated by IRS nonprofit regulations. They may lend to consumers, generally to support home ownership or home rehabilitation activities, business owners or other nonprofits. Funding typically comes from banks, foundations, corporations and the government (CDFI Coalition 2015a, b).

To become certified as a federally recognized CDFI, which is a requirement for applying for CDFI funding awards, entities must have a primary mission of promoting community development; provide both financial and educational services; serve and maintain accountability to one or more defined target markets; be a legal, non-governmental entity at the time of application, with the exception of Tribal governmental entities (CDFI Fund 2015).

While there are nearly a thousand certified CDFIs, there are hundreds more who either do not meet the certification criteria, or do not wish to become certified. While some CDFIs are subject to federal oversight, such as banks and credit unions, many are unregulated at the federal level beyond the IRS 501(c)3 requirements. There is no required review system for CDFIs; however, many voluntarily choose to become rated through the CDFI evaluation system known as Aeris (formerly called the CDFI Assessment and Rating System, or CARS).

CDFIs accumulate their capital from many sources, including banks, government, insurance companies, religious institutions, foundations, and individuals. The Community Reinvestment Act (CRA) is one of the main motivators for banks to invest in CDFIs. The federal CDFI Fund, administered by the Department of Treasury, is an important source of capital for certified entities. The funds are awarded on a competitive basis and require a match of non-federal funds.

CDFIs are different than traditional financial institutions in that they are often willing to make loans that the private sector will not. To meet the financial needs of underserved individuals, organizations, and communities, CDFIs must understand the communities that they serve and form relationships with multiple stakeholders. This helps them learn of and understand the credit needs and risks of the area. CDFIs often partner with other organizations to achieve their mission and expand their impact (CDFI Coalition 2015c).

Budgets/Assets. According to the CDFI Fund, as of January 2016 there are 1012 certified CDFIS with total assets of $108 billion (CDFI Fund 2016). The Opportunity Finance Network (OFN) reported in 2014 that its 222 CDFI members reported over $7.6 billion in total financing outstanding and nearly $3.8 billion provided in the form of direct loans and investments (OFN 2014).

Staff Size: The average staff size of all types of CDFIs is 24 people (OFN 2014). CDFIs operate at the local, regional, state and multi-state, and even national level. The budgets of CDFIs vary widely, with annual average revenue at $6 million, and with $17 million in assets (OFN 2012).

Program Mixture: As noted, most CDFIs operate loan funds with 25% of all lending going towards housing organizations and 24% of all individual lending going to housing. Lending for community services comprised 17% of all lending, while 12% went to business lending. Consumer and micro-enterprise lending comprise 9% and 3%, respectively. Some CDFIs are also active in real estate development and housing counseling. Seventy-four percent of all lending goes to benefit low-income individuals and communities (OFN 2014).

Income Levels Served: On average, 73% of members' clients are low income, 48% are people of color, and 48% are female. In addition, CDFIs can also be active in planning, project management, development, advocacy, services, and management (OFN 2014).

HISTORICAL OVERVIEW

From 1971 to 2006, the National Congress for Community Economic Development (NCCED) , the former national trade association of CDCs, conducted a national community development census every few years to capture the accomplishments and growing impact of CDCs, as well as other nonprofit housing and community development organizations. The first community development census was called *Against All Odds*, and it reported community development accomplishments through 1987. The report was issued in 1988, and additional community development census reports were completed in 1991, 1994, 1998, and 2005. The National Alliance of Community Economic Development Associations (NACEDA) continued the community development census project in the aftermath of NCCED's demise, and published one additional census, *Rising Above*, in 2010. No additional census has occurred since 2010.

The findings from these reports capture the growth and impact of community development from an organizational and programmatic perspective for nearly a quarter of a century. The reports were designed to include a wide range of community development organizations, since community development is broader than any one type of organization. For example, the first census used the term "community-based development organizations" (CBDOs) to be more generic than CDCs. The goal of the census has been to capture the breadth of community development organizations and their accomplishments. Consistently, CDCs have been the most frequent respondents to the six community development census surveys. The three census surveys conducted in the 1990s included an increased number of regional housing development organizations (RHDOs) and community development financial institutions (CDFIs).

EARLY HISTORY

Community development practice emerged out of the political, social, and economic ferment at the national and local levels in the 1960s, notably the Civil Rights Movement, which increasingly focused on economic injustices due to the intended and unintended consequences of federal and local policies, as well as explicit and implicit racism.

Community-based development was a response to underlying structural policies and economic forces that had negatively impacted low-income communities, mostly communities of color. Distressed urban neighborhoods and isolated rural communities had been disinvested and lacked economic and political resources, and were often highly segregated by race. Federal policies including Federal Housing Authority (FHA) made it virtually impossible for people of color to receive home mortgage loans. Housing segregation was alive and well in the USA throughout this decade (Pietila 2010).

Furthermore, federal transportation policies, notably the Interstate Transportation Act, financed highways that cut through and tore up inner-city neighborhoods and encouraged suburban development and sprawl in the 1950s and 1960s. Many rural areas saw a lack of investment in education and basic infrastructure, leading to an out-migration of talented youth. Financial institutions declined to invest in certain neighborhoods, a practice referred to as "redlining." And, local government policies, from zoning decisions to funding practices, also contributed to the negative impact on disinvested communities (Bhatt and Dubb 2015).

Michael Harrington's book, *The Other America* (1962), described the effects of poverty on the American population. The civil unrest in the 1960s caused by racial injustice illuminated the disparate conditions in

America. Policy makers and other leaders could no longer ignore the impact of poverty in the USA. The Kennedy Administration started supporting poverty alleviation strategies through the Appalachian Regional Commission (ARC), and the Economic Development Administration (EDA). Both of these initiatives sought to create jobs for economically poor regions and areas of the United States. This was the first time that the federal government funded anti-poverty strategies that were oriented toward improving the economic conditions of low-income communities (Halpern 1995). Today, this approach is referred to as community-based development. The emergence of community-based approaches to redevelopment through federally backed programs offered these communities an opportunity to take control of their own development process. Community development was viewed as a way to plan, develop, and invest in the human, physical, and economic potential of the community.

The growing Civil Rights Movement had an even greater impact on what became community development than federal policy as it mobilized local leadership, especially from the faith-based community. This community activism spawned community-based organizations just as the government was launching the War on Poverty (Parachini 1980).

President Lyndon Johnson called for a War on Poverty in 1964. This led to the formation of the Office of Economic Opportunity (OEO), which was created to implement President Johnson's goal of eliminating poverty. The following year, Community Action Agencies (CAAs), nonprofit organizations with community-based leadership, became the primary vehicle for OEO to conduct the War on Poverty. These agencies were to be controlled by the people living in low-income communities, which was a new, untested structure for delivering services. Mayors and other local community leaders became threatened over the potential power of CAAs, due to their ability to direct and fund changes in urban communities. Local officials were able to convince members of Congress to introduce and pass several legislative amendments, known as the Green amendments (Parachini 1980). These amendments required that one third of CAA board of directors be composed of local elected and administrative officials. As a result of the Green amendments, CAAs were subsequently weakened politically, and subsequently have focused on social service delivery and early childhood development through Head Start for the past 50 years.

In addition to supporting to CAAs, numerous other federal government programs were created in the 1960s. Historian Robert Halpern referred to the 1960s as the era of overwhelmed initiatives for neighborhoods

(Halpern 1995). His point was that numerous programs and policies were being developed that had neither the capacity nor the resources to make significant progress during the War on Poverty. There was a major difference between promise and performance during this time period. It was in this aggressive, but unfocused environment that set the stage for CDCs.

Several senior OEO officials and two prominent US Senators from New York, Jacob Javits and Robert Kennedy, recognized that a major void existed in the War on Poverty: The campaign lacked an economic development strategy and there was a dearth of programs. Senators Javits and Kennedy met with community leaders and professionals in the Bedford Stuyvesant neighborhood of Brooklyn, an overwhelmingly African-American community, and helped them launch an organization that became the prototype of what is now called a community development corporation (CDC). Bedford Stuyvesant Restoration Corporation (BSRC) developed affordable housing, started a job-training program, and convinced IBM to locate a major plant in its neighborhood that would employ over 400 individuals (Halpern 1995). Senators Javits and Kennedy introduced an amendment to the Economic Opportunity Act (EOA) in 1966 to establish a community economic development program at OEO, which was referred to as The Title VII or Special Impact Program (SIP). In 1968, SIP made two initial grants to Bedford Stuyvesant Restoration Corporation (BSRC), and Hough Area Development Corporation (HADC) in Cleveland. By 1971, OEO made 37 grants to urban and rural CDCs throughout the USA (Blaustein and Faux 1973).

GROWTH AND EVOLUTION OF CDCs IN THE 1960s AND 1970s

As discussed earlier, it is important to recognize that the Federal Government did not create CDCs in the mid-to-late 1960s. Rather, OEO funded local organizations that were in the process of becoming CDCs. Many of these organizations sprang from the ashes of destruction and the growing civil rights movement. In his book *Communities on the Rise*, Stewart Perry, one of the initial OEO senior staff supporting and funding CDCs, stated: "Like many other inventions, even in science and technology, the CDC movement was not invented just once but more or less simultaneously in a number of different black ghettos in America, where desperate need, combined with ingenuity, opportunity, and talent, brought forth the new institution. This innovation—distinct from others that were appearing in this time of social foment and social creativity—appeared to bring together all elements of the black inner-city, even attracting blacks who had migrated to the middle class in the suburbs" (Perry 1987).

CDCs were clearly organic in formation, as demonstrated by a study of 128 CDCs in the early 1990s (Vidal 1992). The study found that over 90% of CDCs operating at that time were started by individuals and small groups. Additionally, over 50% of the 128 urban CDCs in that study had roots in other community-based activities, and more than one third of the CDCs founded before 1975 received momentum from community uprisings (Vidal 1992). During the late 1960s, CDCs were supported by their communities, OEO, and the Ford Foundation.

OEO and its successor agency, the Community Services Administration, funded between 40 and 50 CDCs on an annual basis throughout the 1970s, with most of the CDCs receiving multi-year funding. The Title VII CDCs received significant operational and project based funding, enabling them to pursue a more comprehensive approach to community development including job creation, business development, housing, job training, and human services. The first-generation CDCs were characterized by the breadth of programs and initiatives they pursued due in part to accessing large federal funds (Zdenek 1990). Additionally, CDCs were originally conceived as organizations that would have the capacity to plan, develop, respond, and initiate varied community development strategies (Shiffman and Motley 1990). The Title VII program required that CDCs develop an overall economic development plan (OEDP) for their target community (Parachini 1980). The US Economic Development Administration (EDA) also required their grantees to complete OEDPs.

The Title VII program had a strong focus on economic development with a strategy of starting and managing businesses. Early CDCs ran into trouble when they attempted to start community-owned businesses, as they had limited management experience and had not assessed the market potential (Zdenek 1987). Many of these businesses failed. CDCs were then encouraged by OEO leadership during the Nixon and Ford Administrations to invest in other businesses with entrepreneurs who had management and product expertise, as well as develop major real estate projects (housing, commercial, and industrial). With such partnerships, CDCs started to achieve more long-term successes through business investments, housing, and commercial real estate projects.

Other federal agencies and programs were also providing direct funding to CDCs in the late 1970s including the Department of Housing and

Urban Development (HUD), the Department of Agriculture Rural Development Loan Fund, and Sect. 111 planning grants. One of the challenges with many of the federal programs that supported CDCs is that over time, government funding became more categorical and narrow, making it difficult for CDCs to be comprehensive which drove a shift toward housing (Mayer 1984).

There were some exceptions to this trend. In the late 1970s, the Carter Administration encouraged neighborhood-based community development work through the creation of a neighborhood office at HUD, and a National Commission of Neighborhoods (Mayer 1984). The neighborhood office at HUD, with the support from CDCs and community activists, persuaded Congress to approve the Neighborhood Self-Help Development Program. This program funded over 100 CDC-type organizations in 1980.

More and more of the CDCs launched during this period were able to take advantage of a receptive federal funding climate, albeit one that turned out to be short lived (National Commission on Neighborhoods 1979). The exact number of CDCs is hard to determine during the 1970s since there was no CDC census until 1987. Estimates are that in the late 1970s between 250 and 500 CDCs. With the exception of EDA funding, all the direct federal funding programs in the late 1970s were eliminated during the first year of the Reagan Administration in 1981 (National Center for Economic Alternatives 1981). The Title VII program was replaced indirectly with the HHS Office of Community Services (OCS) Urban and Rural Community Economic Development Fund, a competitive fund for community economic development projects that still exists to this day.

One of the major reasons that CDCs were able to access private financing for their real estate and business development projects was the passage of the Community Reinvestment Act (CRA) in 1977, which required that financial depository institutions that take deposits from a specific geographic area reinvest a portion of those funds in the community. There was a long and troubled history of how both the Federal Government and financial institutions redlined low-income communities, mostly communities of color (Bhatt and Dubb 2015). This started with the Federal Housing Administration (FHA) in 1934 providing federally insured guarantees for home mortgages, increasing the access to homeownership. FHA used a rating system and neighborhoods that were predominately Black received a low rating score thus making them ineligible for FHA guaranteed financing (Bhatt and Dubb 2015). While Federally sponsored redlining ended with the passage of the Fair Housing Act in 1968, financial institutions continued to redline until the Home Mortgage Disclosure Act (HMDA) and CRA passed in the late 1970s.

CRA gave community groups the ability to challenge mergers and acquisitions of financial institutions where the financial institutions did not meet the credit needs of the community. This authority became an important lever in getting banks to support community development. The National Community Reinvestment Coalition, a coalition of community-based organizations focusing on reinvestment formed in 1990, reported that from 1977 to 1991 financial lenders and community organizations negotiated $8.8 billion in CRA credit agreements. The dollar amount of CRA agreements from 1992 to 2007 grew exponentially to $4.5 trillion in potential loans, creating an enormous community development financing market (National Community Reinvestment Coalition 2007Community Reinvestment Coalition 2007).

CDCs Expand in the 1980s

The policy environment for CDCs shifted dramatically from the federal government to state and local government with the election of Ronald Reagan in November 1980. The Reagan Administration succeeded in eliminating or vastly reducing most community development and human service programs where CDCs had received financial support including the Title VII CDC program in 1981. The National Congress for Community Economic Development (NCCED), the CDC trade association, and other community development organizations persuaded Congress to preserve an economic development program at the US Department of Health and Human Services (HHS) as part of the Community Services Block Grant (CSBG), which is still in existence (Zdenek 1990)

An interesting irony is that while there was a reduction of direct federal funding to CDCs in the 1980s, the CDC support system came of age during this time. Many financial and technical resources from philanthropic and bank sources became available to support a growing number of CDCs that were focused primarily on affordable housing production. Two large national community development intermediaries were created in the early 1980s—the Local Initiative Support Corporation (LISC) and the Enterprise Foundation, now called Enterprise Community Partners. At the same time, the federally chartered Neighborhood Reinvestment

Corporation, now called NeighborWorks America, expanded. Together, these organizations provided an array of tools from core operating support and capacity building grants to pre-development and project financing. These large national intermediaries and a number of local specialized community development intermediaries were able to assemble significant private capital and other resources to support local community development initiatives (Pierce and Steinbach 1987). This private sector support was leveraged with public dollars, notably Community Development Block Grant (CDBG) funds that were deployed in a flexible fashion at the local level.

CDCs were well positioned to take advantage of public–private partnerships, an approach that became standard practice and one of the buzzwords throughout the 1980s and beyond. CDCs were well positioned when the Low-Income Housing Tax Credit (LIHTC) passed in 1986 as the major financing program for the production of affordable rental housing. Tax policy, and not federal housing programs, was the primary tool used to encourage community development during the Reagan administration (Pierce and Steinbach 1987). Private investors were looking to partner with CDOs to build and manage housing projects for low-income individuals and families utilizing the LIHTC program. This program had a minimum 15% set aside for nonprofit developers, and in the early days, most of the nonprofit developers were CDCs.

The George H.W. Bush administration in the late 1980s and early 1990s did not depart significantly from the Reagan administration's approach, which limited support of affordable housing and community development. However, the Bush administration did recognize the need for some federal role in housing and family support. With bipartisan support, Congress in 1990 established the Home Investment Partnership program and HOPE (Home Ownership for People Everywhere).

The HOME Investment Partnerships Program (HOME) became a major source of federal funding for affordable housing during this period. It became operational in the early 1990s and provided block grant funding to localities and states for housing production. The HOME statute requires that at least 15% of funds be set aside for nonprofit housing developers that meet certain structural requirements and are officially certified as Community Housing Development Organizations (CHDOs). HOME funds can be used for both rental and homeownership housing production (Zdenek 1993).

Another important development in the 1980s was the growth of CDC associations and networks, as nonprofit organizations turned to state and local government for resources and favorable policies. With a few exceptions, state government policies prior to 1980 were not devoted to housing and economic development. The 1980s saw some fundamental changes in the role of state government. State governments became more activist in nature, and this was reflected in the policies, programs, and growth of state agencies and staff (Osborne 1988). The Reagan Administration's goal of devolution of federal resources to the state and local level, coupled with a major economic recession in the early 1980s, provided the impetus for state governments to play a more active role in housing and economic development. Job creation and economic development became priorities during the 1980s. The new economic development strategy at the state level focused on small business development, enhancing the entrepreneurial climate of the state, and supporting community-based development efforts (Osborne 1988). Housing also became a priority in most states as a result of federal housing cutbacks, a growing shortage of affordable housing, and increased capacity of state agencies, notably state housing finance agencies (Osborne 1988).

A number of state community development associations emerged in the 1980s to take advantage of the more open community development and economic development climate at the state level. State CDC associations grew from three in 1982 to over 20 associations by 1996 (Kelly 1997). These associations helped craft several dozen state programs that fund CDCs and other community development organizations (Mt. Auburn Associates 1993).

NCCED experienced significant membership growth throughout the 1980s and provided policy and technical support to a growing community development field. NCCED also took the lead in helping to organize state CDC associations and networks through providing direct funding and technical support to their members (Kelly 1997). These state associations played a significant role in developing policies, programs, resources, and technical assistance to support the emerging CDC industry in the 1980s with a major focus on small and fledgling CDCs.

Significant progress for CDCs was also achieved at the local level, with many community development partnerships emerging in the 1980s, notably in large urban communities (Vidal 1992: 106). Community development intermediaries played a major role in the partnerships. Local governments started forming partnerships with private sector funders to provide operational and project support to CDCs. Community Development Block Grant (CDBG) funds were the primary source of funding used by cities to support 55% of CDCs (NCCED 1995) . Initial city support of CDC activities was targeted toward housing production, but later expanded to include economic development and comprehensive community development programs (Urban Institute and Weinheimer Associates 1996).

COMMUNITY DEVELOPMENT ORGANIZATIONS GROWTH AND EXPANSION

The first CDC census in 1987 was led by NCCED with financial support and active involvement of national community development intermediaries and other prominent private funders. The community development census found that there were between 1,500 and 2,000 CDCs. The CDCs in the census had developed over 125,000 units of housing with 90% targeted to low-income occupants; developed over 16.4 million square feet of retail, commercial, and industrial space; made loans to 2,048 enterprises, 218 equity investments; and owned and operated 427 businesses. The cumulative job creation credited to CDCs back in 1987 was over 90,000 jobs. CDCs had clearly emerged as a significant presence in several thousand low-income communities throughout the USA, and were seen as a significant force for community revitalization. There was a well-developed CDC production system in many of the major urban centers.

As noted, many community development funders shifted from a comprehensive approach to a more narrowly focused strategy geared toward affordable housing production in the late 1980s and 1990s. This shift happened after federal housing funding dropped in the 1980s, resulting in a growing crisis of affordable housing for low- and moderate-income populations living in urban and rural communities throughout the USA.

The problem of homelessness grew significantly during this period, resulting in federal legislation to address the crisis—the McKinney-Vento Homeless Act of 1987. This Act authorized several programs to address homelessness. The move to affordable housing production was also driven and supported, in part, by the emergence of a large community development intermediaries (LISC, Enterprise and NeighborWorks America) , and a funding system that focused on affordable housing production, notably rental housing production. These organizations supported the dramatic increase in housing production.

1990s INCREASED INFLUENCE AND IMPACT

More and more, community development was being seen as a viable strategy for improving communities throughout the USA by policy makers and funders. For example, CDCs were seen as critical actors in the dramatic resurgence of the South Bronx. Where previously Presidents Carter and Reagan had stood next to rubble, these neighborhoods now had new single-family homes and attractive multi-family dwellings. CDCs and their support system were seen as part of the solution and fabric of the community (Grogan and Proscio 2000).

By the early 1990s, community development organizations continued to proliferate and grow, and the second national community development census/census conducted by NCCED in 1991 found that there were over 2000 organizations. Housing production had increased from 125,000 to 320,000 units of housing in a relatively short period of 4 years.

NCCED sponsored two more community development census surveys—Undertaken in 1994 and 1998, and both censuses showed an explosive growth on the part of community development organizations. From 1991 to 1994, community development groups produced an average of 27,000 units per year. Their housing production capacity jumped to 62,000 units per year between 1994 and 1998.

The 1998 census showed that there were 3600 groups that cumulatively developed 650,000 units of affordable housing; built and renovated over 65 million square feet of commercial and industrial space; and created and retained over 247,000 jobs in low- and moderate-income communities. These numbers clearly demonstrate that community development organizations had become an institutionalized presence within thousands of low-income communities. It is important to note that the census captured a wide range of organizations from small neighborhood-based CDCs with populations of less than 5000 to RHDOs and CDFIs serving low-income constituents in several states. Production numbers continued to grow to an average yearly production of 86,000 units in the years between 1998 and 2005.

As organizations continued to increase their production (housing, commercial, and enterprise development) in the 1990s, they needed to operate in a more business-like manner. The focus of many organizations expanded from community vision and advocacy to management systems, financial sustainability and accountability, and asset preservation. Executives had to learn to manage as well as how to lead. Efficiency and effectiveness became as important as vision and mission.

The community development support system continued to expand significantly in the 1980s and 1990s. A number of national foundations and corporations under the leadership of Peter Goldmark, who was then President of the Rockefeller Foundation, came together in the late 1980s to create the National Community Development Initiative (NCDI), to raise funds from foundations and financial institutions to provide significant operational and project financing support to community development organizations in 23 major urban centers. NCDI was administered by two intermediaries (LISC and the Enterprise Foundation), with certain cities and their community development groups receiving support from LISC, and others from Enterprise. The NCDI, which was renamed Living Cities, had a central role in raising and distributing funding for community development that lasted well into the first decade of the 2000s (Walker and Weinheimer 1998). A few years later, under new leadership, it moved away from its historical role as a major supporter of community development organizations and ended its funding relationship with LISC and Enterprise.

Building upon the CDC track record of physical revitalization of low-income communities in the 1980s, funders started focusing on comprehensive community initiatives with mixed success. The Surdna Foundation established the Comprehensive Community Revitalization Program (CCRP) in 1991 in the South Bronx to support the comprehensive development of CDCs. CCRP funded strong CDCs and encouraged the CDCs to find community partners with specialized expertise in health, early childhood, workforce development, and other related fields. There were notable successes including the creation of five new family health practice clinics in the South Bronx (Miller et al. 2006).

Other major private funders launched their versions of comprehensive community initiatives. The Ford Foundation started the Neighborhood and Family Initiative in Detroit, Milwaukee, Memphis, and Hartford to encourage collaborations. The Annie E. Casey Foundation developed its own comprehensive initiative, the Rebuilding Communities Initiative (RCI), by funding existing community organizations in Denver, Detroit, Philadelphia, Washington D.C., and Boston to lead campaigns for comprehensive renewal and systems change in their neighborhoods (Kubisch 1996). Enterprise Foundation, with support from the City of Baltimore, launched the Neighborhood Transformation Initiative to improve the economic, social, and physical conditions of the impoverished Sandtown-Winchester neighborhood in West Baltimore.

Most comprehensive initiatives were not sustained once the initial funding dried up, with the results that the neighborhoods were not transformed. Foundation funders never planned to provide decade-long funding for these initiatives, and most of these initiatives were unable to expand their funding base or revenue streams.

One of the challenges community development has faced since the 1980s is the difficulty of sustaining long-term comprehensive funding support. While funding for affordable housing has continued to be available through local and federal sources, albeit at declining levels, most disinvested communities also needed job development, workforce training, community infrastructure such as parks and transit, better public schools, and better health care. Each of these is the responsibility of different government agencies which don't necessarily coordinate their efforts and are working within the context of larger macro-economic trends that are difficult to address at the local level (Harvey 2016).

While CDCs continued to grow significantly in the 1990s, this period was also fertile for other types of community development organizations, such as community development finance organizations that got their start nearly a century ago. CDFIs have their roots in self-help credit initiatives, including immigrant guilds, mutual aid societies and African-American sponsored community development credit unions. After the closure of many banks during the Great Depression in the 1930s, the European model of credit unions came to the USA and provided access to capital for those underserved by financial services (Philanthropy NW). All of these mechanisms were created to respond to the lack of traditional banking resources for certain populations, often those with low incomes or communities of color (CDFI Coalition).

The election of Bill Clinton in 1992 was a fortuitous development for community development finance organizations. During a campaign stop in Chicago at South Shore Bank, the nation's first community development bank, Clinton pledged to replicate the bank with the establishment of 100 community development banks. Clinton knew the model well, since South Shore Bank had established Southern Bank Development Corporation in Arkansas with the support of the Clintons and other prominent Arkansas leaders. The South Shore Bank had a significant track record that was important in building political support for what became the CDFI legislation.

Early in Clinton's term, a group of organizations representing hundreds of community loan funds (now CDFIs) worked to turn President Clinton's campaign promise into a reality. The coalition included, among others, community loan funds represented by the National Association of Community Development Loan Funds (NACDLF), now Opportunity Finance Network (OFN) ; the community development credit unions, represented by National Federation of Community Development Credit Unions (NFCDCU); and CDCs, represented by Coastal Enterprises, LISC, and NCCED. The coalition prepared a policy paper to promote the work of CDFIs and describe how the government could best support these entities (CDFI Coalition).

In 1993, Clinton proposed legislation to create a new federal agency that would support CDFIs working in underserved, low-income communities. Congress passed the Riegle Community Development and Regulatory Improvement Act, legislation to support CDFIs in 1994. The US Treasury Department continues to administer the various CDFI funding initiatives. The CDFI Fund, through a mixture of grant funds, tax credits, technical assistance, and certification, has provided the environment for dramatically growing the CDFI field.

Regional housing development organizations (RHDOs) also gained prominence as a good model for executing community development in the 1990s when the Ford Foundation began funding housing partnership organizations across the USA. These partnerships were comprised of board members from the public and private sectors, to ensure sufficient local backing and initial capitalization. While these organizations were rooted in their communities, they weren't tied to one or two neighborhoods. Their footprints typically included an entire city or metropolitan area and their focus was on housing production. With Ford's leadership and financial support, many of the housing partnership organizations became leaders in affordable housing production in their communities. In 1992, 37 of these organizations came together to discuss how they could collaborate and learn from each other. They incorporated as the National Association of Housing Partnerships, Inc., which was renamed the Housing Partnership Network in 2000. Today, HPN has 98 members and its mission is to support and partner with its members to develop innovative solutions that will advance the work and impact of the community development sector (HPN 2015).

The 1990s also witnessed a significant growth of community development associations and networks at the national, state, regional, and local level. In the CDC world, part of this growth was attributed to NCCED, which continued to grow significantly in the early and mid-1990s before beginning a steady decline in the late 1990s that resulted in the dissolution of NCCED in 2006. NCCED's membership grew from 400 in the late 1980s to over 600 dues paying members by 1994 and was well represented throughout the USA. Part of this growth was attributed to NCCED's role in expanding the number of state CDC associations. State CDC associations grew from 15 in 1990 to more than 20 by 2000 (Kelly 1997). The state associations helped raise funds and influence policy at the state level to support CDCs. In Oregon, the Association of Oregon Community Development Organizations was responsible for securing a 5-year grant from the NW Area Foundation to support the nascent CDC industry there, and also benefited from the first legislation backing the creation of CDCs throughout the state, spawning the creation of numerous new organizations.

In addition to membership, advocacy, and technical support that NCCED offered state and regional associations, NCCED played an intermediary role through raising dollars from foundations and government to distribute to associations on a competitive basis. Local community development associations were also forming and growing in the 1990s in a number of cities including New York, Washington D.C., Portland, OR, Chicago, Cleveland, Pittsburgh, Philadelphia, and Miami Dade County. Most of the local associations tended to be smaller than the state associations with the notable exceptions of New York City and Chicago.

COMMUNITY DEVELOPMENT IN THE 2000s

The 2005 census *Reaching New Heights* found that 52% of the households assisted by community development organizations had incomes below half of area median income, which is referred to as very low income. Thirty-six percent of the households had incomes between 50 and 80% of median income, and 10% were moderate income or between 80 and 100% of area income, with only 2% above moderate income. Federal programs require strict funding targets, notably the HOME program and Low-Income Housing Tax Credit program, which together provide a significant portion of the financing to affordable rental housing projects.

Community development organizations have become a significant provider of special needs housing for vulnerable families and individuals. The 2005 census found that 36% of urban groups and 21% of rural groups produced housing for people with disabilities; 26% of urban and 22% of rural groups built housing for the elderly; 27% of urban groups and 13% of rural groups developed housing for formerly homeless residents. Both urban and rural organizations produced some housing for people with substance abuse issues, HIV/AIDS, and for returning prisoners.

The 2010 community development census, *Rising Above,* found that the average housing production per year between 2005 and 2007 was 96,000 units per year. The cautionary note to these numbers is that these production levels occurred just before the Great Recession, and in the years immediately following the recession, affordable housing production plummeted due to tight credit and reluctance of many financial institutions to lend to affordable housing production. The *Rising Above* census also found that community development organizations were fairly experienced, with 65% of the census respondents developing housing for 10 years or more, while only 3% of the respondents were engaging in their first ever development project.

Affordable rental housing has been the primary affordable housing production strategy for CDCs and RHDOs and that trend continues to grow. Sixty-eight percent of all affordable housing production in the 2005 census was for rental housing, and that figure climbed to 78% in the 2010 census due in part to market conditions.

The income level figures in the 2010 *Rising Above* census were consistent with the previous ones showing that half of those served by community development organizations had incomes below half of area median income; 35% were between 50 and 80% of area median income; 12% were from 80 to 115% of area median income; and 3% were above 115% of area median income. This shift to serving slightly higher-income populations reflects, in part, the reduction of subsidies and the production of mixed-income housing developments. Additionally, some organizations elected to broaden their customer base as a strategy to develop more sustainable revenue sources.

Rising Above documented that 37% of community development organizations provided housing opportunities for people with mental and physical disabilities; 28% were engaged in senior housing; 10% in housing for people with substance abuse, and 5% for people living with HIV/AIDS. Twenty-six percent of community development organizations were also involved in permanent supportive housing and an additional 18% were involved with transitional shelter and 7% with emergency shelter. *Rising*

Above did not distinguish between urban and rural organizations in terms of special need housing.

The *Rising Above* census was conducted during the height of the foreclosure crisis, providing the census administrators the opportunity to capture data and analysis on the work of community development organizations in responding to growing crisis in their local communities. Organizations reported that foreclosure rates were low for their own units, but leaders recognized that foreclosure crisis would affect their entire target markets, negatively impacting the value of housing in their communities. A large number of community development organizations started to offer foreclosure mitigation activities, including financial literacy (36%); homeownership maintenance (31%); foreclosure prevention/intervention (27%); credit counseling (26%); predatory lending education (22%); and loss mitigation (13%). The census respondents reported that all these programs and services reached 2.3 million participants in 1 year with the caveat that some of the people received more than one service. The important point is that many organizations responded to the foreclosure crisis before large federal funding sources, such as the Troubled Assets Recovery Program (TARP), became available in late 2008.

The Obama Administration established two major housing programs under TARP to strengthen the housing market and help struggling homeowners avoid foreclosure. The two programs were Making Homes Affordable and the Hardest Hit Fund. Community development organizations accessed those funds until the housing market began to strengthen a few years later.

Given their close connection to the communities they serve, nonprofit community development organizations have historically shown an ability to respond to opportunities or challenges, whether it be special needs housing, green and healthy housing design or foreclosure prevention and mitigation.

COMMERCIAL, RETAIL, AND INDUSTRIAL DEVELOPMENT

Community development organizations have also become important developers of commercial, office, industrial, and community facility space in their communities. The trend toward commercial real estate development has grown significantly since the mid-1990. The 1994 census reported that only 18% of those surveyed had developed commercial, industrial, retail, and community facilities. These percentages jumped to 31% in the 1998 census, and 45% by 2005.

The total square footage of commercial and types of real estate was 64.7 million in 1998 and 126 million by 2005. The *Rising Above* census found an additional 21.2 million square footage of commercial and industrial development space completed between 2005 and 2007. The *Reaching New Heights* census (2005) found that community facility space more than tripled between 1998 and 2005, from 11 million square feet to 37.6 million square feet by 2005. Community development organizations have become involved in constructing day care centers, health-care centers, youth centers, arts programs, and facilities for other social service providers. The Affordable Care Act may lead to some additional community facility opportunities in the health-care field.

BUSINESS DEVELOPMENT, LENDING, AND JOB CREATION

Community development organizations, especially CDCs and CDFIs, have a long history of business development activities including equity investments, lending, and technical assistance to small businesses.

Similar to affordable housing production and commercial projects, community development groups increased their activity in business development in the 1990s. The 1998 census, *Coming of Age*, found that organizations had cumulatively made an estimated $1.9 billion in loans to 59,000 private businesses as of December 31, 1997, with an average size of $32,000. The 1998 census identified 1,144 community development groups that were providing marketing assistance, entrepreneur training, accounting help, and other business services. The net result of the business development and commercial real estate activity was that 247,000 jobs were created as of 1998.

The 2005 census, *Reaching New Heights*, also saw a continued growth in business development activities with over a third of the respondents involved in business development. The business development activity varied and included developing businesses (39%); providing technical assistance (70%); organizing a manufacturing association (30%); and providing entrepreneurial training (52%). When coupled with commercial and industrial development activity, census respondents reported creating 774,000 jobs as of 2005, a dramatic increase.

The 2008 census, *Rising Above*, also found that more than one third of the organizations were involved in business development activities. The census reported on community lending activities and found that groups made 511,000 loans between 2005 and 2007, 115,000 loans for home purchase totaling over $6.6 billion, and 73,000 loans for housing development.

COMPREHENSIVE DEVELOPMENT AND COMMUNITY BUILDING ACTIVITIES

Community development organizations are often engaged in a wide range of community building activities. Some of the common community building activities provided by CDCs either directly or through partnerships with other service agencies include: community organizing, youth programs, job training; community safety, senior programs, arts and culture, individual development accounts (IDAs), homeless services, emergency food assistance; and tenant counseling. These activities can be hard to fund, since much of the public and philanthropic community development money is focused on housing production, commercial revitalization, and enterprise development.

Community development organizations show a tremendous breadth of activities beyond the traditional major initiatives of housing, commercial and industrial development, and enterprise development. Over half of the organizations in the most recent census indicate that they are involved in community organizing and advocacy activities. Most of this work is carried out at a very small scale.

COMMUNITY DEVELOPMENT DIVERSIFIES

The previous decade saw some major changes in terms of the growing influence and impact of CDFIs and RHDOs with CDCs. Although not well documented, it is assumed that the ranks of CDCs thinned significantly in the last several years (Von Hoffman 2013). The voice of the CDC organizations became more diffuse in the early 2000s due in part to the decline and dissolution of NCCED and loss of operating funds, and the resulting dispersion of CDCs into specialized, ethnic-focused associations, such as National Association of Latino Community Asset Builders (NALCAB) and the National Coalition of Asian Pacific American Community Development (National CAPACD). The increasingly diverse and fragmented CDC field has also exhibited a lack of consensus and consistent direction within the constantly evolving community development ecosystem. There are a growing number of voices for community development corporations, and it has been a challenge coordinating these voices on policy at the national level (Zdenek and Walsh 2000). While there are some national convenings that are bringing many of these national organizations together, they are too few and far between to have substantive impact on the field.

At the same time that the CDC voices have become less unified, other community development organizations have strengthened their national voice and influence. The CDFIs have a strong national association, the Opportunity Finance Network (OFN) and the CDFI Coalition; as do the community development credit unions with the National Federation of Community Development Credit Unions (NFCDCUs) . The Housing Partnership Network (HPN) has an active policy office in Washington DC that advocates for policy and administrative changes that improve community development programs and legislation. Community development intermediaries, such as LISC and Enterprise Community Partners, and organizations such as the National Housing Conference, National Low Income Housing Coalition, and the National Community Reinvestment Coalition, also have policy staff who advocate for the housing and community development field, but not always with the same positions or priorities.

Through the first decade of the 2000s, the community development field continued to expand. The most recent community development census sponsored by the National Alliance of Community Economic Development Associations (NACEDA) , *Rising Above*, which utilized 2010 community development census data, found that there were over 4,500 community development organizations. Community Development organizations had cumulatively developed 1,614,000 units of affordable housing, and had built over 21.2 million of commercial, retail, office, industrial, and community facility space.

The federal funding environment in the 2000s tightened, especially with major HUD funded programs, notably CDBG and HOME (NACEDA 2010). It is too early to tell but the CDC field may have plateaued in the number of CDCs, or organizations that self-define themselves as CDCs. This may be caused in part by the fact that CDCs have had limited outreach and impact in suburban communities, the area with the fastest growing overall population, and biggest percentage increase in the amount of poverty (Erickson et al. 2012).

At the same time that public sector resources tightened, the Obama Administration began to place a greater emphasis on cross-sectoral initiatives beginning in 2008. The Obama administration spurred the growth of a series of crosscutting federal initiatives that required a diverse range of community-based institutions and expertise. Examples include: Promise Communities, Choice Neighborhoods, Social Innovation Fund, Sustainable Communities, and Transportation TIGER Grants. Some of these initiatives connect housing, education, and transportation, while others link youth, education, and economic development. This shift moves away from the categorical, silo approach to a more collaborative approach that connects different sectors and institutions to build synergy and stronger outcomes. The Strive Network K to 12 education initiative, modeled on collective impact, example points to the opportunity and success in developing systems that work across initiatives improving outcomes for intended beneficiaries, in this case, students who attend low-performing school districts. Private funders are also emphasizing cross-sectoral initiatives with Living Cities' Integration Initiative as a prime example where community development is connecting transportation, economic development, and public health with organizations working to improve access to healthy food.

One of the major trends in community development over the past 15 years has been the notion of connecting "people to place" and focusing on both the individual and human capacity of the individual as well as the place they reside. Asset building emerged as a major new strategy for community development in the past 20 years, spurred by the work of Michael Sherraden at Washington University in St. Louis who wrote a book, *Assets and the Poor: A New American Welfare Policy*. Sherraden coined the term Individual Development Accounts (IDAs) , which are matched-savings accounts for low-income individuals that can be utilized for post-secondary education, business development or entrepreneurship, and first-time homeownership. IDAs led to an extension of other asset-building strategies including utilizing Earned Income Tax Credits (EITC), and children savings accounts (Sherraden 1991). A number of CDCs, CDFIs, and other community economic development organizations sponsor asset-building programs and often connect asset building to the place-based side of the organization, notably using savings to build a pipeline of future low- and moderate-income homeowners.

Historically, the community development support system was geared more toward the physical revitalization side of community development. However, the work encompasses a wide range of finance and project skills, as well as "high touch" human services and broad engagement with diverse community stakeholders. Professional fields often centralize technical skills (financing, fundraising, data management, information technology, management) and decentralize higher touch services (outreach, case management, and organizing) (La Piana 2000). Workforce development intermediaries and asset building, notably Individual Development Account (IDA) initiatives, involve numerous organizations to effectively deploy centralization and decentralization as a strategy for increasing their effectiveness and impact, involving numerous organizations. Consortiums and networks benefit from focusing on centralized and decentralized services to clearly define roles and responsibilities.

Looking Ahead

The current state of community development is a robust system with an increased variety of actors, some of whom have long histories deeply rooted in the communities they serve. Other organizations are newer to the scene with an agenda that is tied to the specific service that they offer (for example community-based health care). Organizations are beginning to recognize the importance of reaching across traditional silos to partner with each other. This trend will likely continue into the future as the community development sector evolves to meet tomorrow's challenges.

However, the recent changes at the federal level with the election of Donald J. Trump to the presidency puts at risk a number of tools that the community development sector has taken for granted for the past several decades. Trump's intentions to reduce the corporate tax rate has already wreaked havoc on the Low Income Housing Tax Credit program and could affect tax-exempt housing bonds. A lower corporate tax rate will reduce the appetite for tax credits from investors looking to reduce their tax burden. After Trump's election in November of 2016, investors dropped LIHTC pricing by 5–15% in anticipation of the lower tax rate, causing affordable housing projects across the country to face funding gaps (Kimura 2017).

Trump's proposals to weaken banking regulations and fair housing policies could also have bleak consequences for communities. Threats to the Community Reinvestment Act and Affirmatively Furthering Fair Housing rule could mean fewer resources for community development developers and lenders, and fewer opportunities for residents. If the provisions of the Affordable Care Act related to community benefit are weakened, the growing work linking health and housing could be eroded. In addition, domestic programs that provide critical safety nets in the communities served by community development organizations, are at risk of cuts or elimination.

A potential opportunity for the community development sector is Trump's plan to invest heavily in infrastructure. Community development advocates argue that housing is infrastructure and should benefit from these investments. Spending infrastructure dollars in low-income communities could, if targeted properly, have positive benefits in the way of jobs and improved places (Bodaken and Hoffman 2017).

Looking ahead, the times call for diligent advocacy and creative approaches at the local and state level to offset the shifts at the federal level.

REFERENCES

Bhatt, Keane, and Steve Dubb. 2015. *Educate and Empower: Tools for Building Community Wealth*, 57–60. Washington, D.C: The Democracy Collaborative.

Blaustein, Arthur F., and Geoffrey Faux. 1973. *The Star Spangled Hustle: The Nixon Administration and Community Development*, 44. Garden City, NY: Anchor Press/Doubleday.

Bodaken, Michael, and Ellen Lurie Hoffman. 2017. Three Dangers and an Opportunity. *Rooflines: The Shelterforce Blog*. National Housing Institute. http://www.rooflines.org/4770/mobilize_now/. 10 February 2017.

CDFI Coalition. 2015a. What are CDFIs? http://www.cdfi.org/about-cdfis/what-are-cdfis/.

CDFI Coalition. 2015b. CDFI Types. http://www.cdfi.org/about-cdfis/cdfi-types/.

CDFI Coalition. 2015c. What are CDFIs? http://www.cdfi.org/about-cdfis/what-are-cdfis/.

CDFI Fund. 2015. CDFI Certification Factsheet. https://www.cdfifund.gov/Documents/CDFI_CERTIFICATION.

CDFI Fund. 2016. Snap Stat. https://www.cdfifund.gov/Documents/Snap%20Stat%20June%201.%202016.pdf.

Christman, Raymond, Gaynor Asquith, and David Smith. 2009. *Mission Entrepreneurial Entities: Essential Actors in Affordable Housing Delivery*, 10. Affordable Housing Institute.

Erickson, David, Ian Galloway, and Naomi Cytron. 2012. Routinizing the Extraordinary. Investing in What Works for America's Communities. Federal Reserve Bank of San Francisco and Low Income Investment Fund, 382.

Grogan, Paul S., and Tony Proscio. 2000. *Comeback Cities: A Blueprint for Urban Neighborhood Revival*, 15–30. Boulder, Colorado: Westview Press.

Halpern, Robert. 1995. *Rebuilding the Inner City: A History of Initiatives to Address Poverty in the U.S.*, 4–23. New York, NY: Columbia University Press.

Harvey III, Frederick B. (Bart). 2016. Email Message to Author. 11 August 2016.
Housing Partnership Network (HPN). 2015. Member Profile.
Kelly, Kevin S. 1997. *State Association Models for CDCs*, 3. Washington, D.C.:
  National Congress for Community Economic Development.
Kimura, Donna. 2017. *Big Changes Jolt LIHTC Market*. Affordable Housing
  Finance. http://www.housingfinance.com/finance/big-changes-jolt-lihtc-
  market_o. 14 February 2017.
Kubisch, Anne C. 1996. *Comprehensive Community Initiatives: Lessons in
  Neighborhood Transformation*, 8. Montclair, New Jersey: Shelterforce.
La Piana, David. 2000. *The Nonprofit Mergers Workbook: The Leader's Guide to
  Considering Negotiating and Executing a Merger*, 34. St. Paul. Minnesota: W.
  Amherst H. Wilder Foundation.
Mayer, Neil S. 1984. *Neighborhood Organizations and Community Development:
  Making Revitalization Work*, 4. Washington, D.C.: Urban Institute Press.
Miller, Anita, and Tom Burns. 2006. *Going Comprehensive: Anatomy of an
  Initiative that Worked: CCRP in the South Bronx*, 2–13. Philadelphia. PA:
  OMG Center for Collaborative Learning.
Mt. Auburn Associates, and Nancy Nye. 1993. *An Evaluation of the Public Policy
  Initiatives of the National Congress for Community Economic Development*, 3–9.
  Somerville, MA: Mt. Auburn Associates.
National Alliance of Community Economic Development Associations. 2010.
  Rising Above: Community Economic Development in a Changing Landscape.
  Washington DC: NACEDA.
National Commission on Neighborhoods. 1979. *People Building Neighborhoods.
  Final Report to the President and the Congress of the United States*, 9.
  Washington, D.C.: Government Printing Office.
National Community Reinvestment Coalition. 2007. The Community Reinvestment
  Act: Vital for Neighborhoods, the Country, and The Economy, National
  Community Reinvestment Coalition, 4–7, Washington D.C., June 2016.
OFN. 2014. Inside the Membership. http://ofn.org/sites/default/files/
  InsideMembership_FY2014_103015.pdf.
Osborne, David. 1988. *Laboratories of Democracy: A New Breed of Governors
  Creates Models for National Growth*, 158, 244. Boston, MA: Harvard University
  Press.
Parachini, Lawrence F. 1980. *A Political History of the Special Impact Program*, 11.
  Cambridge, MA: Center for Community Economic Development.
Perry, Stewart E. 1987. *Communities on the Way: Rebuilding Local Economies in the
  United States and Canada*, 8. Albany, NY: State University of NY Press.
Pierce, Neil R., and Carol F. Steinbach. 1987. *Corrective Capitalism: The Rise of
  America's CDCs*, 37–42. New York, NY: The Ford Foundation.
Pietila, Antero. 2010. *Not in My Neighborhood: How Bigotry Shaped A Great
  American City*, 3–26. Baltimore, MD: Ivan R. Dee Publisher.

Sherraden, Michael. 1991. *Assets and the Poor: A New American Welfare Policy*, 28. Armonk, New York: M.E. Sharpe.

Shiffman, Ronald, and Susan Motley. 1990. *Comprehensive and Integrative Planning for Community Development*, 271. New York, NY: New School University Community Development Research Center.

Urban Institute, and Weinheimer Associates. 1996. *The Performance of Community Development Systems: A Report on the National Community Development Initiative*, 16–18. Washington, D.C.: Urban Institute.

Vidal, Avis C. 1992. *Rebuilding Communities: A National Study of Urban Community Development Corporations*, 37–39, 106. New York, NY: New School University Community Development Research Center.

Von Hoffman, Alexander. 2013. The Past, Present, and Future of Community Development. http://www.shelterforce.org/article/3332/the_past_present_and_future_of_community_development/2013.

Walker, Christopher, and Mark Weinheimer. 1998. *Community Development in the 1990's*, 19. Washington, D.C.: The Urban Institute.

Zdenek, Robert O. 1987. Community Development Corporations. In *Beyond the Market and the State: New Directions in Community Development*, ed. Severyn T. Bruyn, and James Meehan, 119. Philadelphia, PA: Temple University Press.

Zdenek, Robert O. 1990. *Taking Hold: The Growth and Support of Community Development Corporations*, 7–11. Washington D.C.: National Congress for Community Economic Development.

Zdenek, Robert O. 1993. Investing in Distressed Communities: The Role and Potential of CDCs in Economic Development. *Economic Development Commentary*, 20. Washington, D.C.: National Council for Urban Economic Development.

Zdenek, Bob, and Dee Walsh. 2000. *Coming Together: The Need for a Unified Voice in Community Development*, 22–25. Montclair, New Jersey: Shelterforce.

CHAPTER 4

Understanding the Community Development Ecosystem

ORIGIN OF COMMUNITY DEVELOPMENT

Community development has emerged as an accepted and essential concept in American social policy and practice. Community development is generally defined as an intentional effort to improve the social and economic well-being and sustainability of a specific low- and moderate-income area and/or constituency, and to accomplish that goal through a holistic approach while involving the people who live in the community in the process. Community development is distinguished from other planning processes because it focuses on a unit called a "community," attempts to induce structural and systems change, involves multiple groups and entities, emphasizes participation, and most often focuses on under-invested areas (Cook 1994).

Historically, community development work has been characterized by its adaptiveness to community conditions and needs, especially in low-income communities, many of which are communities of color. The early CDCs in the 1960s and 1970s focused on economic development and comprehensive strategies and the next cohort of CDCs in the 1980s and 1990s shifted their work to stronger focus on affordable housing production and preservation. The community development has never been dogmatic about having a definitive set of principles and theories of practice. Most practitioners used their own sense of the situation to determine their tactics and strategy. Practitioners weren't limited by narrowly defined theories of behavior and social organization to guide their actions; rather,

© The Author(s) 2017
R.O. Zdenek and D. Walsh, *Navigating Community Development*,
DOI 10.1057/978-1-137-47701-9_4

they operated from a place of passion about their communities and a gut sense of what needed to be done (Cook 1994).

The field has continued to evolve over the last two decades, which was described in the previous chapter. While there wasn't a commonly accepted theory of practice for the community development field early on, community development work has been based on an eclectic mix of principles of human behavior with community engagement and economic analysis. For example, community development is participatory and embraces the democratic principle that people have the right to help inform and shape the decisions that affect them and their community. It is also holistic encouraging a multi-sector approach to problem solving and development, acknowledging that economic, social, and political problems and systems are interrelated. The principles of social justice are also critical. As the specific conditions of community development work vary widely and change often, community development practitioners must continually engage in situational theory building and practice, borrowing from a variety of models, theories, and practice (Cook 1994). The best community development leaders are reflective practitioners, in that they act, reflect, and refine their approach to do better. The term "reflective practitioner" was coined by Donald Schon from MIT in his book The Reflective Practitioner.

During the 1970s and 1980s, community development organizations were virtually synonymous with nonprofit community development corporations (CDCs). That is no longer the case. The community development landscape has become increasingly varied with many more types of nonprofit organizations actively engaging in community development work. In addition, a plethora of quasi-governmental organizations and some for-profit development organizations are active in developing affordable housing and other community development infrastructure.

Many mainstream institutions now see the inherent value of revitalized communities and recognize the impact these communities can have on their business's success, as well as their customer and employee base. For example, over the past two decades we have seen some hospitals partner with community development organizations to better address their own missions and business needs. For example, in 2000 an effort to revitalize East Baltimore began. This was an area that in 2000 had a 70% vacancy rate, high infant mortality, high crime, and a poverty rate nearly twice the average of the rest of the city. The anchor institution, Johns Hopkins University, along with the Annie E. Casey Foundation, are the lead investors in a 20 year $1.8 billion mixed-use revitalization project. An impetus for Johns Hopkins was the recognition that the state of the community would impact their ability to recruit staff, faculty, and students. The redevelopment includes new housing and commercial development and the construction of a new school, which is affiliated with Johns Hopkins and an early childhood center, which will serve people living in the community. The redevelopment effort was initially led by a public–private partnership which created a new entity called East Baltimore Development, Inc. (Rienzi 2013). EBDI did much of the initial land acquisition, and is now partnering with community development organizations such as the TRF Development Partners, an affiliate of The Reinvestment Fund, a multi-state CDFI, and Baltimoreans United in Leadership (BUILD) to do some of the development and community organizing work (Sherman 2013). As evident in this example, community development work is best tackled by public–private partnerships and the engagement of diverse stakeholders.

As mentioned in the previous chapter, the Community Reinvestment Act (CRA), which was passed in 1977, required that federally regulated financial institutions invest financial resources in low- and moderate-income communities where they take deposits. Passed in 2010, The Affordable Care Act (ACA) . created a somewhat similar requirement for hospitals that want to maintain their nonprofit status. Nonprofit hospitals are required every 3 years to conduct a community health needs assessment and develop an implementation plan under Section 9007 of ACA. The community health needs assessment encourages hospitals to pursue preventative strategies and partner with community-based institutions to improve health outcomes for patients and residents near the hospital. This requirement provides new or expanded partnership opportunities for community development organizations. The community health needs assessment is relatively new, so it is too early to assess results and impact (Dubb 2013).

As the number of community development organizations expanded throughout the 1980s and 1990s, a network of intermediaries, foundations, and public agencies emerged and began to provide support to these organizations. This community development support system provided valuable financial and technical resources to sector organizations. Funding from these agencies peaked in the early 2000s, and then began to decline as federal public resources diminished. With the exception of short-lived federal funding in response to the foreclosure crisis, capital became harder to access and foundations' interests moved to new philanthropic strategies.

COMMUNITY DEVELOPMENT ECOSYSTEM

Community development theory ordinarily treats communities as systems. Community development work relies on "general systems and on social systems' conceptual frameworks to organize and relate the ideas, intelligence and information uncovered and created in the processes of engagement" (Cook 1994).

Over the last 30 years, the system of public and private players has developed functions much like a biological ecosystem, which is defined as a network of interactions among organisms, and between organisms and their environment. A community development ecosystem is made up of a collection of organizations and institutions that interact with each other and with their environment, while working to improve the livability of a given community. These entities, interacting in a variety of networks, all play a role and their ability to work in sync with each other is essential to their success.

A critical concept within a biological ecosystem is interdependence. Organisms are all interdependent among each other, and within the unique resources and constraints of the local ecosystem. American political and economic culture has an individualistic strain, emphasizing the uniqueness and competitive nature of individuals and organizations that can be viewed in a zero-sum context. The ecosystem model works to maximize the contributions of individual strengths or organization niches to sustain the overall ecosystem. The social system's framework to organize and problem solve is relevant to how community development organizations interact, and speaks to the need for organizations to sharpen their competencies and expertise and seek out complementary organizations to forge alliances and partnerships.

In addition to CDCs, CDFIs, and RHDOs, there are many players in the current community development ecosystem. These include government, financial institutions, philanthropy, and national community development intermediaries, such as Enterprise Community Partners, NeighborWorks America, and the Local Initiative Support Corporation (LISC). Nationally, there are peer networks such as Housing Partnership Network (HPN), Opportunity Finance Network (OFN), National Association of Latino Community Asset Builders (NALCAB), National Alliance of Community Economic Development Associations (NACEDA), and the National Coalition Asian Pacific American Community Development (National CAPACD). There are also city and state CDC trade associations and intermediaries. In some communities, anchor institutions, such as schools, universities, and hospitals, play a role.

Each component of this ecosystem has an impact on the financial health, capacity, and sustainability of the system. When one falters, the others suffer. A case in point is the financial crisis of 2008 and the withdrawal of capital from the system, which resulted in a decline in real estate development and home loans for the next several years. It took years for the system to recover and for capital to be readily available again.

The ecosystem is highly interdependent and benefits from the growth of certain components. For example, the emergence of strong intermediaries and peer network associations in the 1980s and 1990s provided substantial financial and technical support and spurred the nonprofit sector's growth. Research has shown that there is a connection between the state of the ecosystem and the ability of community development organizations to be productive, and intermediaries were a critical component of this system during their heyday in the 1990s (Stoutland 1999; Glickman and Servon 1998).

National and local intermediaries and associations have played an important role in supporting the sector and increasing its effectiveness. For example, NeighborWorks America (NWA), a federally chartered and funded national intermediary and member association, provides financial support for operations and development projects to approximately 245 nonprofit housing organizations across the USA. NWA puts over $60 million directly into the nonprofit sector each year, as well as serves as the leading training organization for the sector. Peer network associations, such as the Housing Partnership Network, have created new business models, such as a member-owned property insurance company, to support its members by giving them more control over the quality and cost of their insurance, which represents a significant business expense, especially for multi-family housing owners. Trade associations, such as the Massachusetts Association of Community Development Corporations (MACDC), have help pass key state legislation to benefit the sector. For example, MACDC advocated for the Community Investment Tax Credit, which provides a 50% tax credit against Commonwealth of Massachusetts tax liability and is designed to support high impact community-led economic development (MACDC 2015). While some of the intermediaries have contracted in size and scope in recent years, they can be credited with providing substantial support to this budding sector during the past three decades. Their support is still very important today and they have grown in sophistication and focus as the sector's needs have become more complex and urgent.

Policy think tanks and academic institutions in a variety of disciplines have also emerged to support the field by advocating for policy that supports nonprofit efforts and creating programs specific to educating a new generation of community development leaders. Researchers have encouraged the community development field to incorporate evidence-based research to determine and evaluate outcomes that build healthy communities (Cytron 2012).

ECOSYSTEM DESIGN

Below is a diagram that shows the key components of the ecosystem, with the residents and businesses of the community at its center, and a brief description of each component's role in this interdependent system (Fig. 4.1).

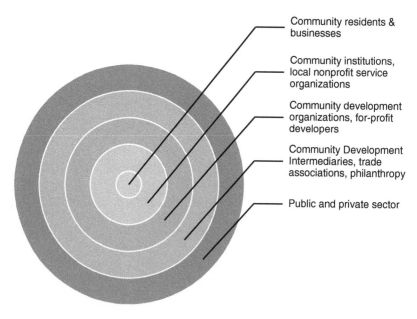

Fig. 4.1 Community development ecosystem

Role of Ecosystem Actors

Community Residents and Business Community: This is the heart and soul of community development work. The very reason the ecosystem exists. The residents identify the important community needs, help determine appropriate solutions, and drive the outcomes and benefits to the local community and the residents.

The businesses that operate in a community are important providers of essential goods and services from healthy food to health care, as well as employment opportunities. The economic vitality of a community is impacted by the financial health and business diversity of the local business community.

Community Institutions (Schools/Universities, Hospitals, Civic Organizations, Churches): Community institutions can be important partners of and leaders in revitalization efforts. Some of these institutions are anchor institutions and drive the economy of the community. Others may have less dominant roles, such as churches, but they still are important community influencers. It is important that communities engage essential institutions as community partners for comprehensive community development. They provide access to important resources and have important community knowledge.

Local Nonprofit Service Organizations: These organizations often offer programs and services that are complementary to those provided by community development groups. Examples include head start centers community action agencies, community health centers, and local area agencies on aging.

Community Development Organizations (CDCs, CDFIs, and RHDOs): These are the engines of community development; the groups on the ground that work with residents and businesses, build networks, create new solutions and ideas, and implement projects to impact communities.

For-profit Development Entities: The most common activity for for-profit real estate development companies is the development of affordable housing financed with the Low Income Housing Tax Credit; however, some for-profit entities have undertaken larger, place-based community development work, most commonly as part of the Hope VI or Choice Neighborhoods programs funded by the US Department of Housing and Urban Development. While they don't typically build for hard-to-house or lowest-income households, well-capitalized for-profits can build at a large scale having a significant impact on communities.

Community Development Intermediaries, Trade Association, and Peer Network Associations: These broader associations provide important technical and financial resources, policy support, and opportunities for learning and advancement at the national, state, regional, and local level.

Philanthropy: Philanthropic organizations such as local and national foundations play an important role in supporting community development work through grants and investments. Philanthropic resources tend to be more flexible than public sector funding streams and historically have provided operating support to community development organizations.

Public Sector (Local, Regional, State and National Government): The public sector plays an important role in facilitating community development through the creation of plans, policies, regulations, and programs. Additionally, the public sector provides financial resources, such as grants and loans, and tax tools such as local property tax exemptions and, at the federal level, the Low-Income Housing Tax Credit and New Markets Tax Credit.

Private Sector (Banks, Corporations, Insurance Companies): This important group provides much of the capital needed to get community development work built and implemented.

Over the past 15 years, the community development environment has been shifting from a CDC-centric approach to a broader array of community development organizations, and more recently a whole set of institutions and organizations in the health, employment, education, food, environmental, and cultural sectors. Community development organizations have also become more hybrid over time, reflecting funding shifts and politics and the needs and priorities of their communities. This has made it more challenging for them to meet their missions and achieve a "quadruple bottom line," which is a term coined to describe the financial demands of developing and maintaining affordable housing while serving resident groups and neighborhoods, in an environmentally responsible manner (Bratt 2012).

The community development realignment is also occurring among funding sources, especially with dwindling public sector resources for community development. The trends and research are clear that public funding of community development is declining, notably the federal Community Development Block Grants (CDBG), and HOME programs. The CDBG program was created in 1974 and represented a consolidation of eight federal programs. The primary objective was to give local governments more flexibility while developing viable urban communities, including decent housing, a suitable living environment, and expanded economic opportunities. However, funds have declined from $5.112 billion in FY 2001 to $3.07 billion in FY 2015, not accounting for inflation (HUD Portal 2016). The HOME Investment Partnerships Program was authorized in the Cranston-Gonzales National Affordable Housing Act of 1990. It was designed as a federal block grant program that provides funds for affordable housing activities that benefit low-income households (Jones 2014). HOME dollars have dropped to $900 million causing some to advocate that the program be combined with CDBG.

The reality of declining funds has led policy makers, public officials, and funders to place greater emphasis on partnerships and collaboration as an essential element of their funding calculus. Funders are going from implicit to explicit encouragement/requirement of partnerships, collaboration, affiliations, and in some cases mergers and acquisitions between organizations. There is a continuum of partnership strategies from memorandum of understandings (MOUs), to joint ventures to acquisitions and mergers. It should be noted that acquisitions are usually between strong and weak organizations, and mergers are among equivalent or complementary organizations (Cramer and Zdenek 2005).

The combination of increasingly diverse organizations and tighter funding creates pressure as well as opportunities for community development organizations to differentiate themselves and focus on their strengths, or core competencies. Community development organizations cannot be all things to all residents, stakeholders, and funders. They need to clearly demonstrate their unique value to their constituencies. This unique value and the special capabilities of the organization, are, by definition, their comparative advantages. By using their competencies to maximize their comparative advantages, community development organizations can better attract the human and financial resources needed to achieve their mission, goals, and outcomes.

This chapter will offer eleven factors/reasons why utilizing comparative advantages to develop effective partnerships can change the community development ecosystem. The factors are divided into external and environmentally driven factors and internally driven factors that pertain to the operation and performance of the organization.

EXTERNAL FACTORS

Factor 1: Increased Complexity

Community development addresses an increasing diversity of challenges, mirroring the trends in the larger society. These challenges and opportunities include addressing persistent social issues such as poverty, health, and education and often require regional solutions that span many political jurisdictions. In the past, community development was viewed as either an urban or rural strategy, but with increased population shifts there has been a noticeable increase in poverty in suburban areas. Community development organizations and practices have expanded to the suburbs, as demonstrated by the last several national community development surveys. The Reaching New Heights survey in 2005 reported that 22% of CDCs nationwide were working in suburban communities. All communities need jobs, affordable decent housing, access to quality education and training, and a physical environment that leads to healthy outcomes for all residents, especially youth and older adults. At its heart, community development connects people and places in a multi-disciplinary way, requiring specialized expertise. As most organizations can't expect to house every specialization required to tackle this tough work, it is necessary to specialize in a few areas and leverage this comparative advantage.

Factor 2: Increased Competition

The growth in both the aggregate number of community development organizations and different types of organizations active in community development, has led to increased competition for resources for programs and projects. There are positive aspects to competition. It can help organizations develop expertise and, if they are successful, a winning track record. The downside is that competition takes time and resources without a guarantee of success. Further, in order to win competitions, some organizations may minimize their true cost of completing a project to appear more competitive and win funding. However, this only leaves them vulnerable to significant financial losses. While many community development programs are funded competitively, heedlessly competing can jeopardize an organization's financial viability.

Thirty years ago, funders had fewer options in finding partners to help them implement their community development plans, but that has changed. The number and types of organizations active in community development has grown. The ability of community development organizations to differentiate through their strengths and advantages will be critical for their continued survival and growth.

Factor 3: Reduction of Public Support to Address Community Development

With the exception of the short-lived boost of federal funds awarded under the American Recovery and Reinvestment Act of 2009 (ARRA) that flowed immediately after the 2008 financial crisis, most community development organizations have seen a steady decline in public sector support in the past decade. A good example is the reductions in federal programs such as CDBG and HOME funds. For example, the HOME program provides that at least 15% of the allocation be set aside for Community Housing Development Organizations known as CHDOs. The definition of a CHDO is a private, nonprofit community-based organization that has the ability to develop affordable housing for the community it serves. Most CDCs fit the CHDO definition and were able to receive HOME funds to support operating expenses and capacity building costs associated with affordable housing development activities. As this money shrank, CDCs felt the pinch (HUD Exchange 2016). The reduction of funds for core operating support has required organizations to become more efficient and focused to remain effective. Some have honed their expertise in a particular area to develop new revenue producing lines of business to support their cost-absorbing work. Developing a comparative advantage that differentiates the organization can help it win new projects or funding, resulting in a new revenue stream for the organization.

Factor 4: Growth of Income and Wealth Inequality and the Spread of Poverty

Today the need is greater, so organizations need to leverage their comparative advantages to do more. The last 30 years have seen a dramatic growth in income and wealth inequality in the USA. While the top 10% experienced significant growth, the remaining 90% of the population experienced flat wages over the past three decades. This growing inequality has had a dramatic impact on the vast majority of citizens, especially those low- and moderate-income families, disproportionately families, and communities of color. According to the Center for Household Financial Stability at the Federal Reserve Bank of St. Louis, median wealth for Hispanics and Blacks is 90% lower than that of Whites (Boshara 2015). What is even more vexing is that the Great Recession wiped out most of the wealth gains since 1989 for Hispanics and African-Americans. Whites and Asians have seen increase in their wealth since 2010, while wealth has continued to decline for Blacks and Hispanics (Boshara 2015).

Median income levels for Hispanics and Blacks are 40% lower, with the implication that these two groups have fewer opportunities to convert their lesser incomes into wealth through homeownership or retirement plans. The data show that the wealth gap is largely unchanged among equally educated, similarly aged whites and nonwhites (Boshara 2015).

Income and wealth inequality also impact educational opportunities. Nearly 80% of students born into the top income quartile between 1979 and 1982 attended college and 54% graduated. Only 29% of students of families in the lowest income quartile attended college, and only 9% graduated. This has a huge impact on communities (Boshara 2015). An even more sobering statistic is that according to Brookings Institution, high school dropouts earned 66% less in 2009 than their counterparts in 1969 (Longman 2015).

Community development has faced a significant worsening of income inequality since the field came of age in the 1970s and 1980s. Poverty was largely concentrated in urban neighborhoods and isolated rural communities, but this has changed. Between 1970 and 2000, the number of people living in high-poverty neighborhoods doubled from 2 million to 4 million and the number of high-poverty neighborhoods, defined as census tracts where over 30% of the households are living below the poverty line, tripled from 1100 to 3100 (Cortright and Mahoudi 2015).

Suburbs have emerged as the fastest growing areas of poverty. In *Confronting Suburban Poverty in America,* authors Kneebone and Berube note that in recent years suburbs have added poor residents more quickly than cities, so that today's suburban communities have more poor than central cities. With more than one third of the total poor population located in suburbs in the USA, the infrastructure to support this population has yet to be built (Kneebone and Berube 2013).

Gentrification is one of the factors at play in the movement of poverty within a metropolitan region. Gentrification can be defined as a lower income area that has experienced redevelopment and reinvestment activity resulting in an increase in rents and home values that causes the actual or impending displacement of residents (Price 2014). According to the 2015 Gentrification in America Report, the pace of gentrification has rapidly escalated since 2000 as compared to the decade of 1990 to 2000. Twenty percent of neighborhoods with lower incomes and home values experienced gentrification between 2000 and 2015, compared to only 9% during the 1990s (Maciag 2015). As neighborhoods become more costly, lower-income residents, especially those who do not own, are often forced to move to lower cost, less amenity-rich areas.

The community development infrastructure is less developed in suburban areas, as demonstrated by the fact that only 10% of community development organizations are located in suburbs compared to 54% in urban areas, as of 2008. Nineteen percent of the total respondents to the 2008 survey reported that they served mixed areas including urban and suburban or suburban and rural areas. There are nonprofit health, social service, and education organizations in the suburbs, but not nearly as many as in the central city and many are not equipped to deal with the demand for help (NACEDA 2010). Suburban nonprofit and services organizations can provide CDCs, CDFIs, and RHDOs an opportunity to partner with organizations that know the local needs, politics, and issues but that could benefit from the expertise offered by the experienced community development entities.

Factor 5: Growth of Multi-sector Issues and Partnerships

Poverty is a multi-dimensional problem and requires the attention of multiple sectors to address it. In most cases, one organization can't do it all and must use their comparative advantages to partner with others. Successful collaborations are generally comprised of organizations with specific, strong competencies. There is a correlation between poor-quality housing, health problems (elevated lead blood levels and asthma triggers from mold and moisture), educational attainment, and economic opportunity. The combination of these problems provides a compelling argument for the integration of housing with health, education, early childhood development, and skill-based training. Effective interventions combine place-based, largely brick and mortar strategies, with people-based services. People and place-based interventions should be viewed as investments. Progress is being made to address these issues through collaborative partnerships. CDCs are starting to partner with Federally Qualified Health Centers; CDFIs are financing early childcare centers whose facilities are built by CDCs; CDFIs have emerged as a major financier of charter schools; and green, universal design building developed by CDCs incorporate health features and safety features for vulnerable populations, notably children under six and older adults. In some low-income communities, over 25% of children entering school have asthma leading to increased absenteeism and falling behind in school (Isles 2014). Social determinants of health have a huge impact on education and economic outcomes for people: Where they live projects the level of health and safety of the residents.

INTERNAL FACTORS

Internal factors are items that impact an organization's operational practices, systems, and performance.

Factor 6: Leadership

Capable, stable leadership is a key for organizations to succeed in today's complex environment, and this includes the senior leadership of the organization as well as the board. Leaders hold the vision for the organization, define the strategy for achieving the mission, and orchestrate their teams to accomplish the work. Successful leaders are competent, responsible, clear communicators and have good interpersonal skills. Translating the vision into actionable items is the chief job of the leader. Effective leadership engages multiple stakeholders both within the organization and outside the organization. The leader serves as a coach and catalyst and builds a culture of shared commitment that helps deepen leadership and develops the next generation of leaders.

Community development organizations need both entrepreneurial leadership and enduring leadership able to forge strategic coalitions (Nanus and Dobbs 1999). Many community development organizations are started by entrepreneurial leaders who often create a strong vision and cultivate supporters to catalyze change. The entrepreneurial leader is in the middle of all decisions, and develops and manages the vast majority of relationships. As the organization evolves, it needs to develop management, systems, and processes. The organization needs to transition from an entrepreneurial style to a more enduring approach, while not losing the entrepreneurial characteristics and vision of the organization. Burt Nanus and Steven Dobbs in their book "Leaders Who Make a Difference"

Chart 4.1   Enduring leadership

From	To
Having a few leaders at the top	Having leaders at every level
Leading by vision	Leading by vision and goal setting
Seeking efficiency	Seeking effectiveness
Leading by allocating scarce resources	Leading by creating strategic alliances
Reacting and adapting to change	Anticipating and creating the future
Being a hierarchical organization	Being a flatter and more collegial organization
Directing and supervising staff and volunteers	Empowering and inspiring teams and internal leaders
Information held by a few decision makers	Information shared widely
The leader as boss	The leader as coach
The leader maintains the culture	The leader as a change agent evolving the culture
The leader develops good administrators	The leader develops future leaders

developed a useful construct of nine key functions enabling an organization to transition from entrepreneurial to enduring organizations. These functions can be adapted to the community development world include (Chart 4.1).

Many of the functions on the enduring organization side lend themselves well to strategic partnerships, but these leadership approaches should not be seen as an either-or (Nanus and Dodd 1999). As community development organization leadership becomes more enduring, the organization tends to place a higher emphasis on partnerships and collaborations with other organizations. By using the team approach and dispersing leadership, organizations can engage more stakeholders.

Factor 7: Specialization

Community development organizations invest significant time and resources in building specialized staff and organizational capacity. Once an organization's expertise is developed and becomes a core competency, it will increase its ability to successfully achieve its goals and can use this advantage to attract resources and opportunities.

Increased diversity and competition requires that organizations have sharpened areas of expertise, referred to as specialization. Specialization has been occurring in real estate development for a number of years, especially with projects that utilize tax code and bond financing. Community development organizations have also moved into new areas of affordable housing from supportive housing to energy-efficient housing. These projects require a team of specialized accountants and lawyers to structure the project and ensure that the project is in compliance with the legislative and administrative statutes.

The comprehensive nature of community development is another reason for organizations developing deep expertise in core work and program areas. In today's environment, myriad activities/projects are beyond the capacity of any one organization to master. Specialization is also a useful strategy as community development practitioners expand to incorporate education, health employment, arts and culture, on top of the traditional real estate and community development programs. Community development organizations can build upon their expertise and offer resources and value to other sectors. Organizations need to find partners who have complementary expertise, skills, and resources.

Factor 8: Business Management Systems for Infrastructure and Operating Systems

The growing specialization in community development requires sophisticated infrastructure systems, technology platforms, and staff knowledge beyond the capacity of many organizations. Today's workplace demands complex business management systems for information technology infrastructure and operational systems that are operated by individuals and organizations with specialized expertise. This is an area where there is great potential for increased collaboration among organizations that have sophisticated systems to provide "back office" operational support to others. Information, technology, and communication systems are often expensive, difficult to manage, and require constant updating and expansion. Organizations have to devote considerable financial resources and staff support, and have to operate in a continuous learning environment. Infrastructure obsolescence is a huge issue for organizations with limited budgets, and this is another reason that shared infrastructure and operation systems can make so much sense. Technology and infrastructure have to be updated on a regular basis, and new systems often cost more than an organization can afford.

By working with organizations with complementary comparative advantages, organizations can increase efficiency and impact without having to increase staff size and often budgets. Organizations can share services including back office administration, HR, IT, property management, insurance, loan servicing, compliance, and contract management. Shared services and infrastructure can lead to creation of efficient, cost-effective systems that support the next generation of community development work.

Factor 9: Effectiveness

Community development work involves a wide range of technical skills coupled with "high touch" human services and engagement with diverse community stakeholders. Certain organizations are better suited to high-level financial skills, while others are better at outreach and direct services. Assembling the right team with the correct array of skills requires careful management and a significant investment of resources over an extended period of time. Teaming up with other organizations can help maximize efficiencies, improve effectiveness and take advantage of each organization's strengths.

There is a growing trend for professional fields to centralize technical skills (financing, fundraising, data management, information technology, management), and decentralize higher touch services (outreach, case management, and organizing). Workforce development intermediaries and asset-building coalitions such as Assets for All in California and MIDAS in Massachusetts are good examples of organizations and partnerships that involve numerous organizations in utilizing centralization and decentralization tools as a strategy for increasing cost effectiveness and program outreach leading to greater effectiveness and outcomes. The lead administrator in an asset-building collaboration often provides management, fundraising, data systems, and program evaluation, and local partners focus on case management and recruiting asset-building participants. East Bay Asian Local Development Corporation (EBALDC), which will be featured later in this book as a case study, has coordinated and managed an IDA initiative for a number of years with other local community partners (EBALDC 2014).

Making a decision to centralize or decentralize certain functions should not be viewed as a simple technical transaction. Organizations need to determine where their comparative advantages lie and work with other complementary organizations to determine both the shared interest and vision, and centralized and decentralized systems, can lead to greater productivity and impact on the part of each organization. Once there is a willingness to proceed, then the next step is often finding an activity or skill that will benefit the participating organizations. Shared services is often the area that potential partnerships start exploring since accounting, information technology, and human resources systems can service multiple organizations. Shared services should also build around the requisite expertise of the participating organizations. Larger organizations tend to have more complex financing and data management systems that have the capacity to be adapted and expanded to smaller organizations.

Factor 10: Impact

Community development organizations are being evaluated increasingly as to the outcomes they are achieving for individuals and communities as well as the impact they have on larger systems. With affordable housing, the quality of the services and supports for enabling residents to maintain their independence can be critical to achieving positive outcomes for the residents. At a large scale, this can have an impact on the health system of the community. The same is true with community facility loan programs that get charter schools and quality day care centers built. The outputs are the student seats or child care slots, the outcomes are the performance of the children, and the impact is a higher functioning education system in a community.

To tackle significant social challenges, solutions require a comprehensive approach with multiple interventions to achieve the desired outputs, outcomes, and impacts.

A good example of a comprehensive approach with multiple interventions is the strategy of aging in community. Aging in community has emerged as an innovative strategy to enable older adults to age in place with housing repairs, safety features, health supports, and financial and transportation accessibility. Civic Works, a community-based nonprofit located in Baltimore, Maryland, has a mission of strengthening low-income communities in Baltimore through education, skills development, and community services. While largely youth focused, Civic Works launched the Cities for All Ages program (CAA) as an aging in place initiative to offer comprehensive services, fall prevention, and home modification program that has served over 1350 low- and moderate-income older adults over 65 in the past 3 years. The older adults are low- and moderate-income homeowners who are at risk of falling because of disability and/or poor home conditions. CAA is a partnership with Johns Hopkins University

(JHU) CAPABLE initiative, which stands for Community Aging in Place —Advancing Better Living for Elders. CAPABLE is staffed out of the JHU School of Nursing and works to support the ability of older adults to safely complete daily tasks by combining home repair with occupational therapy and pain management through daily activity plans. Another major benefit of the joint CAA and CAPABLE initiatives is that it has reduced social isolation for older adults, and increased their engagement in the community. Older adults can play a vital role in maintaining the community and social fabric of a neighborhood (Kali and Zdenek 2016). In this example, each partner in the collaborative is using its competencies and comparative advantage to build a stronger program an increase the impact of the work.

Factor 11: Collaboration

For the past decade there has been a growing movement by funders and policy makers to encourage collaboration among organizations working toward similar goals. Promise Communities, Choice Neighborhoods, US Department of Transportation Tiger grants and the Sustainable Communities program are all federal programs that promote cross-sectoral collaboration. The Collaboration Prize funded by the Lodestar Foundation and Living Cities' Integration Initiative represents philanthropic efforts aimed at the same end. Collaborations can be structured in many ways and all require a common vision that is performance-driven and excellent communication (Walsh and Zdenek 2011). For some organizations, collaboration is a practiced way of doing business. For example, financing and building an affordable housing development involves working with multiple partners over a multi-year period. However, collaborating across sectors, such as working with health care or academic institutions, is a much newer construct for community development organizations and requires new competencies to do well. With more focus on cross-sectoral solutions to community development issues, organizations will need to gain skills in this area to succeed. They will need to apply their comparative advantages to collaborative efforts.

Embracing a Collaborative Approach

The complexity of the community development ecosystem, combined with web of interrelated issues that impact issues of poverty and community livability, makes it essential that community development practitioners utilize their strengths and combine and leverage their resources and capabilities. By understanding the factors that impact their current and future work and embracing a collaborative approach that maximizes their comparative advantages, community development organizations will be able to be more successful in advancing their cause, fulfilling their mission to build and sustain vibrant neighborhoods for low- and moderate-income communities and their residents.

References

Boshara, Ray. 2015. The Future of Building Wealth: Can Financial Capability Overcome Demographic Destiny? In *What It's Worth*, 37–38. San Francisco, CA: Federal Reserve Bank of San Francisco and CFED.

Bratt, Rachel G. 2012. The Quadruple Bottom Line and Nonprofit Housing Organizations in the United States. *Housing Studies* 27 (4): 438–456. doi:10.1080/0267037.2012.677016.

Cook, James. 1994. *Community Development Theory*, 1, 3, 6, 11–15. Columbia, MO: Extension Division, University of Missouri.

Cortright, Joe, and Dillon Mahmoudi. 2014. *Lost in Place: Why the Persistence and Spread of Concentrated Poverty—Not Gentrification—Is Our Biggest Urban Challenge.* Portland, OR: City Observatory.

Cramer, David, and Robert O. Zdenek. 2006. *A Merger of Equals*, 18–21. Montclair, NJ: Shelterforce.

Cytron, Naomi. 2012. Doing the Math: The Challenges and Opportunities of Measuring in Community Development. *Community Investments* 24 (1): 5–9. Federal Reserve Bank of San Francisco.

Dubb, Steve. 2013. Hospitals Building Healthier Communities. In *Rooflines: The Shelterforce Blog*. Montclair, NJ: National Housing Institute, March 5.

East Bay Asian Local Development Corporation. 2014. *Building Healthy Neighborhoods*. Annual Report, Oakland, CA.

Glickman, Norman J., and Lisa J. Servon. 1998. More than Bricks and Sticks: Five Components of CDC Capacity. *Housing Policy Debate (Fannie Mae Foundation)* 9 (3): 500–501.

HUD Exchange. 2016. HOME CHDO. https://www.hudexchange.info/home/topics/chdo.

Isles Annual Report. 2014.

Jones, Katie. 2014. *An Overview of the HOME Investment Partnerships Program*, 1–11. Congressional Research Service, September 11.

Kali, Karen, and Robert Zdenek. 2016. *Staying at Home: The Role of Financial Services in Promoting Aging in Community*, 9–10. San Francisco, CA: Federal Reserve Bank of San Francisco.

Kneebone, Elisabeth, and Alan Berube. 2013. *Confronting Suburban Poverty in America*, 3–10. The Brookings Institution.

Longman, Phillip. 2015. Wealth and Generations. In *What It's Worth*, 237. San Francisco, CA: Federal Reserve Bank of San Francisco and CFED.

Maciag, Mike. 2015. Gentrification in America Report. In *Governing The States and Localities: Governing Data, February 2015.*

Massachusetts Association of Community Development Organizations. 2015. How it Works. https://macdc.org/how-it-works.

Nanus, Burt, and Steven M. Dobbs. 1999. *Leaders Who Make a Difference: Essential Strategies for Meeting the Nonprofit Challenges*, 259. San Francisco, CA: Jossey-Bass Publishers.

National Alliance of Community Economic Development Associations. 2010. *Rising Above: Community Economic Development in a Changing Landscape.* Washington DC: NACEDA.

OFN. 2014. Inside the Membership. http://ofn.org/sites/default/files/InsideMembership_FY2014_103015.pdf.

Price, David. 2014. 7 Policies That Could Prevent Gentrification. In *Rooflines: The Shelterforce Blog*, May 23. http://www.rooflines.org/3731/7_policies_that_could_prevent_gentrification/.

Rienzi, Greg. 2013. The Changing Face of East Baltimore. *Gazette, Johns Hopkins Magazine.*

Sherman, Natalie. 2013. East Baltimore Development Moves to Next Phase. *The Baltimore Sun.*

Stoutland, Sara E. 1999. Levels of The Community Development System: A Framework For Research And Practice. *Urban Anthropology and Studies of Cultural Systems and World Economic Development* 28 (2): 165–191. http://www.jstor.org/stable/40553357.

US Department of Housing and Urban Development. 2016. HUD History, 15 May 2016. http://portal.hud.gov/hudportal/HUD?src=/about/hud_history.

Walsh, Dee, and Robert Zdenek. 2011. *The New Way Forward: Using Collaborations and Partnerships for Greater Efficiency and Impact*, 10–12. San Francisco, CA: Community Development Investment Center, Federal Reserve Bank of San Francisco.

CHAPTER 5

Community Development Core Competencies

INTRODUCTION: WHY COMPETENCIES?

Community development is a complex and long-term process for revitalizing the physical, social, and economic fabric of a community. Community development requires an array of different skills, knowledge, tools, disciplines, and experiences. It can be difficult and costly to have multiple areas of expertise under one roof. Revenue generation is often limited for certain community development initiatives given the low-income constituency community development organizations serve. Affording a large staff and complex internal infrastructure can be challenging for most community development organizations.

The primary community development organizations featured in this book (CDCs, RHDOs, and CDFIs) often have different but complementary competencies. CDCs tend to be strong in community engagement with diverse stakeholders, planning, and project development. RHDOs have built strong organizational systems and processes, project management, and asset management competencies but because they serve broad geographies may not have the close community ties that CDCs enjoy. CDFIs are adept at accessing and managing capital, providing the right type of financing, and assembling technical assistance to enable community development projects to succeed, but depending on their scope may not be comprehensively involved in a particular community.

Community development organizations that specialize in a few core competencies are able to build their expertise, investment, and learning

© The Author(s) 2017
R.O. Zdenek and D. Walsh, *Navigating Community Development*,
DOI 10.1057/978-1-137-47701-9_5

capacity in these competencies, and partner with other organizations who have different but complementary competencies and expertise. Strategic partnerships can be built around the "value add" that comes from diverse organizations collaborating. The complementary competencies can create synergy leading to more effective results and outcomes.

The community development competencies in this chapter are organized around major categories including: organizational development and management; community engagement; planning; communication; project development; lending; property and asset management; program management; resource development, capital aggregation, and fundraising; collaboration and partnering; and performance measurement. The categories are not meant to be exhaustive since community development encompasses an array of strategies and activities. The goal of this book is to cover the major categories and enable the reader to better understand how to assess and deploy competencies. Within each of the categories identified above, there are a number of sub-competencies. Our goal is to capture and describe many of the community development competencies and sub-competencies in one place to serve as a resource guide for community development practitioners, constituents, and supporters as organizations navigate the increasingly complex community development ecosystem.

ORGANIZATIONAL DEVELOPMENT AND MANAGEMENT

To be successful in community development, organizations must be skilled at assembling an effective board, a highly skilled team of employees, and sophisticated operating systems. An organization's team and systems must be well managed and have sufficient time investments. No matter the size of the organization, fundamental competencies must be in place to be effective. Some of the key organizational competencies are:

a. *Governance*: Successful organizations have engaged boards that are effective at setting policy and overseeing the mission and direction of the organization. Board members may be drawn from individuals representing a range of interests, skills, and perspectives, and ensure the mission, vision, and stewardship of resources are being executed by the staff. Boards can also represent various constituencies of the organization and provide a voice to those issues and concerns. According to "Nonprofit Corporate Governance: The Board's Role," good boards "monitor, guide and enable good management;

they do not do it themselves." To help boards perform well, new board members should receive a thorough orientation that provides them with an understanding of the purpose and scope of the non-profit agency, including its programs, organization, and budget. Board members need corporate governance documents including the articles of incorporation and by-laws, audits and year-to-date financials, a board member roster, committee descriptions, and meeting schedules. Regularly scheduled, well-organized board and board committee meetings should be organized to provide an opportunity for the board to fulfill its fiduciary responsibilities as well as engage in generative discussion that helps the organization set strategic direction and grapple with important issues. One of the most important roles for the board is the selection and regular evaluation of the chief executive.

b. *Human Capital—Staff Recruitment, Development, and Retention*: Organizations want to recruit talented new staff who have the requisite technical skills for the job, and/or potential to adapt and learn new skills with the support and resources of the organization. It is also important that the employee understand the challenges and strengths of the community and how they can contribute to implementing the vision of the organization. Once employees are on board, the focus should be on orienting them to how the organization works and help them acquire the skills essential to growing the capacity of the organization. Organizations need clear lines of authority and responsibility, consistent and transparent communication, and fair treatment of staff. Employees perform best when they have realistic goals and the necessary support to accomplish their work.

Organizations that have strong human capital potential provide pathways for advancement for talented employees, as well as the means to establish strong management systems. Staff retention is also a critical competency for a community development organization, especially in light of the fact that staff salaries are often below comparable salaries in the private and public sector. The combination of salary, benefits, meaningful work, and professional advancement is an important factor in helping retain staff.

c. *Learning Organization*: In *The Fifth Discipline,* Peter Senge states that the most significant organizational trait for the entire organization is that it learns from its experience and the lessons of others.

To do this, there must be an investment of time, a willingness to admit to and learn from mistakes, an openness to new ideas from leadership, and a culture of continual improvement. Staff at all levels of the organization needs to be involved in this process in a meaningful way. Learning organizations encourage employees to develop themselves and provide financial resources to support employee learning. Organizations need to provide employees time to reflect on the work being done and identify ways to improve at all levels of the organization. Peer-to-peer learning with other similar organizations locally, regionally, and nationally also helps organizations continually learn the latest strategies and practices.

d. *Assessing Core Competencies:* Organizations that are able to assess their own core competencies can better identify appropriate partners who will complement their work. This understanding also helps organizations identify their gaps and helps them to achieve the proficiencies that they need to advance their work. Self-knowledge and an awareness of strengths and weaknesses are just as important for organizations as it is for individuals. Several methods can be used to assess competencies. The work can be done in-house with careful inventory and review of key abilities, or utilization of assessment tools. It may be beneficial to bring in an outside consulting firm to gain a more objective evaluation of core competencies. Third-party assessments can also lead in some cases to certifications that help promote the agency's abilities, such is done by the CDFI rating agency Aeris. The greater the organization's ability to identify its core competencies and leverage them, the greater likelihood the organization will be competent and effective.

e. *Adaptability:* Complexity and change create constant pressure on nonprofit organizations to achieve their mission and objectives. While organizations need strategic direction and planning, they also have to be able to adapt to change both in terms of seeing negative trends as well as positive opportunities that fit within their mission. SWOT analysis (strengths, weaknesses, opportunities, and threats) is a tool that can help community development organizations better understand their environment and identify where they need to adapt and change. Performance measures are also important tools for enabling organizations to make planning and program adjustments. Organizations that are anticipating major changes should communicate openly with staff about what is anticipated and why, allowing opportunities for employees to ask questions and become part of the solution. Often it is helpful to identify "champions" who can help persuade others to adapt to new ways of working.

f. *Capable Leadership*: All effective organizations need strong leaders. Community development organizations have benefitted from entrepreneurial leaders who helped define the nature and scope of their organizations and helped shape the field. Forty-plus years in, many current CEOs have retired or are near retirement age. The sector needs to build a pipeline of people to take their place. It is critical to encourage the development of other leaders throughout the organization. Deepening leadership in an organization is also increasingly important as community development becomes more comprehensive and engages more stakeholders. To successfully develop leadership throughout the organization, focus should be put on identifying potential leaders, providing training and growth opportunities and career ladders to help move people up in the organization. Organizations that encourage and demonstrate leadership development will have a greater likelihood of positive transitions when current leaders depart.

g. *Internal Infrastructure*: Business management systems, including information, financial, communication, and data management systems, are essential as organizations grow and take on increasingly complex tasks. It is not only essential to have sophisticated systems in place but to invest in these systems and the people who use them and to keep them up to date. Smaller organizations may choose to outsource the expertise for systems administration, while larger organizations will find that they need an individual or a team on staff to manage this function. One major challenge in diverse organizations is ensuring that systems are compatible and can communicate with each other. This is helpful for sharing information and data between business lines and with different partners. If the organization expands to multiple locations, there is also the need to have systems and processes in place for communicating regularly and efficiently with remote sites.

The ability to manage staff and resources well is dependent upon the information you have, therefore having effective systems for gathering, storing, and distributing information is essential. Strong information management systems are the building blocks of a good business. They can improve efficiency and the quality of information employees receive. Necessary systems often include: email, instant chatting, intranets, video conferencing, and customer relationship management software.

h. *Financial Management:* The ability to plan, budget, direct, and account for an organization's revenues and expenses on a timely basis is essential for success. Whether the organization outsources the work or keeps it local, organizations need to get the properly trained and credentialed individuals to do the work. The organization's independent auditor can also provide important and strategic advice with regard to financial management. The CFO or finance manager should have proper financial controls in place to handle all of the reporting requirements and standards. Sound financial management also includes assessing capital requirements, projecting revenues and expenses, allocating cash, and procuring goods and services.

Community development projects are at greater risk when they do not have adequate capital, accurate revenue projections, and the ability to procure goods and services in a cost-effective manner. One of the strengths of partnerships is that resources can be shared and risk spread.

i. *Organizational Risk Management:* Community development is a risky endeavor since community development organizations are rebuilding communities that have been disinvested and neglected by the private and public sectors. There are a number of community development organizations that have launched ambitious projects without accurate market studies, resources, support or partners, and these projects have damaged the community development organization, and in some cases have led to the dissolution of the organization. Three of the key competencies in managing risk are: assessing the risk; measuring the risk; and spreading the risk. Assessing the risk looks at both the viability of the project/initiative and determining if it is being adequately capitalized and underwritten. Community development projects often face additional problems and delays can occur. Measuring the risk includes both an internal and external review of factors that could negatively impact the project/initiative, assessing the likelihood of these events unfolding, and determining how they can be mitigated. Spreading the risk means examining how the risks associated with the effort can be shared by others to lessen the impact to any one organization.

j. *Compliance and Reporting*: With a typical organization utilizing funding from multiple sources for projects, programs, and operations, it is important to have strong systems in place that will allow the organization to meet all of its reporting and compliance requirements. The organization will need systems and staff dedicated to tracking expenditures, program utilization, and program outcomes to ensure that they are fulfilling the minimum legal obligations and performance requirements. Internal or external compliance audits can help identify any weaknesses that need shoring up. The ability to comply with funder requirements can influence an organization's ability to get future funding and can impact their reputation.

COMMUNITY ENGAGEMENT AND PUBLIC POLICY

Community engagement is the act of involving local stakeholders in the planning and execution of community development activities. Community development is not just building real estate or community facility projects. Community development engages individuals and communities in developing their own vision of a healthy and sustainable future, while considering the larger context of the metropolitan and/or regional conditions and needs. Community stakeholders can be residents, business leaders, government, civic organizations, and/or local institutions. These individuals and organizations need to help define and direct the planning and development work in their community to ensure that it is relevant and beneficial to the community as a whole. That said, meaningful community engagement is not necessarily easy. Determining the appropriate methods for outreach and participation takes careful planning and consideration. Different methods of communication need to be tried and tested to ascertain the best ways to gain meaningful participation.

Some of the core elements of community engagement are:

a. *Local Knowledge and Expertise*: Community development requires a deep knowledge of the community, especially its strengths, assets, and leadership. Residents bring knowledge of the history of the community and what has/has not worked in the past. They are aware of emerging leaders and trends. Community development requires the engagement of local stakeholders (residents, businesses, civic organizations, institutions and government) to understand local dynamics and to build strong support. This information can be obtained in several ways, including surveys, focus groups, one-on-one outreach and networking at community meetings. Owners of multi-family rental housing can survey residents or do needs assessments when new residents move into the property. Community development organizations that pursue more comprehensive strategies may choose to develop quality of life plans where residents, community leaders, and business leaders identify basic service needs from access to fresh food to a community health clinic. The Comprehensive Community Revitalization Program in the South Bronx required that each of the five CDC partners complete a quality of life plan with at least 200 participants, and the plans led to new initiatives (Miller and Burns 2006).

b. *Political Relationships and Support*: Strong political relationships are essential for raising resources to revitalize the community. It is important to have relationships at the local, state, and national level. Effective political relationships are important for planning and zoning issues as well as securing local funding and support for the initiative. Political relationships can be important when seeking scarce financial resources for local community development initiatives, especially in an increasingly competitive environment. There can be beneficial partnership opportunities between smaller place-based CDCs and larger regional housing development organizations or CDFIs to expand access to political relationships. Community development organizations have to be careful in developing and managing political relationships with elected officials and their staff as changes occur during election cycles. Organizations have to be careful not to appear overly partisan, but at the same time need to be perceived as having strong local political support from key stakeholders and residents. An effective support base is important toward the long-term growth and sustainability of the organization.

c. *Advocacy and Public Policy*: Advocacy is important for organizing and building power to represent the interests of lower-income communities for quality services, housing, schools, facilities, jobs, businesses, etc. Low- and moderate-income constituencies and communities may have weaker political, social, and economic resources and it can be helpful to organize and advocate for resources. Strong advocacy is crucial to marshal the support necessary to improve the quality of life.

Strategic partnerships between community organizing entities and community development organizations can leverage the competencies of each to attain benefits for the community. Exercising political muscle and influence can create greater support on the part of elected officials, who may prove critical to ensuring that funds are committed for the project. Political support can help raise or target funds, as well as reduce barriers which are often in the form of regulations and approval processes that may lead to time delays that increase the project cost and reduce the financial feasibility of the project. Engaging an organization's political supporters in the planning process can help build their knowledge and support of the project, and create local champions who can help reduce barriers and attract support that generates essential resources.

Advancing specific policy initiatives is also an essential competency for community development organizations. Monitoring and commenting on public policy can be very important in supporting community development work. Policy work in particular is most effective when done in collaboration with like-minded organizations. Community-based development organizations should be active with local, state, and national coalitions and associations.

d. *Resident, Business, and Institution Engagement*: Effective engagement of residents, local business and institutions will lead to a stronger planning and visioning process and support for initiatives and projects that directly benefit the residents. In today's world, most complex urban and rural challenges take a multi-sector/cross-sector approach, necessarily involving multiple interests and organizations. As organizations enlarge their geography, they can expand from urban to suburban and rural, which requires different development strategies and resources. Navigating these relationships takes skill and savvy. Training and capacity building support are essential for growing strong residential leadership that can advocate for the best interests of the community. Training leaders takes time, and requires an investment in both strengthening current leaders and developing the next wave of leaders.

e. *Community Networking*: Successful community development efforts understand, utilize, and build community networks. Community networks connect the fabric of a community, and local community development organizations can be well positioned to play a leadership role in local community networks. Community networks can be formal such as schools, hospitals, businesses, and informal including block clubs and resident volunteer organizations. Community networks provide both formal and informal organizations the chance to connect to community opportunities and resources. As John McKnight and Jody Kretzmann pointed out in *Building Communities from the Inside Out*, neighborhoods have dozens of associations and informal networks that can be deployed toward strengthening the community. Comprehensive development initiatives are a good way to connect various networks in a neighborhood toward building a common agenda.

f. *Stakeholder Development*: Community development organizations work with many components of a community and the organization's work intersects with a variety of different sectors including land-use planning, health, education, transportation, housing, crime prevention, recreation, and arts and culture. The community development organization needs to be competent in working with diverse stakeholders to advance their goals as well as ensuring that community development priorities are included in the goals of other sectors. A growing number of local and state community development associations are partnering with environmental justice networks, early childhood advocates, aging organizations, and public health networks. The Building Healthy Places Network, which represents health professionals interested in community development, works with a number of community development networks. For organizations serving a broad geography, organizations need to be strategic about how they interact with their various stakeholders. Utilizing board members to help with some outreach can be helpful when staff time is limited.

PLANNING

Community engagement helps set the stage for planning through better understanding priorities and opportunities of community residents and their numerous partners. There are three types of planning processes that are essential to successful community development efforts: (1) strategic planning, (2) community planning, and (3) project planning. It is necessary to understand the community's economic and social dynamics when embarking on each of these planning efforts. For example, the fact that many low-income communities have weak economic markets can make the ability to obtain new investment in community development projects and activities challenging. One of the goals of community development is to strengthen local markets so that residents have access to capital as well as livable homes, basic goods and services, health care, education and employment.

a. *Strategic Planning*: Strategic planning is the act of determining the most effective strategies for achieving stated goals. Community development organizations are challenged with having to address multiple issues. The process of developing a strategic plan, based on a thorough environmental scan, and agreement on vision and mission and action, is essential for keeping the organization focused and successful. Learning when to say yes and when to say no is an important characteristic of successful organizations. Strategic planning requires the engagement of the board and staff, since different perspectives and knowledge provide valuable insights in determining the most effective decisions and strategies. Staff, board members, and other key stakeholders need to be part of the strategic thinking that leads to a clear direction and the identification of the resources and partners needed to achieve the plan. While good strategic plans are visionary, they need to be aligned to current capacity and resources, as well as a realistic assessment of future capacity and resources.

b. *Community Planning*: Community planning considers the physical, social, and economic aspects of development in a local community and uses this information to develop an action plan to improve the quality of life in the community. It focuses on resources and opportunities that exist within a community and how to build upon a community's strengths. Community plans also identify limitations and missing resources, raising a series of questions about how to access expertise, resources, and partners. The plan can help identify what type of partners are needed and what skills and expertise these new partners will bring to the community planning and development process. Residents, businesses, and other grassroots leaders should be engaged in the community planning process. Community planning can be focused at a variety of geographies, from a multi-block area to an entire region.

c. *Project Planning*: Project planning is what is done to execute specific projects identified in a strategic or community plan. Project planning can be very technical and generally requires the participation of a variety of people with specific expertise, such as legal, financial, design, and construction. Community development organizations can engage specialists in project planning from a variety of professions, since there are differences in project planning for affordable housing, commercial revitalization, and community facilities.

COMMUNICATIONS

Effective communication, both internally and externally, is critical for keeping stakeholders, staff, and the public informed and to gain support for the organization and specific initiatives and policies.

a. *Internal Communications*: As organizations specialize and grow; there is a need for regular and effective communications among the staff, consultants, board members, and volunteers. Staff needs to understand the programs and initiatives within the organization and how to communicate the results and impact with external audiences.

b. *External Communications*: Community development organizations typically interact with a large number of stakeholders. Clear and regular communication will increase understanding of the work of the organization. This can be done through newsletters, speaking engagements and press releases, as well as social media and an up-to-date Web site. To be effective, organizations need to communicate with their diverse external audiences in a timely and powerful way.

c. *Storytelling*: Effective community development work impacts both people and place, and can be transformational for individuals who benefit from it. Having community residents tell their story is a powerful way to communicate the successes of the organization to stakeholders and the broader community. People relate to stories and successes. Storytelling can also create more community development champions who will help spread the word of the organization's mission and work.

d. *Communicating Impact*: Understanding, utilizing, and communicating data is essential to developing effective community development programs and policies. Data knowledge and communication is a competency that helps others understand the impact of the organization's work. For example, Isles Inc., a CDC serving Trenton and surrounding Mercer County in New Jersey, partnered with researchers at Princeton University to do groundbreaking research and demonstrations on the impact of childhood lead poisoning that led to Governor Christie in April 2016 announcing a commitment of $10 million to address the threat of lead in older homes.

e. *Robust Web site with Interactive Links:* Web sites have emerged as one of the best sources for information about an organization. They are easy to access and can provide both timely and comprehensive information on an organization as well as serve as a tool for constituents to access resources. Web sites need to be updated regularly and be easy to access and follow, with links to other important resources and information.

f. *Social Media:* According to Morten Hansen and Herminia Ibarra, who are leading information and management researchers, social media and technologies have made connectivity easier, making collaboration central to organizational performance (Ibarra and Hansen 2013). Social media has become the most frequent means of communication among younger community leaders and professionals. Social media is capable of reaching a very large public audience, both within a community and beyond. The frequency and quality of social media hits can draw awareness and support for an organization and its mission and programs. Social media is time-sensitive and needs regular attention and fresh content.

g. *Marketing:* Community development organizations interact with diverse audiences and markets. These organizations need to understand their market(s), which can range widely. Marketing needs to be geared toward the various audiences of the organization in an effort to influence their participation, commitment, and support.

Project Development (Real Estate)

Project development represents the various phases of the development of a specific project, from inception to completion. The project development process requires myriad skills including land assemblage, design, financing, construction management, and lease up. Development projects can be new construction, acquisition and/or acquisition and rehabilitation. They can be single purpose, such as residential rental, or multi-purpose, such as mixed-use, mixed-tenure, and/or mixed-income. The more facets to the development, the more complicated it is to complete and the more skills needed. Some of these skills may be handled in-house, while other project development skills may need to be contracted to other organizations or firms specializing in the work.

Community development projects are complex and often take several years to complete due to the difficulty of accessing public and private capital, resulting in considerable expenses incurred by community development organizations before they secure the appropriate financing. If an organization is only going to be developing a project every few years, it may be better to partner with a development entity and not do the development work in-house. Major components of project development include:

a. *Real Estate Development Team*: The development team is composed of all of the disciplines necessary to complete a project. This can include architects, lawyers, accountants, bankers, engineers, construction managers, contractors, brokers, and property managers. Organizations that have completed multiple projects tend to have larger project development staff and relationships with outside professionals that are part of the development team. It is expensive to maintain a large in-house development team, so unless there is a lot of activity and projects under development, organizations should look at contracting the work out or partnering with others to get the work done. It is also essential to assess the strengths, capacities, and limitations of potential development partners, as well as their track record and history of working together.

b. *Project Management*: The project manager's job is to coordinate and guide the work of the development team. The project manager coordinates the schedule and performance of the development team members. Effective project management requires a highly experienced individual with a track record of experience and technical know-how. A proven project manager is invaluable in terms of identifying and minimizing potential problems that can occur in the project development phase. The knowledge and success in completing projects on time with minimal cost overruns is a skill that can be exported or imported to other organizations.

c. *Needs and Market Analysis*: Market analysis is the rigorous analysis of local economic and market conditions. Local markets operate within a regional environment, and understanding the regional markets is critical for the success of any community development initiative. Home ownership projects are challenging in high-cost real estate markets and commercial real estate projects may not have adequate market capacity to succeed in a weak market, or if there is strong competition nearby. Market analysis can help determine project viability.

d. *Feasibility Analysis*: Feasibility analysis determines the economic, political, and social viability of a proposed project. The analysis should determine if there is adequate income and revenue from the project to cover expenses. It should also determine if the project will achieve its objectives, assess the community and political support (or opposition), and identify the resources available to implement the project. Larger organizations often have the internal capacity or ready access to consultants, to perform the feasibility analysis, whereas smaller organizations may not. Proposed community development projects can learn from the experience of others to avoid potential mistakes and learn key success factors.

e. *Land Assemblage and Site Control*: Land assemblage can be time-consuming and require significant resources which often must be advanced before all of the project funding is secured. Property acquisition requires a high degree of sophistication, including legal, zoning, and environmental knowledge. It is often necessary to borrow pre-development funds to gain control of the site or property. With large projects, partnering with others on site acquisition can provide a way to share the cost and risk. Community development coalitions, networks, and partnerships can play an important role in establishing and preserving land use policies and tools that benefit community development, such as inclusionary zoning which places requirements for housing low- and moderate-income households.

f. *Project Financing*: Development projects require acquisition, pre-development, construction, and permanent financing, which can be structured as either equity or debt. The debt can be "hard" which means that it needs to be repaid per the loan agreement, typically on an amortized basis, or "soft" which means that it is paid back only under certain conditions. Community development real estate projects may have between five to ten different funding streams, requiring significant expertise on the part of the community development organization. In addition to banks and the public sector, community development financial institutions (CDFIs) can be an excellent source of financing for community development projects, and can also help attract other financial sources.

It is essential to adequately capitalize the development work and build in contingency funding to bridge the organizations through unexpected setbacks or unforeseen expenses. The financial scenarios of projects can be quite complex and require financial expertise on the part of the organization.

LENDING

CDFIs, as well as some CDCs and RHDOs, provide capital for a variety of entities to help a community achieve its community development goals. Lending may be for real estate, such as community facilities and residential and commercial property development, working capital, or consumer or small business loans. To be a competent lender, an organization must have the following capacities:

a. *Deal Structuring*: To lend, an organization must be able to assess the capital needs of their borrowers, whether they are individuals, businesses, or organizations; determine the appropriate products and services; and have the capacity to deliver these products and services. Staff must be able to negotiate, structure, assess risk, and recommend terms and conditions of loans. Loans must be fully documented and closed, and comply with whatever regulatory covenants are attached to the money. Being successful as a lender also requires that organizations market their products and identify qualified potential customers. Building a pipeline of steady lending opportunities is essential to making the lending program financially successful.

b. *Underwriting*: It is necessary to have the financial skills to assess a proposed transaction and the ability for the deal to work as proposed so that the loan is successful. This requires a basic understanding of pro formas, financial statements, and business plans. In affordable housing development, the real estate project is underwritten, but so is the sponsor/developer. The underwriter must be able to assess the eligibility of a borrower to receive the loan by undertaking a detailed and systematic analysis of a potential borrower's credit-worthiness and the feasibility of the project for which the capital is needed. During the underwriting process, a determination will be made regarding the credit needs, the quality of the collateral that will be used to support the loan, and the borrower's ability to repay. Upon completion of an underwriting process, typically the lender's credit committee will review the proposal and will either approve or reject the loan request.

c. *Capital Aggregation*: Prior to lending, the organization will need to assemble the capital needed to make the loans. CDFIs are not credit unions or banks, but rather are non-depository entities, their funds typically come from a multitude of places. Banks, foundations, the public sector, corporations, and individuals are all sources of capital for CDFIs. Creating a loan pool may require raising capital from many sources, and/or using some funding to leverage or guarantee other sources. Assembling and managing the required capital is complicated, time-consuming, and compliance intensive. It is important to understand lending objectives before you request or accept capital for a fund so that the structure of the capital meets your needs. For example, short-term capital will work for making construction loans but not as well for home mortgages that have a long amortization period. The organization needs to be able to calculate the spread and volume necessary to cover the organization's cost of lending.

d. *Work Outs*: When loans are in trouble, a workout specialist is needed to analyze what is causing the problems and is charged with developing a new loan structure that will allow the loan to be repaid, perhaps at a slower rate, lower interest rate, or with other mitigating factors. A work out specialist needs to be able to determine the probability of the loan being paid back or if it should be written off as uncollectable. When a loan cannot be full repaid, the work out specialist will need to take action to recover as much as possible.

e. *Loan Administration and Servicing*: It is important to ensure that there is an appropriate system in place for loan documentation and funding, and for collecting and tracking payments. This may be outsourced or the lender can use special software to track repayment, balances, etc.

f. *Asset Management of Loan Portfolios*: Once the organization has several loans, it is necessary to manage the quality and profitability of the portfolio. The asset manager will create regular reports about loan performance and identify which ones are experiencing problems. Loans are risk rated and a watch list is developed for troubled loans and more frequent monitoring is conducted. The asset manager works to manage credit exposure and also ensures that there are adequate loan loss reserves that will be tapped in the event that a loan must be foreclosed upon. The asset manager must have a thorough understanding of all regulatory compliance requirements and be familiar with numerous government and private programs.

PROPERTY AND ASSET MANAGEMENT

Property management is an essential competency to the success of the community development project, as well as the sustainability of the organization that has committed significant resources and assets. Property management places community developers in the position of being landlords and bill collectors in their community, in addition to numerous other roles they play. For organizations with a legacy of community advocacy, this will take a new mind set and business model. Property management is a discipline requiring extensive data management, legal knowledge, regulatory compliance, and understanding of complex software systems. The major property management activities include:

a. *Property Management and Maintenance.* The property needs to be well preserved with rents collected on time and quality services provided to the tenant. Managing affordable properties is a low-margin business and it is important to maximize efficiencies by understanding optimum staffing levels and minimizing turnover time and loss of rental income. Property management and maintenance requires sophisticated skills and knowledge of procurement practices, tenant/landlord law and myriad regulations. Not all tenants keep property in good condition, resulting in major expenditures to keep the units or facility in good condition. Properties that decline lose their market value quickly, and this can be challenging in a low-income community with a soft market and depressed prices.

Property management can be done internally or under contract, and requires significant staff and systems capacity. The skills and knowledge for managing commercial property is different from managing residential property. Property management lends itself to partnerships and resource sharing. There is also a scale dimension; it is more cost-effective to manage larger properties since there are fixed costs that are more difficult to absorb with small properties.

b. *Tenant Selection.* Tenant selection and retention is critical to the long-term viability of the residential, commercial, or community facility that the community development organization undertakes. There are many rules and regulations related to marketing and selecting tenants, and certain organizations have the capacity and expertise to do this in-house, while others contract with private firms for this work. Most public sector financing for affordable housing comes with requirements for housing-specific incomes and sometimes has requirements for targeting special populations, such as the elderly, formerly homeless or persons with disabilities. It is important to develop selection criteria that both meet the mission goals of the property and ensure a safe and livable community. It is often helpful to partner with a service agency to provide added support to high-need residents. Having clear, consistent criteria for each property is important, understanding that not every property will have the same criteria depending on the funding and/or social purpose of the property. For example, a property for formerly homeless residents will not be able to demand the same rent-to-income ratio as a property for working families.

c. *Asset Management and Preservation.* Asset management broadly defined is a system that monitors, maintains, and maximizes a portfolio of real estate for its intended purpose over the long term. An asset management strategy needs to be in place so that building systems can be replaced in a measured way that preserves the long-term use and economic value of the building. Community development organizations that are active with the acquisition of older properties will find that capital needs of the property asset can be a significant task. Funds need to be accrued to address the roof, boiler, and other large systems that may need significant repair or replacement. Asset management and preservation can be done in-house or contracted out, but ultimately the property is the owner's responsibility and thus it is in the owner's interest to monitor the building's performance and condition.

d. *Asset Disposition.* Some real estate projects lend themselves to being sold because they either do not meet the mission and goals of the organization or because they are posing a financial drain on the organization. Generally, if a property has received public money, it is highly regulated and disposing of it can require multiple approvals. However, when it is appropriate and possible to dispose of a particular property, the cash generated can be used to advance the mission of the organization in other developments or programs.

e. *Resident Services.* Residents in affordable housing developments are often in need of, or eligible for, an array of services that bolster their social and economic future. Offering services at the residential site can be very effective to help make residents successful in their tenancy and improve their social and financial well-being. Services can be offered on site, at a central location, or through partners in the community. Support services are especially important when housing special needs populations, including formerly homeless individuals and families. Resident Service staff should work closely with community resources and social service providers to ensure that residents have access to an array of services that meet their needs. If providing services off-site, it is important that the facility is in a location that is easily accessible to residents. Bundling services at the location is an ideal way to assist low-income residents in their quest for greater economic independence.

PROGRAM/BUSINESS LINE DEVELOPMENT
AND MANAGEMENT

It is critical to have effective program management skills to successfully execute a program regardless of whether it is a health, housing, economic development, environmental, educational, or social service program. Each of these types of programs requires its own technical expertise that may be best met through a collaborative partnership with an expert in the specific field. Program and business line development requires an understanding of the goals and objectives of the program and the ability to plan the various program components. Implementing a successful program requires a clear timeframe, budget, adequate and capable staff, targeted marketing, competent execution, and evaluation. Program management also requires sound communication and negotiation/problem-solving skills. Program management skills are an essential capacity for most community development organizations.

a. *Idea Generation, Program Conception, and Initiation.* During this phase, the idea for the program should be vetted against the organizations goals and resources as well as an assessment of risk versus reward. Not only should the idea be strong and fit within the mission of the organization, there must be adequate staff and funding to fully develop and launch the program. If necessary, fundraising for the program should begin in this phase.

b. *Program Development and Planning.* This phase is where an organization defines the goals for the program as well as its scope and objectives. Creating a written plan and/or business plan clearly identifying all phases of the project is necessary to ensure good execution. All funding resources should be locked in for program launch. It is helpful to have staff who are willing to champion the program.

c. *Program Launch.* Using the business plan as a blueprint for moving forward, the organization needs to focus on a quick and effective launch. Dragging out new program execution can result in several problems, including increased costs, missed opportunities for action, and/or losing out to a competitor.

d. *Program Execution.* Once the program is up and running, the organizations must provide oversight to ensure that performance and budget targets are met. Regular reporting on performance objectives and problem solving to adjust the program where needed are activities that are undertaken in this phase.

e. *Program Close and Evaluation.* If a program has a sunset, it is important to have an evaluation tool in place to document results and evaluate effectiveness. This is important as it can help inform future efforts and also be critical to reporting outcomes to supporters.

Resource Development, Capital Aggregation, and Fundraising

Community development requires capital and typically this capital is obtained from a wide variety of sources and, as such, is a time-consuming process that takes skill and business acumen. Community development organizations generally need money for core operations, as well as specific projects and lines of business. Nearly all funding comes with rules and requirements.

Earlier sections of this paper discussed the decline in many federally funded community development programs, such as HOME and CDBG. Assembling the required capital to stay in business and pursue your mission is one of the top tasks of community development organizations. Pursuing new funding sources provides an important opportunity for partnership strategies among diverse community development organizations.

Some of the major funding sources for community development include:

a. *Federal, State, and Local Government Programs*: There are a number of federal funding programs that explicitly mention CDCs and CDFIs or are targeted for community development work in low- and moderate-income communities, including: the Office of Community Services Community Economic Development funds (OCS/CED), the Community Development Block Grant (CDBG), the HOME program, and the Low Income Housing Tax Credit (LIHTC). The CDFI Fund at US Treasury Department provides money to CDFIs and other community development organizations through an array of financing tools including New Market Tax Credit (NMTC), and the newly launched CDFI Bond Guarantee Fund, enabling CDFIs and other community development organizations to significantly leverage their resources. A number of state governments have funding programs for CDCs and, in some cases, Regional Housing Development Organizations (RHDOs). Some local governments have also created housing trust funds, bonds, and other funding to support housing and community development work in their community.

b. *Foundations and Corporations*: These two funding sources have played an important role in the growth and evolution of community development. Foundations have seeded community development initiatives, and some have provided long-term funding or funded the same program for multiple years, but the latter is less common. Foundations typically like to fund new ideas and initiatives with a specific start and end date. This is a difficult requirement for community development projects that require a multi-year effort.

Corporations tend to fund in geographical and program priority areas, and a number of them, notably insurance companies, have long-standing funding relationships with community development organizations.

c. *Financial Institutions*: Financial institutions are heavily involved in community development finance due, in part, to the Community Reinvestment Act (CRA), a federal act passed in 1977 to encourage commercial banks to invest in low- and moderate-income communities. CRA was designed to help financial institutions meet the needs of borrowers in those communities. Financial institutions provide loans, equity investments, and grants for housing and community development projects. They are an essential component of community development finance in the USA and tend to focus on markets where they have a large presence and need to invest to meet CRA requirements.

d. *Intermediaries.* The growth of community development in the 1980s and 1990s was fueled by the emergence of national and local intermediaries. These intermediaries, typically nonprofit organizations supported by government, bank, or philanthropic funding, were able to assemble private and public dollars and target those resources to CDCs and related organizations in key geographic areas throughout the USA. Intermediaries focused their support on CDCs and RHDOs undertaking development projects in low- and moderate-income communities. Beginning in the mid-2000s, several large intermediaries began shifting their focus due to changes in their funding stream. With a major drop in support from Living Cities, a consortium of several major foundations, and the demise of the Fannie Mae Foundation, some intermediaries shifted their focus to non-housing activities. National intermediaries still play a role and provide significant grant and investment capital to the sector; however, they are not the primary drivers for community development that they were in the 1980s and 1990s. In some markets, local intermediaries still play a very important role in supporting community development activity.

e. *Community Development Financial Institutions.* CDFIs have become an increasingly significant source of funding in community development. They are mission-focused organizations that offer an array of flexible financing tools, such as pre-development loans, acquisition loans, construction loans, permanent financing, and equity-like investments in nonprofits, specific real estate projects, and businesses. They assemble their funds from a variety of different sources, and a recent positive development is that a number of them have become members of the Federal Home Loan Bank system, increasing their access to long-term capital which they can use to support CDCs, regional housing development organizations, and nonprofit agencies that are developing housing, business enterprises and micro lending, charter schools, health centers, child care, and other community facilities.

f. *Individuals*: Historically, most community development organizations have not focused on raising money from individuals and local businesses, as compared to other nonprofit organizations, but that is changing. More and more, community development organizations have developed robust individual giving programs, raising hundreds of thousand dollars from individual and business supporters. Additionally, the growing field of social impact investment represents a new opportunity for community development organizations to pursue individual and business support. Social investors represent individuals and firms looking to identify and invest in social enterprises that make a specific impact. In addition to a public benefit, individuals and social investors are also looking for a financial return on their investment. There is a growing movement to bring social investors to opportunities provided by community development organizations, and some organizations are creating specific investment opportunities and bringing them to the market. This will likely be an increasing source of capital for organizations in the future.

Collaborations and Partnerships

Collaboration should be viewed as a competency in community development in light of the growing complexity of community development and the breadth of issues and sectors that need to be engaged to effect change. All types of community development organizations need to work well with others no matter their size or aptitude.

The following characteristics are essential for effective collaboration:

a. *Shared Vision*: Successful collaborations begin with a shared vision and purpose that the leadership embraces, and that is explicitly tied to performance results. Gil Robinson Hickman in *Leading Change in Multiple Contexts* articulates that common vision in a collaboration requires a "mindfulness" if partners are to understand the context for a collaboration, and the consequences or costs in launching a collaborative effort. Effective collaboration will not occur without shared vision.

b. *Shared Leadership and Decision Making*: Herminia Ibarra and Morten Hansen define collaborative leadership "as the capacity to engage people and groups outside one's formal control and inspire them to work toward common goals—despite differences in convictions, cultural values, and operating norms" (Ibarra and Hansen 2013). Collaborative or shared leaders are passionately curious, modestly confident, and mildly obsessed with the significance of the collective mission over their own professional goals (Abele 2013). Shared leadership creates a decision-making process that leads to performance agreements and effective partnership implementation.

c. *Shared Participation*: Just as decision-making needs to be shared, the same applies to shared participation. The goal of shared participation is to convince people and organizations that believe they don't need to work together that they will benefit by doing so. This requires an organizational commitment and buy-in among leadership and staff (Abele 2013). Each organization in a partnership regardless of their size must commit resources to the collaborative effort in the form of funds, staff time, and other in kind support. The question of resources needs to be addressed early in the partnership effort so that everyone is committed and has "skin in the game."

d. *Innovation*: One of the major reasons that organizations collaborate is to share knowledge and develop innovative strategies that are beyond the capabilities of one organization. Effective collaborative efforts engage the ideas of key partners in the partnership process. Communities of practice are one way to do that. Communities of practice that are inter-disciplinary and involve multiple organizations usually take the long view in terms of knowledge and practice; lead the direction of the new initiative or product; bring together experts to provide innovative solutions to difficult problems; and manage and expand knowledge to solutions and problems that not have yet been anticipated, an important role for research and development efforts (McDermott and Archibold 2013).

e. *Accountability*: Organizations that participate in collaboration must be accountable to each other. It is not enough to attend meetings and verbally participate. Individual members have to be accountable to the larger collaboration goals, if they are not, then consequences have to be established and implemented, including the possibility of asking an organization to leave the collaboration.

f. *Performance Goals and Measurements*: Performance measurements are at the heart of collaboration, and must be determined by the members and adhered to in meeting the goals and outcomes for the collaboration. Performance goals and measurements are what hold the collaboration together since one of the major reasons for forming collaboration is to improve impact and benefit more low-income individuals and communities.

g. *Constant Communication*: Ongoing communication is critical to the success of any collaboration, and it should happen with frequent personal communication that is clear and open, and encourages discussion and consensus. While e-mails and texting are useful, these methods are not as effective at building relationships as in-person communication. Relationships are the "glue" of collaboration. Open communication increases the likelihood that issues and differences can be resolved.

h. *Everyone Benefits*. The partnering organizations need to benefit at some point in the collaboration. One of the major concepts in organizational change theory is to secure initial victories and accomplishments, and to build from those successes and gain momentum. Not every participating organization will benefit initially. All active members of collaboration need to benefit over time in order for the collaboration to prove its value and importance.

Performance Measurement and Evaluation

Community development organizations are under great scrutiny to make good use of limited funds to achieve significant change within their community. Funders and policy makers place emphasis on effectiveness, performance and impact. In evaluating community development work, organizations need to track their outputs (what they do), their outcomes (the effects of the work), and their impact (how the work affects the bigger issues). Larger organizations are generally able to operate at a bigger scale which can increase outputs, outcomes, and impact. The concept of scale has drawn greater attention in the past few years, as funders seek solutions that have a broad result. Scale is harder for smaller organizations to achieve and, thus, they may need to seek out collaborative opportunities to show increased results.

No matter what size the organization is, it is expected to measure outputs and outcomes and evaluate actual performance against programmatic goals. To be effective at evaluation, organizations may need to engage outside consultants or technical help if the organization lacks these skills in-house. Data collection and analysis, and performance measurement are two important components of most evaluations.

a. *Data Collection and Analysis:* Data are essential for being able to determine the viability of a project and its effectiveness as far as who is served, who benefits, cost reasonableness, and the sustainability of the initiative. At the outset of new projects, organizations need to determine what data are needed to determine project success (or failure). As community development organizations have varying levels of data collection and analysis expertise, they should look to partner with organizations that have strong data management capacity. For example, the Success Measures Project at NeighborWorks America has developed indicators and outcomes that community development organizations can use to measure the effectiveness of the project. Once data are collected, they must be reviewed and analyzed so that it can help inform management decisions. Understanding what data are needed and what they mean is essential for organizations attempting to document and communicate their impact.

b. *Performance Measurement:* One of the major assumptions of community development work is that it will lead to an improved quality of life for the residents. The best way to demonstrate this is to have programs that focus on documenting the tangible changes in the lives of the residents. The residents may learn new knowledge and skills, raise their income and savings levels, or live in decent, affordable housing and have better health and safety outcomes. Programmatic outcomes can be complicated to document. Doing so may require working with a third-party research organization. It may also require collaboration among several organizations to get the necessary data to who impact.

SUMMARY

There is a broad array of competencies that can be deployed for executing community development projects and programs, and the number of competencies and sub-competencies keeps growing as the community development field becomes more multi-sectoral. To better understand and apply these concepts, we have enclosed a "competency chart" that lists all of these competencies and their relevance to the three types of community development organizations featured in this book. The "competency chart" was first presented in the original working paper, *Comparative Advantages: Creating Synergy in Community Development*, written by Robert Zdenek for the Federal Reserve Bank of San Francisco. We have updated and expanded the chart in this chapter.

Chapter 6 will focus on how to adapt the competency chart from theory to practice. This knowledge is helpful in analyzing the challenges, success, and lessons from the case studies in Chap. 7.

REFERENCES

Abele, John. 2013. *Bringing Minds Together*. On Collaboration, 32, 39. Cambridge, MA: Harvard Business Review Press.

Ibarra, Hermina, and Morton E. Hansen. 2013. *Are You a Collaborative Leader?* On Collaboration, 10. Cambridge, MA: Harvard Business Review Press.

McDermott, Richard, and Douglas Archibald. 2013. *Harnessing Your Staff's Informal Networks*. On Collaboration. Cambridge, MA: Harvard Business Review Press.

Miller, Anita, and Tom Burns. 2006. *Going Comprehensive: Anatomy of an Initiative that Worked: CCRP in the South Bronx*, 38–40. Philadelphia, PA: OMG Center for Collaborative Learning.

Advancing Community Development Through Competencies and Comparative Advantages

Introduction

Chapter 5 demonstrated that there are a wide range of community development competencies, and that many of these competencies are technical and highly specialized. In this chapter, we share a community development competency chart that identifies which competencies are most predominant with the three types of community development organizations featured in this book (CDCs, RHDOs, and CDFIs).

We also discuss the rationale for organizations to utilize and leverage their primary competencies in order to have a comparative advantage in the community development ecosystem. A strong comparative advantage will make an organization more competitive and increase its "brand" and reputation in the community. Not maximizing core competencies can result in a less effective, less focused organization.

Competencies can be leveraged as comparative advantages when participating in collaborations and partnerships. These partnerships require working with diverse organizations within the community development ecosystem. We provide an overview of the myriad collaboration and partnership opportunities and strategies that community development organizations can pursue. We will then discuss three major community development models that successful community development partnerships have deployed and the synergistic benefits from collaboration and partnership.

© The Author(s) 2017
R.O. Zdenek and D. Walsh, *Navigating Community Development*,
DOI 10.1057/978-1-137-47701-9_6

103

The last section of this chapter focuses on the criteria utilized to select the case studies that are featured in Chap. 7. The case study criteria help identify challenges, opportunities, and lessons from the case studies that all community development organizations can use to navigate the future community development ecosystem. The case studies are also designed to show the comparative advantages that the lead organizations have sharpened over many years to make them effective and desirable partners.

COMMUNITY DEVELOPMENT COMPETENCY CHART

The community development competency chart is designed to provide a quick overview of community development competencies and the relative strengths of the three types of community development organizations featured in this book. The chart identifies whether each competency is a primary, secondary, or optional competency for each of the three types of organizations. When a competency is shown as "optional," it means that it may or may not be an important skill for the organization, depending on the specific role that the organization has in its community. For example, few CDCs and RHDOs do lending, while virtually all CDFIs lend, so lending is a primary competency for CDFIs, while storytelling may or may not be an important communication competency for CDFIs.

The chart is meant to be illustrative and suggestive of potential partnership opportunities. Local community development practitioners need to assess the competencies and capacities of their local organizations to determine their comparative advantages. For example, it may be advantageous for a large RHDO to partner with a small CDC that can help them learn important information about a particular neighborhood. Or, a CDC may choose to partner with a CDFI that can provide financial resources. The chart shows areas where complementary partnerships could occur based on the relative strengths and capacities of CDCs, RHDOs, and CDFIs.

A blank copy of this chart can be found in the Appendix. Organizations can use this chart to assess their relative strengths. It may be instructive for staff and board members to complete the chart independently and then compare notes on how they've ranked the organization to determine where they have agreement and where there may be areas for further work (Chart 6.1).

Chart 6.1 Community development competency chart

Comparative advantages (primary, secondary, optional)

	CDC	RHDO	CDFI
Organizational Development and Management			
Governance	Primary	Primary	Primary
Human Capital	Primary	Primary	Primary
Learning Organization	Secondary	Secondary	Secondary
Assessing core competencies	Secondary	Secondary	Secondary
Adaptability	Secondary	Primary	Primary
Capable Leadership	Primary	Primary	Primary
Internal infrastructure	Secondary	Primary	Primary
Financial management	Secondary	Primary	Primary
Organizational risk management	Secondary	Secondary	Primary
Compliance and reporting	Secondary	Primary	Primary
Community Engagement and Public Policy			
Local knowledge and expertise	Primary	Secondary	Secondary
Political relationships and support	Primary	Primary	Primary
Advocacy and public policy	Primary	Primary	Primary
Resident, business, and institution engagement	Primary	Secondary	Secondary
Community network	Primary	Secondary	Primary
Stakeholder development	Primary	Primary	Secondary
Planning			
Strategic planning	Primary	Primary	Primary
Community planning	Primary	Secondary	Secondary
Project planning	Secondary	Primary	Primary
Communications			
Internal communications	Secondary	Secondary	Secondary
External communications	Secondary	Primary	Secondary
Storytelling	Secondary	Optional	Optional
Communicating impact	Secondary	Primary	Primary
Robust website with interactive links	Secondary	Primary	Primary
Social media	Primary	Secondary	Secondary
Marketing	Secondary	Primary	Primary
Project Development (Real Estate)			
Real estate development team	Secondary	Primary	Primary
Project management	Secondary	Primary	Secondary
Needs and market analysis	Secondary	Primary	Primary
Feasibility analysis	Secondary	Primary	Primary
Land assemblage and site control	Secondary	Primary	Secondary
Project financing	Primary	Primary	Primary
Lending			
Deal structuring	Optional	Optional	Primary
Underwriting	Optional	Optional	Primary

(continued)

Chart 6.1   (continued)

Comparative advantages (primary, secondary, optional)

	CDC	RHDO	CDFI
Capital aggregation	Optional	Optional	Primary
Work outs	Optional	Optional	Primary
Loan administration and servicing	Optional	Optional	Primary
Asset management of loan portfolios	Optional	Optional	Primary
Property and Asset Management			
Property management and maintenance	Primary	Primary	Secondary
Tenant selection	Primary	Primary	N/A
Asset management and preservation	Secondary	Primary	Secondary
Asset disposition	Primary	Primary	Secondary
Resident services	Primary	Primary	N/A
Program/Business Line Development and Management			
Idea generation	Primary	Primary	Primary
Program development	Primary	Primary	Primary
Program launch	Secondary	Primary	Primary
Program execution	Secondary	Primary	Primary
Program close and evaluation	Secondary	Secondary	Secondary
Resource Development, Capital Aggregation and Fundraising			
Federal, state, and local	Primary	Primary	Primary
Foundations and corporations	Primary	Primary	Primary
Financial institutions	Secondary	Secondary	Primary
Intermediaries	Primary	Primary	Secondary
CDFIs	Optional	Optional	Primary
Individuals	Primary	Primary	Secondary
Collaboration and Partnerships			
Shared vision	Primary	Primary	Primary
Shared leadership and decision making	Primary	Primary	Primary
Shared participation	Primary	Primary	Primary
Innovation	Primary	Primary	Primary
Accountability	Primary	Primary	Primary
Performance goals/measurements	Secondary	Primary	Primary
Constant communication	Primary	Secondary	Secondary
Everyone benefits	Primary	Primary	Primary
Performance Measurement and Evaluation			
Data collection and analysis	Secondary	Primary	Primary
Performance measurement	Secondary	Primary	Primary

A Rationale for Comparative Advantage and Leveraging Core Competencies

There is a strong rationale for organizations to utilize and maximize their core competencies to be effective partners and achieve comparative advantage. Not doing so can result in a difficult and or increasingly expensive management strategy as it is challenging for one organization to possess all the necessary competencies. There are many reasons to utilize and maximize core competencies to achieve comparative advantage including:

Strong comparative advantage and focus is a more effective approach and achieves stronger brand recognition
Organizations that hone their expertise will develop a strong reputation for their abilities and thus will become more competitive for resources and opportunities. Organizations known for certain abilities will become the "go to" agencies in their community development ecosystem for certain types of projects, resulting in better odds for impact and success.

Too many competencies can stretch the organization's capacity and compromise achievement
Developing and maintaining a set of core competencies requires a significant investment on the part of the community development organization in terms of financial, human, and organizational resources. To support organizational development of these capacities, organizations must have flexible and patient operating and working capital, and this type of money is generally hard to obtain. In addition to accessing the appropriate funding, organizations pursing additional competencies need to build their staff and organizational capacities. Hiring the professional talent to succeed in community development is time-consuming and challenging given the sub-market wages many nonprofit organizations pay. Attempting to expand an organization's competencies can draw away from the core mission of the organization, resulting in unmet goals and poor performance. Therefore, it is important for organizations to fully understand what core competencies are essential for their business model, and focus on developing those.

Community development competencies require increased technical knowledge and an investment to become proficient
Each sector that is part of community development ecosystem, including housing, public health, arts and culture, business development, etc., have their own technical knowledge and resources that have become

increasingly complex over time. Affordable housing production and management involves finance, development, construction, management, asset preservation, and compliance functions to ensure that the housing development is consistent with housing policy and regulations. The public health sector is also very technical and ever changing, as we're reminded with the recent passage of the Affordable Care Act (ACA) and the requirement for hospitals to perform community assessments. Technical knowledge keeps accumulating and expanding, placing significant pressure on all organizations to master core competencies and areas of expertise. The ability to master specific technical knowledge can be an important factor in contributing to new partnerships and collaborations.

Individual competencies create different types of comparative advantages that can be leveraged in an environment that values comprehensive community development

In the 1980s and 1990s, community development intermediaries tended to reward CDCs and RHDOs for their real estate development production and capacity, notably affordable housing development. This emphasis has starting to shift to a focus on a more comprehensive approach to community development that considers the physical, social, economic, and health determinants and priorities of a community. Competencies such as community engagement and planning are seen as just as significant as real estate development capacity to the overall community development ecosystem. This enables smaller community development organizations to build their comparative advantage vis-à-vis other larger community development organizations with real estate and financing capacity.

Funders are starting to shift their funding priorities to community development outcomes that require a broader range of competencies

As we saw in Chap. 3, community development made a major transition from focusing on economic development in the 1970s to emphasizing real estate development and affordable housing in the 1980s and 1990s. As previously noted, this was due in no small part to the fact that funders built a strong infrastructure and system for funding affordable housing production through national and local intermediaries, and tax credit financing. National funders, such as Living Cities and the Annie E. Casey Foundation, began to embark on a new direction, focusing on multi-sector initiatives and systems change at the city level. Funders, including intermediaries, have not abandoned affordable housing production, but some have placed a new emphasis on sustainable development and partnerships.

Housing production is not viewed as the end product but as a vital component of a sustainable community.

There is a clear shift in funding priorities within community development toward a comprehensive approach that emphasizes housing, health, education, and economic development. This has implications for comparative advantage strategies, since real estate competencies and capacities were viewed as more valuable in the past and rewarded to a greater extent by the funding ecosystem. One of the challenges and tensions in community development today is that community engagement, planning, and human services can be seen as less significant than project development and management skills. Funding strategies have been more aligned to the perceived "hard development skills" than the "softer" advocacy and service programs. The broadening of community development has the impact of changing the value of a number of the competencies including rewarding those new competencies with more financial and technical support. Additionally, these new sectors and competencies will bring in new funding streams from the health, environmental, and education sectors helping to strengthen the sustainability of community development.

COLLABORATION AND PARTNERSHIPS

Collaboration has become more significant for community development organizations since they are finding it necessary to connect to other sectors and/or reach new partners within the community development sector in order to make meaningful change in communities. Complex, entrenched problems cannot be solved with a single solution by a single organization. Community development and housing organizations are finding the need to align themselves with the health, education, and employment sectors. Collaboration can also be an important strategy for spreading risk among organizations through increasing the resources available to implement the effort.

With the advent of the Obama administration, a shift began in the federal government's policy agenda, with the goal of better coordinating public resources for greater impact. Several federal programs, such as Promise Communities, Choice Neighborhoods, Tiger grants, and Sustainable Communities initiatives, represented this new direction. The new programs sought to move away from categorical programs in separate silos, to a collaborative approach that connects sectors and institutions to build synergy and achieve greater outcomes. Moving from a silo approach to a cross-sector approach is not easy. Success to date has been varied and is still a work in progress, as borne out in the case studies.

Collaborations can be structured a number of ways to be efficient and capitalize on an organization's competencies, depending on the goal or strategy trying to be achieved. Certain functions lend themselves to being centralized, such as back office functions, and finance and human resources, while others are most impactful when decentralized, such as program delivery, case management and community outreach. Generally, there are three common types of collaborative structures. These models can be combined and change as the work evolves (Walsh and Zdenek 2011).

Hub and Spoke: In this model, a centralized entity provides services to a network of decentralized organizations that provide related services that are best delivered where the customers are located. This model often has a highly technical centralized function with a high touch decentralized delivery system. The expensive technical services are provided by the organization with those core competencies, while the service delivery is distributed to agencies with social service skills.

Cross-sector Collaborative: In this model, several groups with expertise in different sectors come together to bring visibility and resources to a large, often complex, issue. The goal can be policy driven, where groups create a common agenda that builds political power to influence public decisions and generates resources that transcend traditional boundaries, such as neighborhoods or cities. Cross-sector collaborations can also be used to leverage knowledge, where one group accomplishes more by leveraging its expertise with complementary services offered by one or more other organizations. Cross-sector collaboration can also be used to tackle large, complex issues that impact multiple sectors and require the expertise of several organizations and/or institutions to affect change.

Service Specialization: In this collaborative model, each organization involved assumes a lead role for one facet of a comprehensive program, allowing organizations to utilize their core competencies. The group of organizations collaborating can set the overall goals and monitor program outcomes, or this can be assigned to one of the organizations that have this as its expertise.

To be effective with any of these models, there are several factors that contribute to success (Walsh and Zdenek 2011):

A Common Vision That is Performance Driven: It is critical that the groups begin with a common vision and purpose that is embraced by the leadership. To achieve this, significant groundwork must have been laid to develop a common language and clarify objectives.

Effective Communication: Personal and frequent communication among the organizations in the collaborative is key to discussing issues and building trust. It is also critical to keep external stakeholders informed and up to date on strategy, implementation, and outcomes.

Mutual Benefit: In successful collaborations, everyone wins.

Mutual Responsibility: In effective collaborations, everyone is responsible for success. All parties need to commit resources, preferably through a binding performance agreement.

Leadership: Collaborations that succeed have at least one person who is committed to making the effort work. There can be more than one champion, but strong, consistent leadership is essential.

Developing a Continuum of Services and Products: Effective collaborations lend themselves to a continuum of products and services that can strengthen the economic, financial, and social well-being of families and communities. Community development organizations need a clear understanding of the competencies they offer. This is especially true for multi-sector collaborations that combine real estate, health, education, and employment. Expertise and competencies are the glue of multi-sector collaborations.

Building Economies of Scale: Shared services and joint projects can lead to greater economies of scale offering savings in reduced overhead and ability to reach more constituents and communities. Economies of scale make organizations more sustainable over time.

Strengthening Marketing Capabilities: Small- and medium-size nonprofits often have limited marketing capacity, and many prospective clients or potential funders are not aware of the services of the organization. A coordinated and shared marketing campaign including a branding strategy can generate greater outreach, client usage, and new financial resources.

Understanding New Fundraising Resources: The previous set of competencies focused on resource development and fundraising. Collaboration and partnerships can offer access to funding sources beyond the reach of an individual organization and/or sector. For example, Medicare part C has a pilot program called Money Follows the Person, that could combine Medicare funding streams with affordable housing streams. Another example is the Department of Education. It has a Charter School Finance Fund that can support the work of CDFIs. Looking to new funding sources in other sectors can help organizations achieve their goals.

THE COMPARATIVE ADVANTAGE CRITERIA

To better understand how community development competencies can be used in effective strategic partnerships, below we offer a series of case studies. These feature organizations that use their competencies as comparative advantages in community development collaborative initiatives. We share compelling examples of community development organizations that find the right partners with complementary competencies and capacities in order to achieve outcomes that result in an approach that strengthens individuals, families, and communities. The criteria utilized to identify the case studies included two or more of the following requirements:

1. Strong organizations that understand their competencies and partner with a variety of partners. We looked for organizations working in collaborations that incorporate major community development strategies—housing, commercial revitalization; employment; health; environment; education; or financial capability.
2. Organizations that had been in strategic partnerships that were in existence for at least two years, and had the potential for an additional three to five years.
3. Collaborations that were in diverse geographic locations, including large cities, small towns, metropolitan regions, and rural or suburban communities.
4. Unique funding models and new approaches to collaborative initiatives.

The case studies in the next chapter provide an opportunity to test the competencies and evolving capacities of CDCs, RHDOs, and CDFIs in the community development ecosystem. The community development land-scape is adding new players, strategies, and initiatives that are cross-sectoral combining fields such as housing, health, environmental remediation, education, employment, and safety. The changing environment offers new challenges and opportunities. These case studies provide a lens to what is becoming "the new normal of community development."

Reference

Walsh, Dee, and Robert Zdenek. 2011. *The New Way Forward: Using Collaborations and Partnerships for Greater Efficiency and Impact*, 4, 10–12. San Francisco, CA: Community Development Investment Center, Federal Reserve Bank of San Francisco.

CHAPTER 7

Case Studies of Partnerships Utilizing Comparative Advantages

As noted in the previous chapter, this book features seven case studies that illustrate CDCs, RHDOs, and CDFIs using their competencies to comparative advantage to tackle complex community development issues. Some of the cases examine special initiatives that were created to address a specific problem. The Community Loan Center, Fairmount Indigo Line, West Cook County Housing Collaborative are each examples of this. Other cases are about changing business models to become more effective and/or expand geography, as represented in the NWSCDC, REACH–ACE merger, and Fahe cases. Finally, one case, featuring EBALDC, is about expanding partners to more fully meet mission objectives. The EBALDC case is an example of this. At the end of each case study, we provide a chart that shows which competencies each partner in the case brought to the table. We also provide a summary of lessons learned for each case.

THE COMMUNITY LOAN CENTER AND CDC OF BROWNSVILLE CASE STUDY

The Situation and Context

The Rio Grande Valley of Texas is an area with a rich history and fertile soil. The availability of irrigation and the arrival of the railroad at the turn of the twentieth century, along with immigration from Mexico, fueled the area's growth. The first American settlement in the area was Brownsville in 1846, which served as a Fort during the Mexican War. The valley includes

© The Author(s) 2017
R.O. Zdenek and D. Walsh, *Navigating Community Development*,
DOI 10.1057/978-1-137-47701-9_7

four counties covering more than 4000 square miles. It is peppered with 39 small city areas and over 2000 colonias, which are unincorporated, unregulated communities, generally with substandard housing and little infrastructure, found along the border (Vigness and Odintz 2016).

The economy of the area with the introduction of the "maquiladora," or twin plant, concept of manufacturing—with labor-intensive work done in Mexico where labor is less expensive, and support facilities on the US side —has been growing steadily for about 30 years (RGV Texas.com).

Brownsville's port is at the end of a deep, long channel connecting to the Gulf of Mexico. It has become a center for the US ship-breaking industry and offshore oil rig manufacturing, represented by two large employers for the area. However, the cyclical nature of these businesses causes employment to fluctuate. Tourism has also grown as an economic force in recent decades.

Today, the population in the Valley is over 1.3 million people and is predominately Hispanic, with a high percentage of individuals under the age of 35. Compared to other urbanized areas, the Valley is very poor in spite of its manufacturing and agricultural base. Historically, the area has ranked at the bottom in per capita income, educational attainment, employment, and health and housing conditions (Miller and Maril 1979).

In the Valley, payday lending (short-term, high-cost low-dollar loans) and auto title loans have taken a large toll on the population. Springing up on many corners of the community, these lenders are taking money out of the local economy and leaving a wake of credit damage, which negatively impacts the future borrowing capacity of many households.

The proliferation of payday lending is relatively new in Texas since it was prohibited until 2001 when state legislators gave way to payday lending companies and passed legislation adopting regulations for it. By 2010, there were 3500 payday lenders operating in Texas, and not many of them adhere to the regulations enacted by the state. This is because by registering as Credit Access Businesses (CAB) under the Credit Services Organizations Act, payday lenders in Texas have been able to skirt the regulations and charge higher fees.

Payday loans and auto title loans are targeted at low-income people who have limited access to traditional credit and who need extra money to meet expenses between paychecks. These types of loans can have a devastating impact on families as the high cost of the loans can turn small loans into major debts for borrowers. Payday lenders are so prolific in Texas, that some communities have passed zoning ordinances to limit where payday lender stores may locate, and some have capped rates and loan amounts (FEDPAYDAY.com 2014).

About 10 years ago, a group in Brownsville, comprised of community leaders from the local utility, two banks, the university, the United Way, and the Community Development Corporation of Brownsville, was meeting regularly to discuss how to improve the economic vitality and health of the community. Called the kaffeklatsch, this group represented some of the key players in the community development ecosystem of the Rio Grande Valley. The kaffeklatsch discussed the issue and agreed that payday loans were a major contributor to the problem (Duffrin 2015).

In the Rio Grande Valley, payday lenders cannot charge interest, but they can charge a fee. The fee is charged at the time the loan is made, and in the RGV payday lenders typically charge $240 for every $1000 borrowed. Every time a loan is extended past its initial 14 day term, the borrower must pay the fee again. More than half of the borrowers extend their loan once, and many do it multiple times, equating to fees of $700 or more on the $1000 borrowed. In the state of Texas in 2013, 3585 payday and title loan lenders did $5.94 billion in lending, with nearly $1.5 billion in fees charged and just under 37,000 cars repossessed (CDC of Brownsville 2015; Office of Consumer Credit 2015).

In late 2006, the kaffeklatsch became aware of an opportunity to get grant funds from Freddie Mac to address this problem. Freddie Mac had embarked on a national campaign called, "Don't Borrow Trouble" to discourage borrowing from predatory lenders, those lenders charging high fees and interest rates. The funds were to be used for a local marketing campaign that would discourage people from borrowing (Duffrin 2015).

Nick Mitchell-Bennett, now CEO of the CDC of Brownsville, was participating in the group and spearheaded the effort to apply for the grant. The CDC of Brownsville, a private, nonprofit community development organization, has provided quality affordable housing to the citizens of the lower Rio Grande Valley since 1974, and was well positioned to lead this effort.

However, after receiving the grant, but prior to finalizing and launching the campaign, the group came to the realization that a "just say no" approach to borrowing wasn't going to address the fundamental problem, which was that community members who used payday lenders did have credit needs, and these needs weren't going to go away. The grant was returned to Freddie Mac, and the group changed course, setting about to create an alternative short-term, small-dollar credit product that would not damage the community (Mitchell-Bennett 2015).

The first step in the process was research. The payday problem wasn't unique to Texas or the Rio Grande Valley, and there were others across the country who had worked to develop alternatives, or "good" payday lending products. But after digging around and looking at various programs it became apparent that the "good" payday lending programs tended to be small, subsidized, and not scalable. A different solution was necessary.

For a new lending product to work, the loan repayment needed to be structured so that the borrowers could make the payments without much difficulty. A critical piece of the research was to talk to potential borrowers to find out what form of repayment would work best for them. The conclusion was that an amortizing loan, rather than a loan with a large lump sum payment, would make it much easier for the potential borrowers to absorb the expense and repay the loan (Mitchell-Bennett 2015).

Program Design

The group set about creating a new vehicle that could provide small-dollar, short-term loans designed to address lower-income individuals' short-term cash needs without causing extreme financial hardship. A solution was needed that would not require a brick-and-mortar, storefront presence, as the group determined that would be too costly. Instead, the group decided to create a fully automated, franchised system and work through major employers to reach potential customers. They believed that this model would build on the core competencies of each of the partners and position the program in the best way.

There were several clear requirements for the new short-term, small-dollar loan product. It needed to be fairly priced with reasonable terms and competitive with other small-dollar loans in the market. The lending program also needed to be scalable and replicable, and able to generate enough income to cover its operating costs (Mitchell-Bennett 2015).

After considering a range of products, the group arrived at a loan that would range in size up to a maximum of $1000 or 50% of a borrower's monthly gross pay. The loan would be repaid through payroll deductions over a 12 month period. There would be relaxed underwriting, no collateral, and no prepayment penalties. An origination fee of $20 and 18%

interest rate would be used to cover expenses. In contrast to the profit-motivated payday lenders, the total cost to the borrower would be about $122 per $1000 borrowed versus $700-plus from the payday lender. The end result: a product that was employer based, highly automated and efficient, and cost neutral to the employer. Employers could offer the product as a benefit to employees (Mitchell-Bennett 2015; Duffrin 2015).

Collaborative Partners and Core Competencies

Launching the business took longer than expected. While the CDC of Brownsville had competence and a comparative advantage in developing effective financial literacy and lending programs, they did not fully anticipate what it would take to obtain a lending license from the state for the CLC online system. It took a year, and developing the right software was also a lengthy process. After hiring a consultant to identify the best "off the shelf" product for the new business, the best that could be found was a system that could only do 85% of what was needed. This software, though inadequate, was used from 2011 until 2014 until a new custom software was created. Getting the perfect software was not easy but was essential for expanding the program. Thanks to a chance conversation, Mitchell-Bennett was able to tap a friend with software design expertise who agreed to create the software in his spare time, at no charge, in return for a small fee on each future transaction.

The launch of CLC was aided by a $600,000 grant from the US Treasury. The group worked with the RGV Multibank, which is a joint venture of eight banks, certified by the United States Department of Treasury as a Community Development Financial Institution (CDFI) and administered by CDC of Brownsville. RGV Multibank established the subsidiary, the Rio Grande Valley Community Loan Center (CLC), to implement this creative and seminal payday lending program.

Two organizations are engaged in the operations of Community Loan Center. The CDC of Brownsville manages the CLC, originates, and services all loans and develops the software and intellectual property. Texas Community Capital (TCC), a nonprofit loan fund and affiliate of the Texas Association of Community Development Corporations, sublicenses the software and intellectual property to local CLC lenders, recruits new local lenders into the business, and creates program guidelines as well as co-branding and marketing material. It is also a licensed lender and provides CLC services in areas throughout the state of Texas that aren't covered by a local CLC (CDC of Brownsville 2015).

While TCC had been around for some time as an affiliate of the Texas Association of CDCs (TACDC), it hadn't been very active prior to its involvement with the CLC. The leadership of the TACDC saw the partnership with CDC of Brownsville as a way to give purpose to TCC and address a very pressing problem in the state. Given TCC's affiliation to the TACDC, it had access to a broad network of community development organizations concerned about the economic health and vitality of their communities. This network was fertile ground for finding local sponsors for the CLC franchise. According to TACDC CEO Matt Hull, they got involved because the TCC needed a purpose, they believed strongly in the mission, and they were willing to work hard to make this new idea work (Hull 2015).

TCC has helped establish several local CLCs as franchises in other markets around the state. The local CLC role is to recruit employers, raise loan capital to fund the loans that they make, and become licensed as a lender via the Texas OCC. The franchise pays a $10,000 fee and splits the loan fees with the RGV CLC. To date there are six local CLCs—three CDFIs and three CDCs. It is not essential that the franchise have consumer lending experience, for in the CLC model, it is the employer that is underwritten, not the borrower. Each local CLC makes financial literacy counseling available to borrowers, but it is not mandatory that borrowers utilize it (Hull 2015).

Each local CLC needs the equivalent of one FTE to manage the program, with the primary duties being marketing the program and signing up new employers, and raising money for the loan pool. Thus far, most lending money has come from banks, corporations, foundations, and individuals.

The collaborative has been very fortunate to receive donated legal services from the University of Texas School of Law Community Development Clinic. The clinic helped the group think through the legal structure, develop contracts and franchise agreements. Each CLC signs a services contract that sets out roles and expectations and a licensing agreement for the software. Another partner in the collaborative, Texas Appleseed, a nonprofit organization dedicated to promoting social and economic justice for all Texans, has raised money to pay for an evaluation of the CLC program by Texas A&M University.

Some of the key components that make the CLC program successful are an online application, employer portal, financial partner portal, and an administrative portal. The custom software has been designed to make the process as automated and streamlined as possible.

Each partner in the collaborative brings a different set of competencies to make the program work. Below is a chart highlighting where each group's strengths lie.

Core Competency Matrix

Chart 7.1 highlights the key competencies that each of the organizations utilized in this collaboration.

Accomplishments to Date

In the first year of the program, CLC made 792 loans. As of November 2016, the CLC network of lenders has originated nearly 18,000 loans totaling $14.7 million. The program has expanded into Dallas, Houston, Laredo, Austin, Brazos Valley, Waco, and Longview in Texas; Fort Wayne and La Fayette in Indiana; and, Baltimore, Maryland. There are plans to move into several other locations over the next 5 years. CLC is working with 125 employers covering 65,000 employees. Loan losses are at a modest 3.5% network wide (Mitchell-Bennett 2016).

A survey of borrowers completed in April 2015 provides insight into who is benefiting from the CLC product. Based on the responses of 452 borrowers from around the state, the mean age of the borrower is 41 years of age, and 57% are female. Of the respondents, 55% are Latino/Hispanic, 24% are Black, and 11% are White. Nearly 67% of the borrowers had incomes under $50,000 a year, with 3% under $20,000. The income profile of these borrowers, while still low, is higher than the payday loan applicants, where 43% the borrowers have incomes under $20,000 a year (Consumer Financial Protection Bureau).

Most borrowers in the survey had both a checking account (91.4%) and savings account (64.8%), but only 16.2% state that they have enough savings to cover a car repair or other unexpected expense. Only 11.9% reported that they have enough money to pay for 3 months' expenses in an emergency. Most (68.8%) had 401k, IRA, or other retirement funds. A slight majority rent (51.8%). Of those who know their credit score (46.5%), 70% are rated below 619, which is considered a poor credit score.

Chart 7.1 CDC of Brownsville—Community Lending Center Competency Chart

Competency	Organizations						
	CDC of Brownsville	Rio Grande Valley Multibank	Texas Community Capital	Community Loan Centers	University of Texas CD clinic	Texas A&M University	Texas Appleseed
Organizational Development and Management	X	X			X (Legal)		
Community Engagement and public policy		X	X	X			X
Planning	X		X				
Communications	X			X			X
Project/Business Development	X		X				
Lending		X	X	X			
Property and Asset Management							
Program/Business Line Development and Management	X		X				
Resource Development, Capital Aggregation and Fundraising	X		X	X			X
Collaboration and Partnering	X	X	X	X			
Performance Measurement and Evaluation						X	X

Program Goals

The immediate goals for the CLC program are to get ten more licensed CLC lenders and to make 16,000 loans in 24 months. The long-term goal of the collaborative is to build a sustainable social enterprise for nonprofits that is scalable both locally and nationally.

Plans are underway to have a thorough program evaluation completed. Working with Texas Appleseed, CDC of Brownsville has contracted with a researcher at Texas A&M to do a year-long study of over 400 borrowers of the CLC. The study is broken into three parts addressing: (1) Who is borrowing? (2) Assessing after 6 months how is it going with the loan and how was the money used? (3) Assessing whether this product changed the borrowers' lives for the better in any way, such as has it improved the individual's credit score or helped the borrower develop better budgeting skills? The program will also be evaluated based on the number of loans originated, total capital lent to borrowers, total loans originated per location and per employer, the rate of delinquencies, rate of defaults, and number of CLCs operating. Estimates on savings per borrower and community will also be calculated.

What Was Learned

According to Mitchell-Bennett, who acted as the lead "quarterback" for the effort, they were "building the plane while they were flying it." Given the originality of the model, every step of the process involved innovation and learning. Thus far, some key lessons learned are:

- *Volume is critical.* In order to make the program work financially, there needs to be a constant flow of business. This means that the nonprofit franchise managing a CLC needs to do constant marketing. Nonprofits typically don't have expertise in this area. CDC of Brownsville hired a sales person from Sam's Club to help the nonprofit franchises build these skills.
- *The benefits must be clear and the system easy to use.* Business owners typically love the product, but this is not necessarily so for the human resources staff. The owners see it as a benefit and the HR staff see it as more work. As a result, there is a need to educate the businesses about the broader benefit of the giving employees access to affordable short-term cash.

- *Picking the right businesses is essential.* In this business, it is important to underwrite the business more than the borrower. Employers with high turnover or a cyclical employment pattern can wreak havoc on loan repayments when employees leave before the loan is fully repaid. The collaborative has learned the importance of picking large, solid employers to balance out employers with less stability. Initially they worked with the Brownsville ship-breaking companies, but when there were no ships to break, employment plummeted and there were high loan losses. On the other hand, local government, large hospitals, and school districts have fairly stable employment and large numbers of employees with modest incomes. School districts in Texas pay their teachers just 10 months of the year, so short-term loans in summer months are a great benefit.
- *Choosing the right partners with the right competencies for the collaborative and the franchises is essential.* The local CLCs don't have to have an expertise in lending, but they do have to be mission driven and have a desire to replace exploitive payday lending with a better product.
- *Good software is essential to business model success.* For the system to be low cost to operate, it is critical that the software work flawlessly and be easy to use for the borrower and the employer. There is a need for constant tweaking to keep the system working and to address issues that pop up when working with employers with a variety of accounting systems.
- *The collaborative approach with multiple organizations was essential* to gain a statewide reach and access competencies not held by the CDC of Brownsville or the RGV CLC, but it can, at times, slow the process due to the number of parties involved.

CONCLUSION

In today's global economy, the causes of the problems that plague a given community are generally much larger than any one organization can tackle, yet that doesn't stop mission-driven, entrepreneurial organizations from trying. When Nick Mitchell-Bennett and his kaffeklatsch colleagues decided to tackle the payday lending problem in the Rio Grande Valley, they assembled a group of disparate organizations who created a new business model. Each organization leveraged their competencies to solve the problem. They risked significant capital and persevered through multiple setbacks. Each member of the collaborative played, and continues to play, an important role. They are utilizing their competencies and strengths to make the effort successful. The results thus far are promising. The CLC system provides a meaningful alternative to predatory payday lending in Texas. To continue, and extend beyond Texas, the durability of the collaboration and the ability to become financially self-sufficient will be critical for success.

WEST COOK COUNTY HOUSING COLLABORATIVE CASE STUDY

The Situation and Context

As the foreclosure crisis rocked the nation after the financial collapse of 2008, many communities found themselves facing great devastation and tens of thousands of vacant housing units. In the Chicago metropolitan area, the crisis hit hard, with 405,155 foreclosures in a 4 year period between 2008–2014 (Woodstock Institute 2016).

The Chicago metropolitan area, defined as the Chicago-Joliet-Naperville, IL-IN-WI Metropolitan Statistical Area, has approximately 9.6 million people comprised of 3.3 million households. The racial composition, according to the 2010 census, was 52.8% Non-Hispanic White, 22.1% Hispanic, 16.7% Non-Hispanic African-Americans, and 6.4% Asian. Other ethnic groups such as Native Americans and Pacific Islanders made up just 2% of the population. The average cost of a home in 2012 ($207,100) and the average household income ($59,261) were near the national averages (American Communities Survey 2012). The poverty rate in 2012 hovered at 15%, equivalent to the national rate (US Census Bureau).

In spite of many local and national efforts to address the foreclosure problem, including the Home Affordable Modification Program, the Hardest Hit Fund, and the Cook County Mortgage Foreclosure Mediation Program, the Chicago inventory of foreclosed homes was the largest in the country in 2011 (O'Shea and O'Shea 2011).

As the crisis abated, neighborhoods in downtown Chicago and those in the north began to prosper, but those in the south and west did not. While the Great Recession and foreclosure crunch were major contributors to the distress in these communities, they weren't the only factors. Vacant homes have plagued some of the city's neighborhoods for decades, the result of years of disinvestment and economic and social disparities (Gallun and Maidenberg 2013).

One of the factors that exasperated the foreclosure problem in the Chicago area was that Illinois is a judicial foreclosure state, meaning that state courts must process foreclosures. This is a lengthy process and in many cases foreclosure resolutions could take as long as 2 years (Gallun and Maidenberg 2013).

To help alleviate this issue, in 2013, the Governor of Illinois signed a bill to fast-track foreclosures. Though foreclosure filings began to drop compared to earlier years, the number of foreclosures still put Chicago as the second worst city of the nation's 10 largest metro areas, according to RealtyTrac (Gallun and Maidenberg 2013).

The six-county region did not start to recover until 2014. That year there were just under 14,000 foreclosure filings, a 38% drop from the prior year, and the lowest number since 2007, according to the Woodstock Institute.

Metro-wide Housing Challenges

Prior to the foreclosure situation, many parts of the Chicago metro area were experiencing a growing deficit of affordable housing. During the 1990s, the suburban housing markets were not keeping pace with job and population growth. Jurisdictions took a variety of approaches to address the problem, resulting in inconsistent housing policy across the suburban communities (Longworth 2011). The lack of affordable housing, especially in areas where jobs were growing, resulted in negative impacts for employers, employees, and transportation infrastructure (Snyderman and Dever 2013).

During this period, the Chicago Metropolitan Agency for Planning and its Metropolitan Mayors Caucus (MMC), a membership organization that includes nine councils of government and 272 municipalities, as well as the Metropolitan Planning Council and Chicago Community Trust, provided research and policy direction on issues of regional significance.

In recognition of the housing affordability issues and housing-jobs imbalance, the Mayors Caucus' Housing Taskforce was launched in 2000 (Snyderman and Dever 2013). The MMC is a 501(c)6 tax-exempt organization that is supported by member dues and foundation grants and operates by consensus (Clements 2015). The MMC developed housing goals, which resulted in a Housing Action Agenda that promoted a balanced housing strategy for the region. After a few years of tackling the agenda town by town, it became clear that strategies for addressing the jobs–housing imbalance needed to be done across jurisdictional boundaries (Longworth 2011).

When the foreclosure crisis came, MMC redirected its focus from the jobs–housing balance challenge to combatting foreclosures. Given the collaborative approach of MMC, it was well positioned to launch an effort to work across jurisdictions to reduce the massive foreclosure inventory.

The planning work done by the MMC was complemented by a parallel effort undertaken to execute solutions to the foreclosure problem. In 2003, under Chicago Mayor Daly's direction, a Home Ownership Preservation Initiative (HOPI) was created to analyze and propose solutions to the problem of high foreclosure in impoverished neighborhoods. This group was expanded in 2007 to work regionally, becoming RHOPI, and included a unique partnership among the public, nonprofit experts, and practitioners. RHOPI, in addition to researching problems and solutions related to the foreclosure crisis, promoted a practice of cross-sector, inter-jurisdictional collaboration. According to Allison Milld Clements, Director of Housing Initiatives at the MMC, there were many communities hit by large numbers of foreclosures that did not have the capacity to apply individually for the resources that were becoming available to combat the crisis (Clements 2015).

As federal resources became available through the American Recovery and Reinvestment Act (ARRA) and Neighborhood Stabilization Program (NSP), communities were encouraged by MCC to work together, and take a collaborative approach to address the problem (Clements 2015; Longworth 2011).

The Collaboration

In the West Cook County communities of Bellwood, Maywood, Forest Park, Oak Park, and Berwyn, the foreclosure issue was significant and by 2010 the number of filings in these five communities was outpacing many of their neighboring suburban communities (WCCHC 2014). Together, these five towns have a total population of just under 166,000 with roughly 60% of the homes owner-occupied. The communities are not demographically or economically homogenous. Oak Park was the wealthiest of the five communities with the highest home values. While Oak Park is diverse ethnically, the other communities were predominately minority—either African-American or Hispanic. The level of foreclosures also varied among the communities with Berwyn having 2.5 times the number of foreclosures of Oak Park (Longworth 2011).

They all shared a common challenge and desire to mitigate the negative impacts of foreclosure. For them, the crisis was real and threatening, as it impacted their tax revenues and the livability of their communities. Each city had specific core competencies that they could use to confront the crisis, but no one city had every competency that was needed. In the city of Berwyn, one in five properties went through foreclosure, impacting nearly every block in the community. While some suburban communities did not take a proactive approach to the foreclosure problem, these five communities all wanted to take action to improve the situation (Summers 2015). The then-Mayor of Oak Park made this work a priority. He encouraged the neighboring suburbs to come together and apply for federal funds and directed his staff to contribute time to the collaborative, even though the Oak Park community had not been hit as hard as the other areas and would not be eligible for some of the federal funding. Oak Park's leadership recognized that it was in their self-interest to see their neighbors' housing markets improve (Clements 2015; Grossman 2015).

The availability of the Neighborhood Stabilization Program (NSP) funds to combat foreclosure in 2009 led to the formation of the West Cook County Housing Collaborative (WCCHC), which applied for the funding. Each community had different strengths and competencies, but they all had one thing in common: the lack of staffing and expertise to advance foreclosure mitigation measures on their own. Together, they were able to get philanthropic support from the Chicago Community Trust and Grand Victoria Foundation, to hire a coordinator to manage the planning, application, and implementation process. The nonprofit community development organization IFF was selected as the WCCHC's coordinator (Snyderman and Dever 2013). MMC acted as the fiscal agent for the collaborative (Clements 2015).

The WCCHC was one of three inter-jurisdictional collaboratives in the Chicago metro area that began in response to the foreclosure crisis. Each collaborative was structured slightly differently, with the WCCHC the only one that initially picked a nonprofit community development entity as its coordinator.

The WCCHC coordinator IFF is a mission-driven lender, real estate consultant, and developer whose mission is to help communities thrive by creating opportunities for low-income communities and people with disabilities (IFF 2015). With headquarters based in Chicago, IFF has been a key community development player in the metro area since 1988.

Beginning in about 2007, IFF began to work with suburban jurisdictions on housing issues. IFF attended RHOPI meetings and participated in discussions about housing issues. The suburban communities at that time lacked an active, high-capacity nonprofit affordable housing developer, and IFF's initial foray in this geography was to create a senior housing development in a western suburb. IFF also did some community development lending in Oak Park and Berwyn. When the opportunity arose to coordinate the collaborative, IFF was well positioned to do the work. They had the competencies needed to facilitate a collaborative effort, and the real estate and financing know-how to address the issue (Neri 2015).

According to Berwyn Assistant City Administrator Evan Summers, IFF was a natural fit for what was needed. The collaborative knew it wanted a nonprofit to lead the housing work and IFF had the knowledge and competency to navigate the housing finance world. They knew what resources were available and had the ability to secure them and put them to good use for the collaborative. While the various pots of funds had use stipulations that made their distribution uneven among the municipalities, the WCCHC worked with IFF to find resources to help each community. The group operated under the principal that they were in this together, and that if one neighbor failed, everyone suffered (Summers 2015).

Another benefit of the WCCHC, according to Summers, was that the collaboration served as a "de facto housing department" where the municipalities could bounce ideas, crunch data, and find out what others were doing to get new implementable ideas.

When the WCCHC issued the request for proposals for the coordinator's role, IFF saw it as a significant opportunity to help implement comprehensive community change. By strategically deploying expertise in research, planning, lending, and development, IFF could bring much more to the job than a single individual could who would likely not have all of these skills. The WCCHC agreed and engaged IFF in 2009 (Neri 2015).

Included in IFF's responsibilities as the coordinator is the facilitation of the WCCHC steering committee, which is comprised of elected officials from each jurisdiction and the working group which is comprised of staff. The role of the steering committee is to set overall direction while the working group handles strategy and tactics. According to IFF, representation has been pretty consistent with both groups over the length of the collaboration, although the level of interest has varied as the individuals filling the elected positions change (Ansorge and Bell 2015).

Putting the Competencies to Work

In the beginning, there were many strategy meetings to determine what should be done to mitigate the foreclosure crisis. However, given the complexity and limitations of various funding sources, the strategy had to be adapted to utilize available funding. The group placed a priority on renovating vacant single-family homes, which was the biggest issue in three of the five communities, the exceptions being Forest Park and Oak Park (WCCHC 2014).

The NSP funding, which was distributed by the Illinois Housing Development Authority (IHDA), was the initial resource obtained by the collaborative and key to launching its work. While the collaborative applied for money to renovate foreclosed single-family homes, the majority of funding awarded by the state to WCCHC was for multi-family housing preservation. Thus, the group had to refocus its strategy accordingly, and used the $3.2 million to renovate a 26-unit foreclosed building in Maywood and renovate three single-family homes.

Of the five communities, the city of Berwyn had the highest foreclosure rates and, as a result, received a direct allocation of NSP funds from IHDA. The city used the $4 million to renovate 27 single-family homes and is now recycling the repaid money for additional renovation. They managed the funds with their staff, who had experience managing other federal block grant programs. Initially they tried to use a lottery to sell the renovated homes, but realized that people wanted a more traditional approach, so they switched to using an experienced real estate broker (Summers 2015).

IFF worked closely with two nonprofit organizations on the single-family acquisition and rehab strategy, Breaking Ground and North West Housing Partnership. Breaking Ground is an NSP-approved developer and general contractor. They acquire foreclosed properties in need of rehab, assess the work required, bid out the work, and manage the construction process to completion. Breaking Ground uses the construction to provide employment to graduates of a program they run aimed at teaching inner-city youth building construction skills (Breaking Ground 2015). North West Housing Partnership is a multi-faceted nonprofit whose mission is to create and implement programs to promote economically diverse housing (NWHP 2015).

Creating a large pool of buyer-ready households to purchase the homes repaired under the various programs was one piece that was missing in the collaboration. According to IFF, this limited the number of homes that were ultimately improved. While the Oak Park Neighborhood Housing Center provided home buyer education and ensured that buyers met the criteria for the subsidy programs, no entity was focused on the demand side of the problem to greatly increase the number of qualified buyers. At the height of the foreclosure crisis, in areas with a damaged housing market, creating demand for the newly renovated homes was one of the biggest challenges (Neri 2015).

After Hurricane Ike, the federal government allocated Community Development Block Grant Disaster Recovery Program funds. The money, which was provided to address flooding damage, became available from the Illinois Department of Commerce and Economic Opportunity (DCEO) (MPC, MMC and MPC 2013). IFF applied for a grant on behalf of the WCCHC to repair homes in targeted communities. The grant was structured so that it wasn't restricted to just flood-damaged homes. This allowed the collaborative to create a $4.2 million revolving fund to renovate homes in three of the five communities that were eligible for the funding. Once the monies are repaid, they can be re-used for renovations in all five communities. Subsequently, an additional $3 million was granted from the Illinois Attorney General, which could be used in the two communities that did not qualify for the Disaster funds.

During the Disaster funds allocation process, the DCEO made a determination that IFF could not both administer the funds and act as a developer, even though they had been allowed to play a dual role when administering the NSP money. As a result, other developers were brought into do the renovation work, adding another layer of coordination and complexity to the process. IFF provided technical assistance to these firms with a goal of completing about 100 homes.

As coordinator, IFF was always on the search for new sources of funding that could advance the collaborative's priorities. In 2010 they applied for and were awarded a HUD Sustainable Communities Challenge Grant to create a transit-oriented development loan fund and create comprehensive plans for four of the WCCHC communities. One community, Maywood, already had a current plan and therefore participated in the comprehensive plan piece of this effort.

IFF also had the very important but unglamorous job of managing all of the government paperwork, including certifications and audits. In a large collaborative with many partners and multiple funding sources, these essential administrative tasks need attention.

Accomplishments to Date

Since 2009, WCCHC has received $396,750 in philanthropic funds from three sources—the Chicago Community Trust, the Grand Victoria Foundation, and JP Morgan Chase Foundation. These funds were used to support the work of WCCHC, including the coordinator's role. WCCHC estimates that it has leveraged $14.4 million in public and private funds to advance the collaborative's work (WCCHC 2015). To date, 72 units of housing in homes with 1–5 units have been renovated and sold and 26 units of multi-family housing have been renovated and leased for a total impact of 98 units of additional affordable housing added to the communities.

Future Goals

The foreclosure crisis has abated, and in some of the communities, such as Berwyn, the home prices have bounced back to pre-crisis levels, while Maywood and Bellwood still have a way to go (Summers 2015). As a result, the priorities for the collaborative and the level of engagement are in transition. The WCCHC has continued to meet, recently signing a new intergovernmental agreement, and they have identified several housing issues that they wish to tackle in each community. They are looking at pooling resources to perform certain functions and they are continuing to engage IFF as the coordinator. Getting a quorum at meetings, which is required under open meeting laws, has become more of a challenge, and the collaborative is reducing the frequency in which they meet in hopes of countering this trend. IFF will continue to lend funds and develop property, but if their role becomes solely administrative, there may not be a need for them to stay active with the collaborative (Ansorage and Bell 2015).

Core Competencies

Each member of the collaborative brought specific competencies to bear. While each partner has many competencies, the chart highlights the key competencies that were essential to their role in this collaboration.

Core Competency Matrix

Chart 7.2 highlights the key competencies that each of the organizations utilized in this collaboration.

What Was Learned

- A crisis and money can motivate.

While the Chicago metropolitan area has a rich history of regional planning and had begun to work collaboratively across jurisdictions to address the foreclosure crisis, the crisis and related funding opportunities were a primary impetus for the creation of the WCCHC.

- Clear intent must be present over time.

Now that the crisis has subsided and the majority of the related funds have been spent, there is less of an urgency or drive to work together. Both the steering committee and working group have cut back on the frequency of their meetings and the ability to get a quorum has been sometimes challenging. While the group has recently recommitted to working together and has identified some new goals, the common sense of purpose is not as strong. Furthermore, there have been some changes in political representation in communities, which has resulted in a shift in priorities.

- More can be accomplished working together than working alone.

The success of the WCCHC to attract and expend funds would not have happened had the communities not come together and hired a coordinator that had the necessary competencies to lead this work for them. The collaboration also allowed each jurisdiction to get more done to address the foreclosure crisis in their community.

- Take advantage of existing efforts.

The collaborative was able to benefit from the efforts of the regional planning work of MCC and funding from national sources.

- Look for funding in unusual places.

The recovery money for Hurricane Ike and Sustainability grant for transit-oriented development provided additional resources that advanced the work of the collaborative. If the WCCHC had only relied on NSP money, it would not have accomplished nearly as much.

Chart 7.2 West Cook County Housing Collaborative Competency Chart

Competency	Organizations					
	IFF	Five participating communities	Oak Park Neighborhood Housing Center	Breaking Ground	North West Housing Partnership	MMC/MCP
Organizational Development and Management	X	*	X	X	X	
Community Engagement and Public Policy		X	X			X
Planning and Public Policy Communications	X					X
Project Development (Real Estate)	X		X	X	X	
Lending	X					
Property and Asset Management				X		
Program/Business Line Development and Management	X	X		X	X	X
Resource Development, Capital Aggregation and Fundraising	X	*				X
Collaboration and Partnerships	X	X		X	X	X
Performance Measurement and Evaluation	X	X				X

*Oak Park had a role in managing grants and fundraising

- Regulations can impede collaboration.

The WCCHC faced some obstacles in working together when funders put certain restrictions on the use of funds. Fortunately, with IFF as the coordinator, the WCCHC was able to submit proposals that had a multi-jurisdictional benefit. But had IFF not been in place, they would have been forced to compete with each other or submit duplicative proposals. Equally challenging were funds that required the applicant to be a public entity, and funds with geographic restrictions, which caused uneven access to each funding source.

- More can be done with a coordinator with multiple competencies.

As mentioned, two other multi-jurisdictional collaboratives were created to address the foreclosure, but only the WCCHC selected a nonprofit organization to serve as the coordinator. While IFF was happy to partner with others throughout the process, if necessary, they were able to draw upon multiple competencies to deliver what was needed to the collaborative. Their resource development, lending and developer competencies, as well as their ability to facilitate and lead, were key to the WCCHC's level of accomplishments. By comparison, the South County Collaborative changed tactics, and hired IFF to coordinate implementation of a grant due to lack of progress under the prior arrangement using a single individual as the coordinator.

REACH Community Development—ACE Merger Case Study

The Situation and Context

Portland is the largest city in the state of Oregon, located at the confluence of the Columbia and Willamette Rivers. It has a population of approximately 632,000 and is predominantly White (76.1%), with 9.4% Hispanic, 7.1% Asian, 6.3% African-American, 1% American Indian and Alaska Native, and 4.2% other (US Census Bureau 2016).

In its early years, Portland was a port town and hub for the timber industry. It has undergone several economic transitions and now serves as a major center of high tech with its Silicon Forest and sportswear companies. While a beacon for "hippies" in the 1970s, Portland has become one of the most popular cities in the USA, attracting young professionals who seek both its outdoor and hipster lifestyles (Pdxhistory.com 2013).

During the 1970s, the city of Portland made some significant changes to the way that it involved citizens in local government decision making. While neighborhood activists had been gaining clout by inserting themselves in major public policy decisions during the 1960s and 1970s through programs like Model Cities, their involvement wasn't sanctioned by local government. With the passage of SB 100 in 1973, which stipulated that every city in the state of Oregon develop a comprehensive plan, neighborhood groups were granted the right to initiate the creation of district planning organizations that would be allowed to participate in the comprehensive plan process which would guide future development in their community. Many of the guidelines that were created for the district planning organizations were used by the city of Portland a few years later when it created the Office of Neighborhood Involvement (ONI). ONI, among other things, provided citizens with a formal process for commenting on the city's land use and planning decisions. This formal method of community involvement, operating through a citywide system of neighborhood associations, helped galvanize the voice of community activists on a number of urban issues (Office of Neighborhood Involvement 2016).

During the 1970s, as Portland's suburbs continued to grow, the city's inner neighborhoods were experiencing decline (Goodling et al. 2015). The Buckman Neighborhood in inner southeast Portland was not immune from these symptoms. Many of its Victorian homes had been recently demolished to make way for plain, low-rise apartment buildings enabled by a recent change in the local zoning. When a large apartment building was proposed on a parcel that the community wanted to develop as a park, a few members of the Buckman Neighborhood Association (BNA) intervened. They formed a partnership and developed 12 new row homes that fit in with the older homes in the community. In 1980, the association held its first community congress and discussed the changes impacting the neighborhood. The school district had decided to close the local high school and BNA members responded by forming a community development corporation called REACH. REACH stood for recreation, education access, commerce, and housing. The group, led by BNA activists, proposed that the school district turn over the high school to them for development as a multi-use facility. The school district declined, but REACH persevered and went on to purchase and renovate vacant homes in the neighborhood (Buckman Community Association 2007).

Since REACH's incorporation in 1982, it has grown dramatically. It began as a community development corporation working in six neighborhoods and today is a Regional Housing Development Organization (RHDO) working in a two-state metropolitan area. While its primary mission continued to be the creation of affordable housing, REACH's lines of business expanded over the years. During the 1990s, REACH worked with community members to create and implement three comprehensive community development plans in neighborhoods that were experiencing disinvestment and decline. At the same time, REACH began to offer resident services to children and adults living in its housing. These services included "Youth$ave," a financial education and matched-savings program for children, as well as several asset-building programs for adults. In 1995, in response to a rising number of homes that had fallen into disrepair, REACH created a free home repair program for senior and disabled home owners. By 2012, REACH had developed or preserved over 1600 units of housing and had 100 staff (REACH 2016).

In Portland, the 2008 recession hit real estate markets fairly hard. Portland's revenue decline due to the loss of property value and related tax income dropped $64 million from 2007 to 2009 (The Pew Charitable' Trust 2013). Housing starts slowed dramatically and prices fell or remained flat. The real estate market didn't begin to improve much until 2013/2014 when rents increased an average of 9% over the previous year (Holmstrom 2016).

Many nonprofit community development organizations in Portland experienced a reduction in resources for affordable housing development from both public and private sources. However, organizations with strong balance sheets, like REACH, were well positioned to offer good investment opportunities to investors and lenders still active in the market. As a result, REACH had a healthy development pipeline and related developer fee income (REACH 2009–2012).

Small community development organizations did not prosper during this period. Unable to attract private banks and investors to participate in their real estate deals, many small community development groups had to reduce staff or look for partnership opportunities with others. Affordable Community Environments (ACEs), a small CDC based in Vancouver, Washington, which is part of the larger Portland metropolitan area, was struggling financially. In 2008 they experienced a financial crisis and were able to survive the immediate problem by raising some funds to bridge the anticipated developer fees and reducing staff and expenses. However, they needed to generate new real estate development deals to earn fees to support their operations. At the time, they had a portfolio of five apartment communities containing about 200 units of affordable housing (Leonard et al. 2013). ACE's Executive Director explored the possibility of partnering with other Vancouver nonprofits with similar missions, but did not find an organization that was a good fit.

Program Design and Goals

In 2011, REACH's Executive Director was in the midst of implementing their strategic plan, which called for growing the geographic footprint, affordable housing production and impact. REACH explored many avenues for expansion, including developing new partnerships with organizations and institutions in other sectors, such as the regional transit company, which resulted in a mixed-use development along a new rail line.

REACH also explored collaborations and mergers, including one with a smaller organization that was experiencing a leadership change. REACH had considered expanding across the state lines into Vancouver, Washington, as this area had a great deal of need and few entities engaged in affordable housing development. However, REACH recognized that to be successful working in Vancouver, they would need community and political support, and historically Portland and Vancouver had a civic rivalry that might make this challenging.

After hearing the Executive Director of a small CDC based in Vancouver talk about their financial challenges at a local housing conference, REACH's Executive Director thought that there was the possibility of a mutually beneficial collaboration and approached ACE's Executive Director with a proposal to explore a partnership.

ACE's financial model relied on the development fees generated from new affordable housing projects, and as noted, they had struggled financially in recent years. In the post-recession environment, ACE's leadership recognized that as a small organization, their ability to obtain and compete for financing for a steady stream of new development projects was questionable. They were committed to finding a solution where their portfolio of housing would continue to operate.

On the other hand, REACH came out of the recession financially strong and had recently secured a pipeline of projects to build in the Portland metro area. However, Oregon's financial resources were limited and working in another state would open up a whole new funding stream.

The "ingredients" of a good collaboration were apparent. REACH had financial strength and programs that would be beneficial to Vancouver residents, while ACE had a solid track record and strong ties to the community and local leadership. Both organizations had similar missions and were committed to meeting the affordable housing needs in the communities they served.

After two exploratory meetings, the Executive Directors of both organizations agreed to begin a serious exploration of a merger. They began by surveying their boards and staffs to identify issues and concerns. They developed a timeline of activities and sought grant funds to help support the merger work. They were successful in getting funding from NeighborWorks America and Enterprise Community Partners for a consultant to facilitate deliberations, and for technical assistance and legal advice needed to conduct the transaction. Enterprise Community Partners also prepared a write-up evaluating the partnership upon completion.

Together, REACH and ACE hired a consultant to facilitate discussions between the boards of directors and to develop the merger plan. Due diligence work was split up between the organizations. Due to the complexity of affordable housing finance, it was determined that ACE would become a subsidiary of REACH; that way, the ownership structure on ACE's properties would not need to change.

After nearly 2 years of conversations, joint board meetings and due diligence and legal work, the organizations "merged" with ACE becoming a subsidiary of REACH and maintaining its status as a Washington non-profit corporation and Community Housing Development Organization (CHDO).

Accomplishments to Date

The REACH by-laws were changed to include representatives from Vancouver and SW Washington and the ACE board. The ACE board continues to provide strategic direction for ACE activities in SW Washington.

Two ACE board members joined the REACH board. The ACE portfolio was preserved and management of it was taken over by REACH's property management team.

The staff of ACE was invited to join REACH's staff; two chose to join and one left the organization. The Executive Director of ACE became the housing development director for the Vancouver/SW Washington geography. Since the merger, one acquisition rehab project of an existing affordable apartment community was completed and one new construction project for seniors is under construction.

Collaborative Partners and Core Competencies

Both organizations brought key competencies that complemented each other. REACH leveraged their financial, programmatic and organizational strength, while ACE leveraged its strong community credibility and a good reputation. REACH had an experienced property management staff, while ACE outsourced this work. REACH had an extensive resident services program and ACE had a goal of expanding what they could provide their residents. ACE had strong relationships with several community organizations and leaders, and local governmental bodies. ACE had been successful in raising money to support their work. REACH was a newcomer to the Vancouver and Washington funding scene. By joining together, each leveraged their competency to advantage and it was a win–win for both organizations (Enterprise 2013).

Core Competency Matrix

Chart 7.3 highlights which competencies each group used in the collaboration in this case study.

What Was Learned

- Collaborations take time. Even with both organizations supportive of the effort to join arms, the process took 2 years. Organizations embarking on such efforts need to plan adequate time and money to conduct the due diligence and legal work necessary to complete the "merger."
- Conducting a survey of staff and board up front was very helpful. It identified issues that were of concern to both that may have not been apparent to the Executive Directors leading the merger. It was also helpful for the boards of both organizations to have social time to get to know each other before diving into negotiations.
- Hiring an independent consultant to negotiate deal points was extremely helpful to building trust and overcoming reservations.
- Cultural differences between organizations regarding work styles and expectations need to be discussed and understood. Blending cultures is one of the biggest challenges to melding two organizations.

Chart 7.3   REACH-ACE Merger Competency Chart

Competency	Organizations			
	REACH	ACE	Enterprise Community Partners	Neighbor Works America
Organizational Development and Management	X	X	X	X
Community Engagement and Public Policy		X		
Planning	X	X		
Project Development (Real Estate)	X	X		
Lending				
Property and Asset Management	X			
Program/Business Line Development and Management	X			
Resource Development, Capital Aggregation and Fundraising	X	X	X	X
Collaboration and Partnerships	X	X		
Performance Measurement and Evaluation	X		X	

While REACH and ACE did not differ greatly, the culture of a very small organization has different characteristics than a large one with more formalized processes.

CONCLUSION

The REACH–ACE collaboration was successful because the leaders of both organizations took the time to understand the issues, involve key stakeholders, and work through difficult technical and cultural issues. The collaboration slowed down somewhat due to a change in leadership at REACH toward the end of the due diligence period. However, because key board and staff had been involved throughout the process, the collaboration survived.

While each organization shared a similar mission and some of the same competencies, they operated at different scales and had enough complementary competencies to create a good, durable partnership.

FAIRMOUNT INDIGO LINE CASE STUDY

The Situation and Context

Incorporated as a town in 1630, Boston, Massachusetts, is the largest city in the state of Massachusetts and the tenth largest metro area in the country. Originally settled on a peninsula, major land reclamation and excavation expanded the city to its current 48 square miles. Today, it is home to over 30 colleges and universities, numerous high-tech companies and medical centers, and the seat of state government. The median household income is $70,967 and it has one of the highest costs of living in the USA (Forbes 2015; City of Boston 2015).

Boston's Massachusetts Bay Transportation Authority (MBTA—known as the "T") operates the nation's fifth largest transit network, consisting of both light and heavy rail rapid transit and regional commuter rail lines (MBTA 2015). The Fairmount line of the metropolitan commuter rail system, which was built in the mid-1800s, runs 9.2 miles southwesterly through several diverse neighborhoods, including Dorchester, Mattapan, and Hyde Park. The line once had 11 stations but over its 60 year life, service has been reduced. Beginning in the 1940s, the passenger service was cut due to disinvestment in the area, which had experienced demographic changes after World War II. Most of the stations closed for commuter service, leaving the residents with limited access (Fairmount Collaborative 2015).

It was not until 1979 that the MBTA resumed some service to two stations at Uphams Corner and Morton St., along the Fairmount Indigo Line. However, the service was infrequent and the fares for service along the line were high, especially for the lower-income households that lived nearby (Fairmount Indigo CDC Collaborative 2015). In 2015, the 180,000 people who lived in the corridor were predominately low- and moderate-income and multi-cultural. The median income for the area is 17% lower than the citywide median at $31,300. The population is quite diverse with 61% African-American and Caribbean, 21% Latino, 9% White, and 1% Asian (TD Bank Project Summary, Foundation Center 2011).

The Collaboration

In 2000, the Greater Four Corners Action Coalition (4CAC) launched a campaign to get more stations and service and to improve conditions for residents along the Fairmount Indigo Line. In 2004, four community development corporations along the corridor joined efforts to support 4CAC to win new stations, improved service, and lower fares. The CDC agenda was to promote and build affordable housing and reinvestment in the surrounding communities (Dubois 2016). This built on their core competencies and leveraged their comparative advantages.

The CDC collaborative included Dorchester Bay Economic Development Corporation (DBEDC), Codman Square Neighborhood Development Corporation (CSNDC), Mattapan CDC (MCDC), and Southwest Boston CDC (SWBCDC). The groups met over the next few years and established a formal relationship focused on transit equity, smart growth, and transit-oriented development (Foundation Center 2011). While 4CAC had been active on the transit issue long before CDCs got involved, the CDCs brought additional momentum and resources to the effort and, due to their track records, brought legitimacy for those investing in the area, which helped to catapult the work (Beleche 2016)

The design for improvements was laid out in the Indigo Line plan. This was the result of community organizing efforts to reactivate the corridor with more frequent transit service. After much negotiation, on the goals of a parallel development effort, a memorandum of understanding (MOU) was drafted to identify goals and desired outcomes. The CDC vision was to "create strong, vibrant, and diverse twenty-first century neighborhoods along the corridor that support strong civic engagement, provide mixed-income housing, access to safe open space, decent paying jobs, and achieve transit equity" (Foundation Center 2011). According to Codman Square Neighborhood Development Corporation Associate Director Marcos Beleche, who was Director of Organizing for Codman at the time, "the collaborative was exciting because it provided an opportunity for young people and adults in the community to access jobs. Prior to the transit improvements, it had been very hard for people from the neighborhoods to get to work" (Beleche 2016).

Six specific goals for the project were identified: (DuBois In2016 and Fairmount/Indigo Corridor Collaborative 2015).

- Transit equity to increase access to the line through 4–5 new stops and increased service.
- Equitable Transit-Oriented Development (ETOD) to create vibrant mixed-income, mixed-use "urban villages" to avoid displacement.
- Increase Economic Opportunities for businesses and job seekers.

- A Green Corridor of sustainable buildings and a Fairmount Greenway of assorted parcels and connecting bike/walking paths.
- Engage the community through grass roots organizing to insure that new services, development, and amenities serve the current and future residents.

The MOU established the goals, principles, and decision-making process for the CDC collaborative. The collaborative decided to work jointly on strategy development, fundraising, fund distribution, as well as sharing some consultants. Each CDC would independently carry out development of its own projects in accordance with the MOU's principles. The MOU clearly stated that the CDCs preferred to collaborate rather than create one large corridor-wide organization (Foundation Center 2011).

As early as 2004, the local CDCs began to purchase property along the line and the Fairmount greenway task force began to plan for a new greenway. A rally in 2005 held in the Four Corners/Geneva Avenue Station area included over 100 people from the original transit groups and also the four CDCs. This action solidified the MBTA commitment to finance four stations along the line (FICC website 2015).

In 2005, the Commonwealth of Massachusetts began extensive capital improvements as part of a legally mandated program to mitigate increased pollution caused by the "Big Dig" project which rerouted 3.5 miles of Interstate-93 underground in the downtown core. By 2007, work was underway to improve the stations at Upham's Corner and Morton Street, and construction began on the first new station at Four Corners/Geneva Avenue in 2009. Construction on two new stations began in 2010 and planning began on a third (Fairmount/Indigo Corridor Collaborative 2015).

By working together, the four CDCs were able to leverage their competencies to accomplish more than they could on their own. By sharing a common goal to improve the neighborhoods along the Fairmount Indigo Line and improve transit access for the residents living there, the collaborative was able to involve local residents and community leaders to ensure that the projects had a community benefit. Aiming to work along a long corridor was a big task, and the collaborative tried to identify issues to work on that involved more than one stakeholder (Beleche 2016).

Each CDC took on specific transit-oriented development projects located near the transit stations in an effort to create new "urban villages" that would be mixed-income, mixed-use communities close to the line

(Fairmount Indigo CDC Collaborative 2015). To achieve the broad goals of the collaborative, the four CDCs that comprised the Fairmount Indigo CDC Collaborative worked with two additional coalitions. One coalition was led by Four Corners Action Coalition, and included other neighborhood organizations, the Conservation Law Foundation, and the Fairmount Indigo Transit Coalition. The second coalition group, the Fairmount Greenway Task Force, was comprised of the 4 CDCs and 6 community partners to create and oversee the greenway plan. The Barr Foundation had granted $600,000 over 3 years to the 10 community organizations to identify priority sites and routes for the greenway. All three networks involved considerable community engagement and organizing to increase the number of local leaders, increase participation, and build power with these transit, development, and environmental initiatives (DuBois 2016).

Codman's Beleche notes that being involved in the collaborative required being flexible and being supportive of the larger vision, not just your own organization's specific goals and tasks. It also meant reaching out to new partners who could bring the expertise needed to address specific components of the vision, like the greenway (Beleche 2016).

Many public and private entities assisted the collaborative by providing either grant or low-cost capital to fund various components of the work. The Boston Foundation was a key supporter, as was the LISC, the Local Initiative Support Corporation, and the Hyams Foundation. The City of Boston and the nonprofit Boston Community Capital were also important supporters.

In 2011, the Fairmount Indigo Line was one of five pilot groups to be selected for a federally funded pilot program called the Sustainable Communities Partnership administered by the Department of Housing and Urban Development, the Environmental Protection Agency, and the Federal Transit Administration.

Also in 2011, Dorchester Bay EDC's "Quincy Corridor" projects and partnerships with Project RIGHT, Dudley Street Neighborhood Initiative, and Quincy Geneva CDC were chosen as one of the first HUD Choice implementation projects in the USA. They were awarded $20.5 M to support an array of community projects and programs including the upgrade of a 129 unit distressed property, a multi-business food production center, several resident efforts to improve public safety and local services, and case management services for local residents (DuBois 2016).

After the completion of the initial planning, and victories with transit funding, multiple acquisitions by the CDC Collaborative, and the selection of pilot segments by the Greenway Task Force, in 2012 the Boston Redevelopment Authority (BRA) convened a second-phase Fairmount Indigo Planning Initiative to help prioritize investments along the line and conduct Corridor Wide planning meetings as well as Working Area Groups (WAGS) with stakeholders in Upham's Corner, Four Corners, and Mattapan. Hyde Park had a previous planning process and was not included in a WAG on this second round (DuBois 2016).

In 2014, the Talbot Norfolk Triangle (TNT) neighborhood within Codman Square was designated as an EcoDistrict, a 2 year immersion program for those actively working to improve the area around the new Talbot Avenue transit station. The goal was to develop a mostly residential triangle with rental, homeownership, and commercial opportunities utilizing eco-upgrades in weatherization, water reuse, green bus stops, and green construction materials and methods (EcoDistrict 2015; Dubois 2016).

Project Goals

The long-term goals of the Fairmount Indigo CDC Collaborative were to create and/or preserve 1500 affordable housing units, develop 780,000 ft^2 of commercial space, and add 800 new jobs, as well as build four new transit stations and develop bike and walking paths on and off streets that would connect the parks and green parcels up and down the line.

The collaborative sets goals and reviews progress annually. They monitor revenue and expenses, progress on development projects, numbers of residents involved in transit advocacy and greenway planning, jobs and businesses created, and important public policy decisions (Foundation Center 2011).

Accomplishments to Date

By 2015, as a result of the Fairmount Indigo Transit Coalition, three new stations had opened, two previous stations were upgraded, ridership was increased 241%, evening and weekend service was added, and fares were lowered to $2.10 which was equivalent to other corridors (DuBois 2016).

In addition, significant public and private investment was underway in the corridor. Specific achievements included the following:

- Completed a successful planning process for the corridor with resident buy-in and support.
- The award of $200M in federal and state funds in 2006, partly triggered by the Big Dig mitigation lawsuit to build four new stations along the corridor.
- Developed a Smart Growth Corridor plan, winning awards from the American Planning Association, the American Institute of Architects, and the Congress for New Urbanism.
- Awarded a "Collaboration" prize from the Massachusetts Nonprofit Network in 2009
- Designated a federal Sustainable Community pilot in 2010 by HUD, EPA, and FTA.
- Completed nearly 800 housing units and 80,000 ft^2 of light industrial and commercial space, with a pipeline of 300+ more housing units.
- Completed planning of the new greenway path and pilot parcels. Finished one pilot parcel, pre-development work on a second, and planning on three other sites.
- Attracted funding from primary funders: The Boston Foundation, the Barr Foundation, the Surdna Foundation, Local Initiatives Support Corporation (LISC), Boston Community Capital, Boston Department of Neighborhood Development, Boston Redevelopment Authority, Community Economic Development Assistance Corp, MassWorks, Mass Department of Housing and Economic Development, Mass Development, Mass Division of Banks, Federal Economic Development Administration (EDA), HUD's Office of Community Services (OCS), HUD Choice, HUD CDBG and HUD 108 funds, EPA Brownfield planning and remediation funds, TD Bank North, CitiFund, Citizens Bank, NeighborWorks, the Overbrook Foundation, Hyams Foundation, and other private donors.

Future Goals

After seeing what the collaborative could leverage by working together, the CDCs in the collaborative were motivated to see if they could identify other, large issues that cut across the corridor. Jobs and workforce development were two issues they decided to tackle. Furthermore, while the transit victories had made the community more livable, they had also made it more appealing and there was a growing concern over gentrification and displacement that the community wanted to address (Beleche 2016).

Specific goals identified for the future by the Collaboration include:

- Focus on attracting more businesses and increasing jobs in the corridor through incentives, zoning changes, and increased financing.
- Creating a coordinated workforce system that connects job seekers, employers, trainers, and new skill builders.
- Developing anti-displacement strategies such as "just cause eviction" laws to slow down condo conversions. Stopping predatory speculators
- Creating more mixed-income housing at primarily low and moderate levels with some market rate homes.
- Building ridership and marketing the line.
- Boosting grass roots arts and cultural engagement, and enhancing public places for improved quality of life.
- Raising or finding sources for significant funding, ownership, and maintenance of the Greenway parcels and paths (DuBois interview 2016).

Core Competencies

Each CDC contributes its primary competencies to the collaborative. In 2006, recognizing that it would be helpful to have some central staff to coordinate the work, the group retained part-time consultants to assist with coordination, fundraising, financial management, real estate assistance, greenway coordination, and organizing. To help leverage the experience and balance sheets of the two older, larger CDCs, DBEDC and Codman formed joint ventures with the younger, smaller Mattapan and Southwest Boston CDCs. In spite of this assistance, the smaller Mattapan CDC closed in 2010.

Chart 7.4 highlights which competencies each group used in the collaboration in this case study.

Core Competency Matrix

Chart 7.4 highlights the key competencies that each of the organizations utilized in this collaboration.

Chart 7.4 Fairmount-Indigo CDC Collaborative Competency Chart

Competency	Organizations					
	Four Corners Action Coalition	Fairmount Indigo CDC Collaborative and central staff	Fairmount Indigo Greenway Taskforce	Boston Re-development Authority	Fairmount Indigo Network	Lead local funders
Organizational Development and Management	X	X				
Community Engagement and Public Policy	X	X	X	X	X	
Planning	X	X	X	X	X	
Communications	X	X	X	X	X	
Project Development (Real Estate)		X	X	X		X
Lending		X				
Property and Asset Management		X				
Program/business line development and management		X				
Resource Development, Capital Aggregation and Fundraising		X	X	X	X	X
Collaboration and Partnering	X	X	X		X	X
Performance Measurement and Evaluation	X	X	X		X	X

What Was Learned

Funding: Together, the groups were able to raise more money than they could have done independently. As the profile of the effort increased, both individual community organizations and the CDC collaborative were able to attract more funding. Building a bigger tent with additional partners helped attract even more new resources. As the various coalition and collaborative efforts gained attention, and additional stakeholders and leaders were attracted to join, there was a risk that resources would be spread too thin, and that some of the core community-based organizations might receive less support. Sometimes, the goals of the profit-oriented stakeholders conflicted with the community stabilization goals of the earlier community groups.

Real Estate Development: The CDCs and the two internal joint ventures worked with both nonprofits and for-profits to achieve mixed-income Transit Oriented Development (TOD) goals, while achieving a goal to work with many minority and female contractors and workers. One of the CDCs hired partner groups to do outreach and monitor involvement to ensure this goal was met.

Building Power: Creating alliances with others helps to grow political power as well as resources. According to Jeanne DuBois, former Executive Director of Dorchester Bay EDC, "The secret sauce is combining grassroots engagement and organizing with housing and commercial development. Organized money and organized people builds more power."

Group Process: Collaboratives with many voices require compromise, especially if you are trying to operate under a consensus decision-making model. In most cases, the CDCs, the organizing groups, and their community members reached agreements on goals, details for projects, economic development goals, and family services needed. While it can become a challenge to keep focused when there are demands to work on a wide variety of goals, the broader networks maintained innovative adaptations and flexible partnerships that accomplished most of the goals. When not all members have equal capacity to deliver, sometimes the stronger organizations needed to step into make sure the work got done.

Leveraging Experience: For some, the experience of participating in the collaborative affected the way their organization considered future work. Marcos Beleche relayed that because of the learning from the Fairmount Indigo Line experience, Codman Square CDC has more interest and confidence to tackle bigger, tougher issues, and to do so by collaborating with others.

Northwest Side CDC Case Study

History and Context

Northwest Side Community Development Corporation (NWSCDC) was founded in 1983 to reverse the decline of the 30th Street industrial corridor in Milwaukee, the home of several major factories that provided well-paying jobs to thousands of individuals in Milwaukee (Snyder and Daniell 2011).

Milwaukee demographics are characteristic of a number of older industrial cities that have experienced economic decline in the past 40 years. The Milwaukee population peaked in 1960 at 741,324 and has declined to 594,833 as of 2010. According to the 2014 American Community Survey, 15.4% of Milwaukeeans lived below the poverty level, with the rate for African-Americans at 38.1% and Latinos at 27.2%, and Whites at 7.4% below the poverty. African-Americans are more than four times likely to be poor in Milwaukee than Whites. The owner-occupied housing rate in Milwaukee is 43%, which is well below the national level. 22.8% of Milwaukee residents over 25 are college graduates and 81.8% are high school graduates.

NWSCDC focus was on commercial and industrial development, and like many other CDCs, their strategy was to acquire and manage large commercial and industrial real estate development projects that created and retained good jobs for area residents.

By 1994, NWSCDC owned about 250,000 ft^2 of commercial property, and did not have the capacity to manage and improve all the properties. This led to a severe cash flow problem derived in parts from inaccurate cash flow projections, and a lack of financial property management skills on the board and staff. The CDC found itself with a budget deficit of $200,000 including money owed to IRS, which was a huge challenge for the organization (Snyder and Daniell 2011).

The financial hemorrhaging of dollars was not unique to NWSCDC in Milwaukee, and according to Snyder and Daniell, the majority of CDCs in Milwaukee folded under financial pressure due to a shift of federal, state, and local resources along with challenging real estate investments and management. The financial condition of NWSCDC in the mid-1990s was not sustainable.

Both the board and staff leadership realized that NWSCDC needed to change their financial and business model by spreading risk. The leadership of the organization changed strategic direction in the mid-1990s away from acquiring and managing commercial real estate projects toward attracting and partnering with major economic development players in Milwaukee and the Midwest. They focused on companies that would either remain or locate in the community and provide well-paying jobs and revenue for the hard-hit residents of the community. According to Alan Perlstein, a long-time NWSCDC board member and President of the Midwest Energy Research Consortium (M-WERC) formerly known as the Wisconsin Energy Research Consortium "Howard Snyder and NWSCDC stepped out of the box from a traditional community development approach to an approach that leverages connections and strategic investments that will keep Milwaukee as a center of technological innovation" (Perlstein interview 2015).

Before shifting their economic development focus, NWSCDC had to divest itself of 250,000 ft^2 of commercial and industrial property. NWSCDC was able to sell most of its real estate portfolio including the historic fire station, which housed NWSCDC's offices. The vast majority of the properties were sold between 1997 and 2003.

In addition, to selling their real estate projects, the CDC eliminated several of its major programs including workforce development, small business incubation management, and property management.

At the same time that they were selling properties, the NWSCDC leadership faced a dilemma of how to restructure a community-oriented real estate development organization to an organization that would not own or manage real estate. The staff and board decided to adopt a new approach that built on their core competencies of community engagement, political support, and advocacy resource development. NWSCDC saw these core competencies as their comparative advantage that would attract major industrial firms through leveraged partnerships and collaboration in business and real estate transactions. Simply put, the CDC did not want to manage or own real estate property.

This new direction had implications for the staff and board. NWSCDC downsized staff from 15 in 1994 to four by 2006 as they closed down programs. The remaining staff under the leadership of Howard Snyder, who has served as Executive Director of NWSCDC since 1984, focused on financing skills, partnership skills, and community organizing. NWSCDC revised the governance structure and procedures of the organization, and decided to expand the board of directors to reflect the new strengths needed for the organization. Board members were recruited with specialized expertise in marketing, law, and human resources, skills that would help the organization assess potential economic partners.

At the staff level, the CDC made some strategic staff realignments to reflect the new direction of the organization. A new position was created for an organizer/strategic planner to engage the community in a neighborhood strategic planning process. Yvonne McCaskill, a long-time resident, retired teacher, and community activist said one of the major goals of the neighborhood planning process is to both make the community stable and ensure that the economic development that occurs in the community benefits existing residents (McCaskill interview 2015). McCaskill stated there are a large number of long-time homeowners in the community who are mostly older adults. Community leaders like McCaskill along with NWSCDC are trying to create new homeownership opportunities for younger families who can benefit from the economic opportunities. Local residents, with support from NWSCDC, helped start neighborhood block watch clubs in 2003 and 2004, and then organized the block clubs into the Century City Triangle Neighborhood Association. The initial goal of the association was safety and community improvements to retain and attract businesses that provided living wages. Previously, the community had several auto manufacturing businesses that contributed to a sizeable black middle class.

The goal for both NWSCDC and Century City Triangle Neighborhood Association is to position the community for investment with employers and manufacturers that provide innovative technology and industrial opportunities. NWSCDC attracted financial support for building Century City Towers, and the neighborhood association has been important in providing community support to the Century City Towers which resulted in the Eaton Corporation moving their manufacturing headquarters to the neighborhood.

Additionally, the CDC and neighborhood association are working together to build new affordable homeownership housing in the neighborhood. NWSCDC developed 47 units of low-income rental housing above the Villard Library, and they have renovated seven homes, and are in the process of rehabbing an additional ten owner-occupied homes.

The collaborations that NWSCDC have created are very unusual strategic partnerships in that they involve firms that have a high degree of technology and an inner-city low-income community with a high level of poverty. The two major areas where NWSCDC operates are among the poorest neighborhoods in Milwaukee, which is one of the poorest cities in the USA. The two neighborhoods are Inner North and Outer Northwest, which have a poverty level of 23.8 and 25.9%, respectively.

Milwaukee has been a long-time national leader in firms that specialize in energy, power, and controls and have firms with large contracts from the US Defense Department. DRS had a long-term plant in the neighborhood, so the issue was whether the plant stayed in the community or moved to another location in the Milwaukee region. NWSCDC convinced DRS to stay in the community through a combination of securing federal funds for renovating their facility and for business operations. NWSCDC has taken a proactive strategy to help keep technology and industrial firms in the community, through strengthening the local environment for these types of businesses. The partnership with Midwest Energy Consortium has led to the creation of the Milwaukee Technology Incubator and Energy Innovation Center (EIC) helping local firms to develop their commercialization capacity to pursue contracts with defense and other government contractors.

Collaboration and Partners

NWSCDC pursued collaborations with both DRS Power and Control Technologies and Midwest- Energy Research Consortium (M-WERC). DRS Power and Control Technologies, the largest employer in the 30th Street corridor, is a multi-national electronics corporation and defense contractor that had purchased the "Navy Controls" business unit of Eaton Corporation (Snyder and Daniell 2011). DRS was interested in NWSCDC because of their access to real estate financing and good political relationships with local alderman, mayor, state, and federal officials. NWSCDC was able to secure a $700,000 grant from the Office of Community Services to finance facility renovation for DRS, which helped keep them in the neighborhood, and also allowed the CDC to co-locate within a 600,000 ft^2 complex. The former executive of DRS Controls, Alan Perlstein, became the new executive of M-WERC. NWSCDC next partnered with DRS to establish the Milwaukee Technology Incubator to develop technology businesses that employ local residents, and they partnered to establish a 1000 ft^2 power and controls test lab for technology businesses. NWSCDC ability to attract new financial resources, political support, and potential employees for the technology firms became a comparative advantage for the CDC, attracting interest of the major firms.

M-WERC is a consortium of four universities, six tech colleges, 50 industry partners, and 20 nonprofit organizations. M-WERC has formed a strategic partnership with NWSCDC to help mentor technology-based businesses; provide financing through the NWSCDC Community Development Financial Institution (CDFI); launch a workforce development program in the power controls and energy; identify real estate space; and help emerging technology businesses access and navigate government support. M-WERC has co-located with NWSCDC, and they sublease office space from NWSCDC in the Century City Towers complex. M-WERC moved their Energy Innovation Center to occupy several floors of the Century City Towers, and to be closer to NWSCDC. The EIC is also a partnership between both organizations, and each organization provides their areas of expertise to support the growth of small businesses.

EIC is critical for start-up technology businesses in both the power control and energy sectors specializing in manufacturing components for submarines, aircraft carriers, and littoral combat ships. Small technology businesses need the innovation center to help grow, and do not have the resources individually to purchase equipment and facilities technology accelerator. Alan Perlstein credits NWSCDC with playing an important mentoring role with start-up firms to help them access financing, benefit from government resources, and connect small firms to skilled employees.

To provide financial support to the growing technology-based businesses in Milwaukee, NWSCDC established a CDFI that was certified by the CDFI Fund in 2000. Since 2000, the NWSCDC CDFI has financed an array of economic development projects and forged partnerships with leading manufacturers that have resulted in the creation of over 500 permanent jobs. Several examples include Nature Tech, a green technology employer; the relocation of Diamond Precision into Milwaukee; and the assisting with the financing of Century City Towers.

The organizations and their core competencies: NWSCDC is the lead organization in the collaboration, and their partners are large economic and industrial development organizations each of which brings their respective competencies and comparative advantages. NWSCDC core competencies that have become their comparative advantage began evolving when the CDC was restructured in the late 1990s, including:

Financing: NWSCDC has built strong capacity in financing through becoming a CDFI, and they have invested equity dollars raised from both Office of Community Services and the CDFI Fund. These funds have attracted and retained major industrial and technology firms including DRS, Milwaukee Technology Incubator, Diamond Precision, and Century City Towers. Their strategy is to offer financing as a critical part of the development for locating major technology firms in their core neighborhood, notably the 30th Street Industrial Corridor. Since 2000, NWSCDC has been awarded 12 Federal Office of Community Services project grants to finance business expansion loans, totaling $7,545,981. These 12 projects have created 985 total jobs (including low-income and non-low-income) during the project periods, and 826 of these new jobs were filled by low-income jobseekers. Two active projects (awards from 2014 and 2015) are still generating new jobs (Ted Wysocki Blog 2016). In addition to federal resources, NWSCDC has strong financial relationships with PNC Bank, Wells Fargo Bank, and the Wisconsin Housing and Economic Development Authority (WHEDA) and the City of Milwaukee.

Property acquisition: NWSCDC has helped major manufacturers acquire properties that the CDC formerly owned, as well as industrial properties in the neighborhood through financing and political relationships.

Neighborhood engagement and knowledge of community: NWSCDC has strong political relationships with local aldermen, mayor and mayoral staff, and other local and national officials. Effective political relationships are essential for raising resources to revitalize the community. It is important to have relationships at the local, state, and national level. These political relationships are key for planning and zoning issues as well as securing local funding for the initiative. Political relationships are increasingly important given the need to attract scarce financial and technical resources for local community development initiatives, especially in an increasingly competitive environment. These relationships can be invaluable in building community support, finding employees, providing protection, and helping to access financing.

Community networks: NWSCDC has forged community development networks that help employers train and hire workers for their industrial and technology positions. Successful community development efforts understand, utilize, and build community networks such as the Century City Triangle Neighborhood Association. Community networks connect the fabric of a community, and local community development organizations are best positioned to play a leadership role in local community networks. Comprehensive development initiatives are a good way to connect various networks in a neighborhood toward building a common agenda.

Client service: CDCs are adept at offering client services to attract and retain a variety of partners, in the case of NWSCDC large technology-based firms that have significant job growth potential and make products that are in demand by important economic sectors.

The other major partners are the technology-based industries that NWSCDC is partnering with including DRS, Diamond Precision, and Midwest Energy Research Consortium (M-WERC). DRS is a multinational electronics corporation and defense contractor that makes power controls for the Navy. Diamond Precision manufactures precision equipment for the defense industry. M-WERC is an innovative education and technology partnership between a number of major universities and over a dozen corporations with expertise in energy, power, and control. The goal of WERC is to attract federal dollars to fund basic research into transformational technologies (Snyder and Daniell 2011). This is often referred to as a cluster approach. The leadership of M-WERC views NWSCDC's value add as their contacts with city, state, and federal economic development groups as well as their knowledge of financial accountability standards required by a 501(c)3 organization (Snyder and Daniell 2011). NWSCDC has played a leadership role in creating this unique industry and academic partnership designed to maintain leadership in Milwaukee in power and propeller distribution utilized by the US Navy and other power sources.

Core Competency Matrix

Chart 7.5 highlights the key competencies that each of the organizations utilized in this collaboration.

What Was Learned

NWSCDC has demonstrated the following lessons from their strategic partnership approach based on a few core competencies that have led to comparative advantages. Rich Gross, a senior housing developer at Enterprise Community Partners and long-time partner and colleague of Northwest Side CDC, commented that "the ownership model for NWSCDC did not work well, and the shift to a partnership model has turned out to be strategic, effective, and sustainable." Rich Gross also mentioned that one of the major implications in transitioning the organization from an ownership business model to partnership model is that the CDC can have less ownership of real estate and investments through a heavily focused partnership approach (Rich Gross interview 2015).

Chart 7.5   NW Side CDC Competency Chart

Competency	Organizations				
	NWSCDC	Century City Triangle NA	DRS, DP, Eaton and MERC	Local and State Government	Feds
Organizational Development and Management	X		X		
Community Engagement and Public Policy	X	X			
Planning	X			X	
Communications	X		X		
Project Development (Real Estate)	X			X	
Lending	X				X
Property and Asset Management		X			
Program/business line development and management	X		X		
Resource Development, Capital Aggregation and Fundraising	X		X	X	
Collaboration and Partnerships	X	X	X		
Performance Measurement and Evaluation			X		

NWSCDC's new business model resulted in the following:

- NWSCDC has demonstrated that a community-based development organization can have a significant impact without owning and/or managing real estate.
- NWSCDC has leveraged their community networks, political relationships, and successful ability to secure federal, state, and local funds to make their neighborhood desirable for large multi-national firms specializing in power, controls, and energy.

- NWSCDC has built upon the comparative advantage of Milwaukee (power, energy, and control businesses) to create a cluster of opportunities through the Energy Innovation Center and M-WERC.
- NWSCDC partnership strategy is built around value add and NWSCDC has attracted capital and technical support to large and small firms in the technology industry.
- NWSCDC has become a nimble organization with relatively small overhead and positioned itself for long-term sustainability.

NWSCDC leadership is committed and relentless in generating new ideas and partnerships that attract significant partners and investors.

Federation for Appalachian Housing Enterprises (Fahe) Case Study

Background and History: Central Appalachia, which includes portions of Kentucky, West Virginia, Virginia, and Tennessee, has been an area of persistent poverty for generations. The area is characterized by mountains, ridges, and valleys, which lead to economic and social isolation. The physical isolation of many of the communities in Central Appalachia results in transportation challenges with goods and services, since the terrain is quite mountainous. This limits economic opportunities. Extracting natural resources, predominately coal, has been the primary economic engine of the region for the past 100 years. There has been a decline in the number of coal miners due in large part to technological advances. Financial capital is difficult to attract to the region, and most of the existing financial capital flows outside the region.

The numerous economic and social challenges in Central Appalachia are beyond the purview of this case study, other than to paint the picture of how difficult it is to overcome economic, social, and housing challenges in the region. President Lyndon Johnson's War on Poverty strategy focused significantly on Appalachia through The Office of Economic Opportunity (OEO), the Appalachian Regional Commission (ARC), the Economic Development Administration (EDA), and other programs. Community-based organizations began to sprout up in Appalachia by the mid-1960s and were supported by the Federal Government through the Appalachian Regional Commission (ARC), Office of Economic Opportunity (OEO), and Economic Development Administration (EDA). These nascent organizations received additional support from the faith-based community including the Commission on Religion in Appalachia (CORA) (Okagaki 2008).

One of the leading organizations that emerged during the late 1960s and 1970s was HEAD Housing under the leadership of Dwayne Yost (Tom Carew interview 2015). HEAD saw the value of partnering with other small community-based, primarily housing organizations in Central Appalachia to encourage more peer-to-peer learning and financial support. Dwayne Yost, and several other community leaders including Tom Carew, who was then Executive Director of Frontier Housing in Moorhead, Kentucky, formed the Federation of Appalachian Housing Enterprises now called Fahe in the early 1980s to be a peer-to-peer network. They recruited a fellow Kentuckian, Dave Lollis, who was a local housing advocate to serve as executive director of Fahe. The early years of Fahe centered on building a peer-to-peer learning network among the dozen organizations that composed Fahe, as well as attracting financial capital for affordable housing to Fahe and its initial 6 members. According to Tom Carew, the glue that enabled Fahe to grow was the trust that was built between staff, board, and members. There was a shared vision and Fahe emerged as one of the leading local advocates for affordable housing and community development in the USA. David Lollis stood next to President Clinton in 1994, when he signed legislation creating the Community Development Financial Institution (CDFI) Fund.

Fahe became a certified CDFI and started lending to its members in 1995. The growth was steady, but there was an increasing gap between the need for affordable housing in the region, and Fahe's production capacity (Okagaki 2008). Dave Lollis retired from Fahe in the early 2000s, and the organization selected Jim King. King, who was the CFO of Fahe in the early 1990s, became a partner in a consulting firm, and then returned to Fahe to serve as the next President of Fahe at the beginning of 2003.

Situation and Context

Between 2000 and 2003, Fahe and their 30 plus members produced 2000 units of housing annually (Okagaki 2008). The production trajectory was flat, and the new leadership team was concerned that Fahe self-sufficiency rate was only 38% from earned income and fees. Jim King and his leadership team were worried that the lack of capital affected long-term sustainability and impact for both Fahe and their members, since Fahe's existence is based on the effectiveness and impact of the local members

(Jim King interview 2015). An external factor that influenced the new leadership thinking was that one of their trade associations, Opportunity Finance Network (OFN), was challenging the CDFI industry "To Change, Grow, or Die." This resonated with Jim King, and reinforced the realization that Fahe had to grow or become less relevant (Jim King interview 2015). The Fahe team saw it as their challenge to change systems and improve processes with their members. According to Pam Johnson, Executive Vice President of Outreach, Fahe needed to lead by example and model the changes for its members.

The turning event or catalyst for Fahe was when Jim King attended the second class of Achieving Excellence in 2004, sponsored by Neighbor Works America and the John F. Kennedy School of Government at Harvard. This program has made a huge positive impact on community development leaders. The Achieving Excellence program was designed by Douglas K. Smith, a well-known organizational consultant and entrepreneur. The core initiative within the 18 month program was that each leader had to develop an ambitious performance challenge and create a process to achieve it. Jim King's challenge was to lead an effort to quadruple the amount of housing produced annually by Fahe and its members from 2000 to 8000 units annually by 2010.

Fach, under Jim King's leadership and with significant technical assistance and support from Doug Smith, developed what was called the Berea Performance Compact, named after the town in Kentucky where Fahe headquarters are located. The idea behind the Berea Performance Compact was to enable Fahe's members to operate at scale in a partnership way. The Berea Performance Compact consisted of five initiatives: multi-family developments; loan servicing; volunteer recruitment; manufactured housing; and mortgage broker services (Walsh and Zdenek 2011). Fahe's strategy was to pick one member with a particular core competency to be the primary aggregator or distributor of the services for other members, and then do a pilot project to standardize what works and then roll out the model for larger scale and impact. Fahe requires each member of the collaborative to strive toward a common performance challenge, so that the lead member and other organizations are vested in the outcomes, and stand to benefit from the successes of the initiative. The five initiatives became Fahe's comparative advantage and expertise compared to other initiatives.

Both Fahe and individual Fahe members have served as the lead compact members for the five initiatives. Frontier Housing is the lead compact member with manufactured housing production and technical support for the initial years of the Berea Performance Compact. The manufactured housing lead has shifted to Next Step, a national network that brings quality manufactured housing to lower-income communities. Community Housing Partners (CHP) has been the compact leader for multi-family development. CHP is doing work with several Fahe members to design and develop affordable housing. In some cases they provide management services and have also been involved in co-ownership in certain circumstances.

Fahe took the lead in the other three initiatives which are loan servicing, mortgage financing, and the green compact. The loan servicing has grown from nearly 800 loans to nearly 7000 on an annual basis. Fahe provides loan service contracts to 39 other organizations. Fahe has expanded the mortgage lending from $6.5 million when the Berea Compact was initiated to the current level of $40 million. Fahe's green compact has no single product; rather, the emphasis is on having Fahe members using national standards for energy efficiency. The original target was to have 70% of their members using energy efficiency standards. Currently, 90% of Fahe members use national energy efficiency standards. As part of the green compact, Fahe launched Power$aver Mortgage, and Appalachia HeatSquad in partnership with Neighbor Works of Western Vermont (King 2015).

As of 2014, Fahe and their now 55 members have increased annual housing production in Central Appalachia from 2000 to over 8725 units per year with the annual level of capital deployed growing from $7 million in 2003 to over $80 million in 2014. It should also be noted that Fahe has carefully expanded to other geographic areas adjacent to their prime location including Northern Alabama and Western Maryland, as well as larger regional cities near their target areas.

Fahe's self-sufficiency rate nearly doubled between 2002 and 2014 from 38 to 68%. This is impressive given the economic recession that impacted projects and fundraising for a period of time (Okagaki 2008).

Program Design and Goals

The program design and goal to quadruple production of housing of the Fahe Membership was supported by the creation of systems and platforms at Fahe including: a mortgage platform that delivered subsidy programs as well as market rate programs; a loan servicing platform that provided back off support to local organizations allowing them to focus on education and counseling of a family, and design and construction of affordable homes; expansion of subsidy programs such as Low Income Housing Tax Credits and other forms of subsidies made available during the economic crisis. Sara Morgan, the COO of Fahe, describes the mortgage platform growth in four stages:

Stage 1   Fahe became a broker and was able to originate market rate housing loans with Fifth Third Bank, and Kentucky Housing Corporation, which is the housing finance agency in Kentucky. This gave Fahe expanded product offerings that weren't constrained by the size of Fahe's balance sheet.

Stage 2   Fahe became an approved FHA and USDA lender, enabling them to garner guarantees and deliver loans with guarantees to investors. This positioned Fahe closer to the decision-making point to access traditional market rate finance. Fahe could underwrite USDA and FHA guaranteed loans.

Stage 3   Fahe became a correspondent lender for JP Morgan Chase & Co., and Flag Star Bank, allowing them to originate, underwrite, and sell loans to both of these financial institutions, in essence becoming a secondary market. Fahe could then blend the subsidies with market rate sources and achieve greater scale.

Stage 4   Fahe established a broker network allowing local organizations, Fahe members and partners, to originate USDA guarantee loans and earn a fee for loans closed. The broker network utilizes the delivery system of a local organization working with the borrower to become credit ready, earning a fee for originating a loan, and maximizing on Fahe's systems to process, underwrite and sell loans to an investor. This establishes a value proposition with the local organization as well as Fahe to enhance delivery of market rate loans.

Fahe had to invest in the mortgage platform and hire experienced financial executive staff including John Rogers, a former Fannie Mae senior lender, to develop the systems and quality control necessary to succeed. The organization invested in mortgage origination software called BYTE. As a result of these initiatives, Fahe became a leader in loan servicing in their region and by 2015 had attracted 33 investors including state housing mortgage finance agencies, Habitat for Humanity, and other partners. The mortgage platform became a major comparative advantage for Fahe and attracted so many diverse financial institutions and resources.

Fahe is meticulous about ensuring that their mortgage origination and services meet industry standards. Their emphasis on quality control and industry standards has enabled them to raise significant pools of capital including three equity funds of $40 million for Low Income Housing Tax Credit (LIHTC) pools of capital. They have also expanded their loan servicing beyond Central Appalachia and are servicing loans in the Mississippi Delta and rural Michigan, and Florida (Morgan 2013). They have the systems and software to service the loans combined with deep knowledge of community development and communities with high rates of poverty.

Another key element to the program design is that Fahe spends extensive time with their 50+ members. They meet twice a year in the spring and fall with all of their members, and have quarterly meetings that they refer to as caucus meetings in each of their four major states (Kentucky, Tennessee, Virginia, and West Virginia). Members in Alabama participate in the Tennessee caucus and Maryland members in the West Virginia caucus. These meetings focus heavily on peer learning and sharing of best practices, training, and technical assistance. They also provide a constant opportunity to share information and build knowledge among the members. Their knowledge and expertise can also be viewed as a comparative advantage.

Fahe has never forced their products and innovations on their members, and they have a strictly volunteer approach to participating with the various Fahe mortgage platform products. Fahe members understand how the products and tools will be utilized, enabling members to increase their housing production within their respective communities. Community Housing Partnership, located in Southwest Virginia, is the lead Fahe member in producing affordable multi-family housing, and they manage over 6000 units of affordable housing. One of their major financing sources is the Low-Income Housing Tax Credit (LIHTC). Community Housing Partnership provides support to other Fahe members, and is able to take advantage of the financial products and resources that Fahe and its members have leveraged including the equity funds that Fahe has capitalized.

The program design for scaling affordable housing in Central Appalachia is based on a value chain model, which focuses on the unique competencies and strengths of each partner (Pam Johnson interview 2015). The value chain model helps improve organizational performance and relies on standard operating procedures that are performance based and improve efficiency over time. Pam Johnson, the Chief Administrative Officer of Fahe, says the goal is to "work smarter not harder," and continue to leverage partnerships with their members and others.

Collaborative Partners and Core Competencies

Fahe is a unique community development intermediary in that it is a membership network of over 50 community-based partner organizations that have a shared vision and mission of providing affordable housing as a strategy for tackling persistent poverty in Central Appalachia. Fahe was built on a foundation of trust, advocacy, and peer learning and exchange of effective practices. This DNA was critical for enabling Fahe to move forward and succeed with the Berea Compact and the housing platforms that they have built over the past decade resulting in an increase from 2000 to 8725 units of affordable housing production per year.

In addition to growing their membership, Fahe has forged some powerful external partnerships with state and federal governments, as well as leading financial institutions that have enabled them to become a SBA and FHA lender and correspondent selling loans to financial institutions, and develop a loan servicing capacity that reaches beyond Central Appalachia.

Several of their key partners point to both Fahe's technical expertise and intangible partnership skills in facilitating affordable housing and community revitalization in Central Appalachia. Jeff Fultz, Market President for Central Bank in Richmond, Kentucky says one of the major reasons that his bank partners with Fahe is that "Fahe is good for my business, but also makes me feel good at night knowing our partnership is helping folks improve their lives." He goes on to say that Fahe's focus is right and he likes, respects, and enjoys participating with Fahe staff and members. They have lengthy conversations periodically, speaking again to the importance of the relational side of collaboration. According to Jeff Fultz, the partnership with Fahe is built upon both housing products and chemistry. Central Bank was a major investor in Fahe's Housing Equity Fund II at $1 million, which is significant for a small bank. Central Bank is constantly looking at financing new Fahe sponsored projects.

Kathy Peters, the Executive Director of the Kentucky Housing Corporation (KHC), the housing finance agency in Kentucky, is another strong Fahe partner. KHC has a 30 year history with Fahe, and they see one of the core benefits of Fahe as their ability to shepherd small community-based organizations that are common in Kentucky to access funding, provide timely reports, demonstrate accountability, and complete housing projects on time. She finds Fahe's financial and technical support of great comfort to KHC, and "she sees them as a progressive, collaborative, and respectful partner." Another important issue she pointed out is that Fahe staff help inspire their members to achieve more in affordable housing and community development in Kentucky.

Jay Kittenbrink is the Senior Development Manager for Episcopal Retirement Housing (ERC), headquartered in Cincinnati, Ohio. ERC is an organization that serves portions of three states (Ohio, Kentucky, and Indiana) focusing on senior housing and the continuum of care. They add a blend of supportive housing services including social activities, social workers and coordinators, and transportation. Recently, they added health clinics featuring nurse practitioners who can issue prescriptions which is a huge benefit to their elderly population. Since Jay started at ERC in 2008, ERC has been actively partnering with Fahe and their Kentucky members. This is Jay's first time working with rural communities and Fahe has been an invaluable partner to ERC. They have financed several projects together, and Jay is impressed with the high quality of the Fahe members in Kentucky. ERC participates actively in the Kentucky Caucus meetings. Jay mentioned that, "partnerships are a core value of ERC and that is a major feature of Fahe, and ERC sees value in bringing people together."

Core Competency Matrix

Chart 7.6 highlights the key competencies that each of the organizations utilized in this collaboration.

When asked to describe Fahe's core competencies, Jim King, the President and CEO of Fahe, stated that the lead Fahe competency is collaboration, which he defines as being performance driven (Jim King interview 2015). Collaboration that is performance based is a comparative advantage of Fahe. He then went on to say that their collaborative strength is based on:

- *Trustworthy*: Fahe delivers what they say they will deliver.
- *Flexible*: Fahe is open to new ideas that their members or partners propose.
- *Predictable*: Fahe provides a high degree of predictability in terms of the systems, processes, and results.

Chart 7.6   Fahe Competency Chart

Competency	Organizations				
	Fahe	Fahe lead partners	Fahe members	Financial Institutions	State Housing Finance Agencies
Organizational Development and Management	X				
Community Engagement & Public Policy	X		X		
Planning	X		X		
Project Development (Real Estate)	X		X		
Lending	X	X		X	X
Property and Asset Management			X		
Program/Business Line Development and Management	X		X		
Resource Development, Capital Aggregation and Fundraising	X	X	X	X	X
Collaboration and Partnerships	X	X	X	X	X
Performance Measurement and Evaluation	X				

- *Successful*: The collaboration results are a success for members, partners, and Fahe.
- *Shared Values*: Fahe and their members have similar values and are all working to improve outcomes for low-income families and help address the persistent poverty issues in their region.

Fahe's core collaboration competency is starting to be expanded beyond a housing production framework to include energy efficiency, healthy homes, and aging in community. This will lead to a whole new array of partners. Other major competencies that Fahe staff identified include:

- *Connecting capital and finance to opportunity*: Fahe's strategy is heavily focused raising and leveraging capital and they have seen an increase in deployed resources from $7 million in 2003 to over $80 million annually in 2014.

- *Loan servicing:* Fahe was able to reduce the delinquency rates on their loan portfolio from 15% in 2008 to 2% in 2015.
- *Financial expertise and leveraging resources:* Fahe has developed a series of financial platforms, products, and services built on strong financial expertise.
- *Capacity building:* Fahe has invested in their members' training and systems.
- *Operating systems:* Designing and managing financial systems is a core competency of Fahe, and they are constantly updating financial, information, and management systems to improve member performance. Sara Morgan the COO of Fahe emphasized that there was a constant need to ask questions and challenge assumptions so that Fahe and its members can make adjustments and create systems and processes more effective.
- *Performance measurement:* Performance measurement is at the heart of the Berea Compact and the work that Fahe does. Performance measurement is essential for assessing the impact of a dispersed network of over 50 members. Fahe is also providing financial services and products to organizations beyond the Fahe membership.

What Was Learned

- Performance-driven goals, data, and measurements are essential for collaborative work. In an effective collaboration, everyone has to be accountable and able to achieve their goals and initiatives that they have committed to implement. Data and measurements help ensure that the goals are being achieved and that low-income residents benefit from the work.
- No margin, no mission. Organizational missions are only as important as the ability of the organizations to implement them. Without funding including earned revenue, projects will not succeed. You can't achieve your mission unless your organization is offering valuable products, and has a sustainable business model.
- Importance of questions. Community development collaboration is a challenging work that brings together organizations with different

skills and strengths. Diverse organizations need to spend time understanding each other's work. Raising questions is a good way to learn about each other and build relationships. One of the strengths of community development is that it is open to exploring ideas and strategies that can lead to new products and systems and questioning the status quo can lead to new approaches and innovations.

- Capital and expertise. To effectively use capital, a high degree of expertise is needed. That is why there is a need for a vibrant network of community partners and external partners who can share their knowledge and leverage their expertise. Community development financing is complex and comes from local, state, federal public, and private sources. This capital requires much technical acumen to both obtain and deploy effectively. Often, partnerships allow organizations with different types of financial expertise to complement each other and obtain more funding than otherwise would be possible individually.

- Lead by example. Fahe staff and board leaders can't expect their more than 50 members to implement their practice and vision unless they model it themselves. This goes back to having trust and being predictable. Fahe staff invest a considerable amount of time and energy in working with their members, including the 18 formal meetings that Fahe sponsors with their members throughout the year.

- Through partnerships, Fahe is able to work smarter, not harder. Fahe is able to leverage their expertise and relationships so that they and their members are more strategic and effective. The outcome is not hard work; it is the ability to be strategic and have impact throughout their network.

- Collaboration is the underpinning of Fahe's work, and by being strategic with collaboration, Fahe will be able to open new doors into other areas that complement their mission and areas of expertise. Fahe is expanding their collaborative work to include health care and energy conservation firms and organizations. They do not need to be health care or energy efficiency experts, but rather be effective partners bringing their deep knowledge of housing finance and community development to the table.

East Bay Asian Local Development Corporation Case Study

Background and History

The East Bay Asian Local Development Corporation (EBALDC) was established in 1975 by local Asian American activists who wanted to convert a warehouse in Downtown Oakland into a mixed-use multi-purpose center. This center became the Asian Resource Center, for retail businesses, medical facilities, and nonprofit organizations, and opened in 1980. The Asian Resource Center became a hub of activity and programs for the community and EBALDC (Fong interview 2015). A consistent theme that emerged from EBALDC's early work is comprehensive development that engages diverse partners initially in Oakland's Chinatown, and expanding over time to other low-income communities in Oakland and Alameda County. Oakland's population as of 2010 is 390,724 with 34.5% White, 28% Black, 17.4% Asian Pacific Islander (API), 25.4% Hispanic/Latino; 18.7% of Oakland residents live in poverty. EBALDC's emphasis has always been on engaging community residents and other major stakeholders toward developing projects that improve the quality of life for low-income residents.

In the 1980s, the organization expanded into affordable housing development and built several major low-income rental and senior housing projects including the Frank G Mar Community Housing project, which provided 119 units of multi-family and senior apartments with ground-level retail and service space. This project was a partnership between EBALDC and BRIDGE Housing Corporation, a regional affordable housing intermediary. A significant majority of EBALDC residential projects have entailed partnerships with other community-based organizations as well as large developers (Josh Simon interview). Lion Creek Crossings is a joint project of EBALDC and The Related Companies of California, the West Coast Affiliate of a very large national real estate developer. This ability to partner with small, regional, and national organizations has helped pave the way for EBALDC's strategic direction of healthy neighborhoods, discussed later in this case study.

EBALDC has continued to develop affordable housing and as of 2015 EBALDC has developed 2053 townhouse and apartment units of affordable housing. The organization has also built 158 units of owner-occupied housing, and manages an additional 1126 units of townhouses and apartments (Building Healthy Neighborhoods Annual Report 2014–2015). While many of these affordable housing complexes are located in or near downtown Oakland, EBALDC's core community, a number of the projects are located in other sections of Oakland, Alameda County where Oakland is located, and neighboring Contra Costa County.

EBALDC has emerged as one of the most comprehensive CDCs in the USA in combining physical revitalization with economic development and asset-building programs, and social services. They have developed over 300,000 ft^2 of commercial space throughout Oakland that brings street-level vitality with critical services including pharmacies and optometrists, childcare and health centers, and food purveyors. Swan's Market is on the National Register of Historic Places, and Preservation Park is a major historic complex and park in downtown Oakland.

EBALDC was one of the original pilot sites for Individual Development Accounts (IDAs) as part of the American Dream Demonstration led by CFED in the late 1990s. They continue to have a significant IDA program and expanded their financial stability and asset-building work through operating Volunteer Income Tax Assistance (VITA) sites that enable low-income residents to have free tax preparation, Earned Income Tax Credit (EITC) refunds, and asset-building products and services (Building Healthy Neighborhoods Annual Report 2014–2015).

EBALDC expanded their neighborhood and economic development work in 2006, adding the Money Savvy Youth financial education program and resident services in their housing developments. Resident services and youth savvy savings brought financial counseling, social services, health, wellness, and other programs for EBALDC to serve local residents consistent with the goals of Family Economic Success. EBALDC housing units and commercial properties were natural locations to offer comprehensive services and financial counseling and savings strategies. Eighty-five percent of EBALDC residents receive housing counseling, and 80% of the same residents report that they have enough money to meet their basic needs (Building Healthy Neighborhoods Annual Report 2014–2015).

Tse-Ming Tam, of the United Way of the Bay Area, has partnered with EBALDC for nearly 20 years with different programs—from Individual Development Accounts (IDAs) to family economic success. He observes that EBALDC is committed to serving economically challenging populations and that EBALDC is relatively unique and effective in creating resident-focused groups that provide constant feedback and influence with designing programs. Tse-Ming worked with EBALDC in the late 1990s on the Life Time initiative program for young adults receiving TANF with EBALDC helping the young adults navigate TANF rules and regulations so that they could stay in college and eventually graduate (Tse-Ming Tam interview 2016).

United Way of the Bay Area invited EBALDC to participate in the SPARK POINT initiative that deploys a service integration strategy to improve financial outcomes. Thirty nonprofits were invited to participate but EBALDC was one of the five nonprofits selected to implement the initiative. As part of the SPARK POINT Initiative, EBALDC used to partner with 20 public elementary schools to offer Monday Savvy Youth to 4th and 5th grades.

The World Health Organization (WHO) and The Atlantic Philanthropies, a major foundation, started encouraging communities and organizations to pursue Age-Friendly Community policies and practices for all ages, notably older adults over 55 years of age. Older adults represent 36% of the population that EBALDC serves through its various initiatives (EBALDC 2015 fact sheet). EBALDC was one of the first CDCs to adopt Age-Friendly Community practices and they received funding from The Atlantic Philanthropies to develop what became the Age-Friendly San Pablo Corridor Initiative, one of the first of its kind in 2011. San Pablo Avenue is a major thoroughfare from downtown Oakland to Emeryville, and traverses a largely low- and moderate-income area. EBALDC moved its headquarters from the Asian Resource Center to 1825 San Pablo Avenue in the middle of the Age-Friendly Corridor to underscore the importance of the San Pablo Corridor. EBALDC has organized a number of older adults who live in the San Pablo Avenue Corridor to establish neighborhood priorities. The priorities that they established include public safety, transit improvements, wellness, and access to fresh, nutritious food. EBALDC has awarded small grants to local residents to work on health, wellness, and community engagement activities. The residents determine the usage and recipient of the funding between $100 and $1000. The total funding available was $7000. A number of the older adults live in EBALDC-owned and EBALDC-managed housing and the organization will continue to develop additional housing and commercial facilities to serve the older adults and residents.

In addition to the San Pablo Avenue Corridor, EBALDC is planning to target its resources to the Havenscourt neighborhood, a low-income neighborhood near the Oakland Coliseum in East Oakland, several miles from downtown Oakland. EBALDC has developed a 567-unit project,

Lion Creek Crossings (LCC). LCC is a transit-oriented development located along major bus lines and one block from the Coliseum BART (Bay Area Regional Transit subway line) station. EBALDC brought onsite two early childhood centers, created an after-school and summer program in partnership with the local public schools. EBALDC established a Family Resource Center at LCC with a computer center, and classroom spaces, and offers benefits assistance, housing counseling, career development and placement assistance, and other supportive services.

EBALDC over time has become a valued partner with leading public sector and nonprofit organizations. The Oakland Housing Authority has partnered with EBALDC because they believe that EBALDC creates better housing outcomes for its residents with the emphasis on service-enhanced housing that improves wellness and health. Eric Randolph of the Oakland Housing Authority relayed that in his experience most of the health indicators in affordable housing do not change or improve, so he is excited that EBALDC is tackling healthy neighborhoods in two major neighborhoods in Oakland—the San Pablo Avenue Corridor and Havenscourt (Randolph interview 2016).

Situation and Context

EBALDC has invested over $200 million in the past 40 years in seven targeted neighborhoods in Oakland and Alameda County to improve the physical, social, and economic well-being of low-income residents. Their work over many years has deepened their awareness of the relationship between poverty and poor health. In 2010, EBALDC's senior management team began discussing the recent research findings from the Alameda County Public Health Department, which tied health disparities and poor health outcomes to physical, economic, and social conditions in many of the neighborhoods where EBALDC worked. The study found that compared to a White child in the Oakland Hills, an African-American child in West Oakland is:

- One and a half times more likely to be born premature or with low birth weight
- Seven times more likely to be born into poverty
- Four times less likely to read at grade level in the fourth grade
- Five to six times more likely to drop out of school.

This study is consistent with a growing body of evidence that one's environment plays a huge role in determining the health outcomes of children, youth, young adults, adults, and older adults. Robert Woods Johnson Foundation, the leading philanthropic funder of health initiatives, states that the zip code where a person was born and raised is sadly the most important determinant of one's health conditions through their "life-course" (Erickson interview 2015).

EBALDC's new strategic direction is a comprehensive "Healthy Neighborhoods" approach that connects social, environmental, and economic factors that determine the length and quality of an individual's life. EBALDC's healthy neighborhood lens will help identify the neighborhood assets and stressors, and determine which stressors (lack of jobs and affordable housing, violence, public safety, and pollution) can be mitigated in a collaborative strategy that builds upon EBALDC's strengths. Healthy Neighborhoods has emerged as a comparative advantage for EBALDC due to their comprehensive development experience and their ability to form effective partnerships.

EBALDC launched its Healthy Neighborhood Strategic Plan in 2013 as a 4 year plan through 2016. The Healthy Neighborhoods Strategic Plan assessed each project, program, and partnership for its potential to create resources and opportunities that enable local residents to have healthy outcomes and vibrant lives. The organization will integrate its core work in housing options, social supports, and income and wealth with other factors and priorities identified by local residents including community gardens, green building design, environmental remediation, transit development, access to health, and school partnerships.

EBALDC's Healthy Neighborhoods Strategic Plan is built upon five core values including:

- Collaboration—Strong partnerships, enabling EBALDC to accomplish more by engaging others.
- Respect—Respect is built with emphasis honoring diversity and listening skillfully to others and involving them in decision making.
- Leadership—Leadership requiring a strong vision, and encouraging people to be leaders and problem solvers in their community.
- Accountability—The organization takes responsibility for its work, honors its commitments, and makes sound financial decisions for the health and benefit of the community.

- Passion—Passion is deriving from an unerring commitment to mission and vision, reflecting the deep commitment to their communities.

Program Design and Goals. EBALDC's healthy neighborhood framework will focus on five major goals, with each goal having a series of 3 year objectives from 2014 to 2016. These goals will cut across all of their projects and programs. The goals are:

1. *Improve the social and financial health of residents, community members, and business owners in Oakland and East Bay.* Some of the key objectives of this goal were neighborhood safety, refining and applying comprehensive programs to Havenscourt and the San Pablo Avenue Corridor priority neighborhoods, and creating and supporting vibrant business districts in target neighborhoods.

2. *Establish new and strengthen existing partnerships to amplify positive change in our pilot and target neighborhoods.* EBALDC expanded partnerships in healthy neighborhoods with health care institutions, schools, financial institutions, public agencies, businesses, for-profit developers, food justice organizations, and other nonprofits. One of the objectives is to assist their partners in building capacity.

3. *Influence and shape local and national policy and planning decisions to reflect a healthy neighborhood vision.* This objective includes refining EBALDC's understanding of the intersection between public health and community development to play an active role in initiatives, and coalitions that impact the health and well-being of low-income people and neighborhoods, and advance advocacy and policies at the local and national level.

4. *Enhance data and systems for evaluating EBALDC performance, efficiency, and impact.* Healthy Neighborhoods requires outcome data measurements that can assess the impact of the pilot. If you don't have the correct outcome measurements, it is hard to determine if the social and health interventions targeted are making a difference. This is a different type of performance measurement system than the traditional community development measurement approach of housing units built, dollars invested, and jobs created. One of EBALDC's objectives is to build upon evaluation areas of expertise including income and wealth, education, housing options, and health and well-being.

5. *Ensure EBALDC's continued operational excellence and impact.* Developing healthy neighborhoods is a complex undertaking that requires significant organizational capacity and an ability to forge partnerships around complex issues. EBALDC will be building upon its track record in creating housing options, providing social supports, and building income and wealth for low-income residents through increasing financial and strategic support from foundations, corporations, financial institutions, and government agencies. To achieve the healthy neighborhoods vision, EBALDC will grow the number of individual and corporate donors to provide long-term flexible financial support to pursue healthy community initiatives. EBALDC will also assess how to use its existing real estate portfolio to expand real estate and services on adjacent sites.

These goals will be implemented in part through the commitments and action areas for the San Pablo Area Revitalization Collaborative (SPARC), the initial target area for the healthy neighborhood initiative. SPARC was formed in 2014 to improve the health and wellness for the 8000 residents living near and along 1.5 miles of San Pablo Avenue, and drew from the experience of the San Pablo Avenue Age-Friendly Corridor which built a collaborative strategy to improve economic, social, and health outcomes for older adults. The next neighborhood where EBALDC will expand the healthy neighborhood initiative is Havenscourt, mentioned earlier in the case profile.

EBALDC, working with an array of local organizations and community leaders, formed an 11-member steering committee for SPARC to coordinate the five major priorities with EBALDC serving as the "backbone organization" in the collective impact model. The ability of EBALDC to serve as a backbone is a major comparative advantage for the SPARC Collaboration. The SPARC steering committee includes representatives from two grass roots local organizations, West Oakland Neighbors Group, and Hoover Resident Action Council, plus other community leaders and health care professionals. The Steering Committee meets every 6–8 weeks (Hall interview 2015). SPARC is concentrating on four priority areas: health, blight, housing, and economic development.

Several of the proposed SPARC actions have a strong health focus including the action to reduce emergency room and hospital visits by residents with high blood pressure. EBALDC and their partners propose to do this through preventive treatment at health clinics, healthier foods, and exercise and health education (San Pablo Area Revitalization Collaborative plan 2015). EBALDC in partnership with Lifelong Medical Care, Sutter Health, and People's Grocery launched a pilot community clinic to provide blood pressure screening and referrals for healthy food, activity, and medication management for 10 weeks for adults living in the SPARC target area. Sixty-two of the 140 residents were screened for hypertension during the 10 week period. Brenda Goldstein of Life-Long Medical Care values the partnership between her organization and EBALDC dating back to when EBALDC acquired the California Hotel, which serves a high-risk low-income population including individuals who were homeless. Life-Long provides social workers and health care professionals and EBALDC performs property management functions.

The other partner in the California Hotel is People's Grocery who planted and maintained a garden in the back of the complex for the residents and other family members. Life-Long stresses the importance of working with affordable housing organizations like EBALDC so that they can combine supportive services and health with quality housing. Ms. Goldstein goes on to say that "a healthy neighborhoods strategy is bigger than health care and community organizing, and neither Life-Long nor EBALDC has to step out of areas of comfort" (Goldstein interview 2016).

Several proposed actions emphasize improving safety by reducing blight and improving streets, parks and abandoned land. Improving the physical environment can improve the perception that neighborhood is more safe and active. SPARC partners including community residents and the Oakland Public Works Department mapped five "hot spots" in the neighborhood where there was blight and lack of safety. They have begun to address these issues through community design projects, such as mural wall paintings, median projects on San Pablo Avenue to clear up trash and make the streetscape more attractive and active. SPARC completed a chalk crosswalk in the fall of 2015 to make it safer for older adults to cross a busy intersection in an area where there is a concentration of senior housing (Hall interview 2015).

Other proposed actions focus on developing additional units of affordable housing so that long-time residents can stay, creating a thriving main street atmosphere through supporting local businesses and encouraging resident entrepreneurs to create more business, and connecting local living wage jobs that then they pay for their housing, healthy food, and other basic needs. One of the exciting economic and health partnerships that is emerging is a community grocery store and urban agriculture farm near several senior affordable housing developments to encourage healthy foods and life style.

EBALDC is planning to continue the healthy neighborhoods work, and they are starting to plan for their next strategic plan that will encompass the period between 2017 and 2020. One of the challenges facing a multi-sector collective impact approach is the issue of alignment both from the perspective of staff and systems from the backbone organization, and the alignment of partners to ensure that everyone brings their knowledge and strengths and is committed to the long-term success and outcomes of the initiative.

Collaborative Partners and Core Competencies

Chart 7.7 highlights which competencies each group used in the collaboration in this case study.

Core Competency Matrix

Chart 7.7 highlights the key competencies that each of the organizations utilized in this collaboration.

EBALDC has been able to achieve a lot using the various competencies including:

- *Mixed-use comprehensive approach.* Using the Asian Resource Center as a hub. EBALDC thinks about the importance of "place making" as a key component of community development, and their comprehensive approach to real estate development reflects that with more recent projects including Swan's Market Place and Preservation Park (Simon 2015).
- *Partners add value.* Individuals and organizations bring important contributions to the table. The partnership is built around the concept Low cost/No cost framework that aligns and leverages all partners' existing work (Fong 2015).
- *Broadening leadership.* This is important for both the lead organization as well as the partners. EBALDC leaders have brought an important variety of skills including long-time former executive director, Lynette Lee known for her openness; EBALDC Senior Management Team's leadership in 2009–2013 to shepherd through the new Healthy Neighborhoods Strategic Plan (Fong 2015).

Chart 7.7 EBALDC Competency Chart

Competency	Organizations				
	EBALDC	UWBA	Life-Long	Oakland Housing Authority	Alameda County Public Health Department
Organizational Development and Management	X				
Community Engagement and Public Policy	X	X	X	X	X
Planning	X	X		X	X
Communications	X				
Project Development (Real Estate)	X			X	
Lending					
Property and Asset Management	X				
Program/Business Line Development and Management	X				
Resource Development, Capital Aggregation and Fundraising	X	X	X		
Collaboration and Partnering	X	X	X	X	X
Performance Measurement and Evaluation	X				

- *Continuous communication.* In managing SPARC, EBALDC chairs monthly meetings with the SPARC steering committee and they communicate on a regular basis with their other partners.
- *Different partnership phases.* EBALDC's initial partnership work was primarily with real estate development projects and they learned that there were three phases: pre-work, development, and operational. The pre-work helps determine the relationships and priorities for the project or initiative; development is assembling the team, designing

the project, and raising the resources; and operational is completing the project and successfully managing the initiative over time to achieve the outcomes proposed (Josh Simon interview 2015).

- *High-potential partnerships.* Nonprofit hospitals have the potential to be strong partners. Hospitals are looking for partners on community health improvement, and have strong community benefits assessment capacity with data. Organizations like EBALDC have a partnership frame that hospitals can plug into.

Data Analysis and Application

EBALDC has learned to use neighborhood data (particularly heat maps) to inform the healthy neighborhoods planning about the existing challenges and assets. These data maps have turned out to be critical when it comes time to deciding what priorities to include in the neighborhood action plans. EBALDC is continuing to use neighborhood data to inform progress of its healthy neighborhoods work.

What Was Learned

1. EBALDC's collaborative work starts with their core values of collaboration, respect, leadership, accountability, and passion. EBALDC has consistently displayed these values for many years.
2. Partnerships come first—importance of relationships before engaging in partnerships and initiatives. Josh Simon states that "the partners come first and the goals come later."
3. Partnerships require many leaders, with leadership roles evolving over time. Leadership roles have to be communicated and clarified on an ongoing basis.
4. EBALDC was able to adapt to the recent economic recession through doubling down on what they do well which is strategic partnerships and focusing on the importance of creating healthy neighborhoods, which are their comparative advantages.
5. EBALDC has been open to change from its early days reflecting the long-term leadership of Lynette Lee, who was EBALDC's Executive Director for over 25 years.

6. There needs to be a long-term view that is grounded in a preventative and developmental approach—"an ounce of prevention leads to a pound of cure." This is an underlying premise of the healthy neighborhoods approach.
7. Support of different community voices is needed. EBALDC started as an Asian American-focused organization, and now reflects the racial and ethnic diversity of Oakland from its board and staff to its residents and clients.
8. Healthy neighborhoods require a long-term shared vision by EBALDC and a diverse array of partners committed to making neighborhoods healthier and sustainable. EBALDC has incorporated the collective action framework to work with diverse stakeholders.
9. There need to be clarity about leadership roles since many leaders are needed. EBALDC serves as the quarterback and backbone for these efforts and has incorporated a collective impact approach.
10. Partners need to stay at the table and there needs to be a supportive structure in place with resources and knowledgeable staff dedicated to building the collaborative strategy. This goes back to EBALDC's core values.
11. In the future, an expanded role of hospitals as anchor institutions should be explored. Possible additional roles include: procurement, hiring, real estate development, and impact investing.

References

American Communities Survey. 2012.
Ansorage, Kate, and Dana Bell. 2015. Interviewed by Dee Walsh, 10 July 2015.
Beleche, Marcos. 2016. Interviewed by Dee Walsh, 19 February 2016.
Breaking Ground. 2015. https://breakingground.net/. Accessed June 2015.
Buckman Community Association. 2007. The History of Buckman. http://www. neighborhoodlink.com/Buckman/pages/38240.
Carew, Tom. 2015. Interviewed by Bob Zdenek, 18 June 2015.
CDC of Brownsville. 2015. Community Loan Center: Affordable Small Dollar Loans. Powerpoint Presentation, March 2015.
Clark, Steve. 2013. Local Loan Program Takes Issue with 'Payday' Label. MGN Online. *The Brownsville Herald*, April 11.
Clements, Allison Milld. 2015. Interviewed by Dee Walsh, 18 August 2015.
Consumer Financial Protection Bureau. What Is a Payday Loan. http://www.consumerfinance.gov/askcfpb/1567/what-payday-loan.html.

Dubois, Jeanne. 2016. Interviewed by Dee Walsh, 3 February 2016.

Duffrin, Elizabeth. 2015. Thwarting Payday Lenders at the Texas Border. NACEDA, 27 April 2015. http://www.naceda.org/index.php?option=com_dailyplanetblog&view=entry&category=people-places&id=6:thwarting-payday-lenders-at-the-texas-border.

East Bay Asian Local Development Corporation. 2014. *Building Healthy Neighborhoods*, 1–15. Annual Report, Oakland, CA.

EcoDistrict Website. 2015. Target Cities Programs. http://ecodistricts.org/get-started/technical-and-advisory-services/target-cities-program/ Accessed 26 Dec 2015.

Enterprise. 2013. Adapting to a Changing Environment: Organizational Sustainability in the Pacific Northwest's Affordable Housing Development Community. http://www.enterprisecommunity.com/where-we-work/pacific-northwest/see-the-work/ace-reach-partnership.

Fairmount Collaborative. 2015. http://fairmountcollaborative.org/, March 20.

Fairmount Indigo CDC Collaborative Website.

Fairmount/Indigo Corridor Collaborative website. Accessed 29 Dec 2015.

FEDPAYDAY.com. 2014. Payday Loans in Texas. FAQ. http://www.fedpayday.com/.

Forbes. 2015. The Best Places for Business and Careers. Boston, MA. At a Glance. http://www.forbes.com/places/ma/boston/.

Fong, Charisse. 2015. Interviewed by Bob Zdenek, 29 November 2015.

Fultz, Jeff. 2015. Interviewed by Bob Zdenek, 4 September 2015.

Gallun, Alby, and Maidenberg, Micah. 2013. Will the foreclosure crisis kill Chicago? *Crain's Chicago Business*, 9 November 2013.

Goldstein, Brenda. 2016. Interviewed by Bob Zdenek, 21 January 2016.

Goodling, Erin, Jamaal Green and Nathan McClintock. 2015. *Uneven Development of the Sustainable City: Shifting Capital in Portland, Oregon*, 12.

Gross, Rich. 2015. Interviewed by Bob Zdenek, 14 December 2015.

Grossman, Tammy. 2015. Interviewed by Dee Walsh, 27 August 2015.

Hall, Romi. 2015. Interviewed by Bob Zdenek, 2 December 2015.

Holmstrom, Chris. 2016. Will Portland's Housing Crisis Become a Housing Bubble? http://koin.com/2016/04/28/will-portlands-housing-crisis-become-a-housing-bubble/, April 28.

Hull, Matt. 2015. Interviewed by Dee Walsh. 21 June 2015.

IFF Website. 2015. http://www.iff.org/.

Johnson, Pam. 2015. Interviewed by Bob Zdenek, 8 June 2015.

King, Jim. 2015. Interviewed by Bob Zdenek, 23 June 2015.

Kittenbrick, Jay. 2015. Interviewed by Bob Zdenek, 9 September 2015.

Leonard, M.A., Leah Greenwood, Brett Sheehan, Suan Duren and Ben Nichols. 2013. Almost a Merger: The ACE-REACH Journey to Successful

Collaboration. Housing Washington Presentation. http://www.wshfc. org/conf2013/presentations/T8.pdf.

Longworth, Susan. 2011. *Suburban Housing Collaboratives: A Case for Interjurisdictional Collaboration*, 7, 11. Community Development and Policy Studies Division of the Federal Reserve Bank of Chicago.

McCaskill, Yvvone. 2015. Interviewed by Bob Zdenek, 9 November 2015.

Miller, Michael Victor, and Robert Lee Maril. 1979. Poverty in the Lower Rio Grande Valley of Texas: Historical and Contemporary Dimensions. Texas Agricultural Experiment Station, Texas A & M University.

Mitchell-Bennett, Nick. 2016. Email Communication to Dee Walsh, 5 December 2016.

Morgan, Sara. 2013. Interviewed by Bob Zdenek, 25 June 2013.

Neri, Joe. 2015. Interviewed by Dee Walsh, 30 July 2015.

North West Housing Partnership. 2015. http://www.nwhp.net/. Accessed June 2015.

Office of Consumer Credit. 2015. https://www.consumeraffairs.com/payday-loans-and-lenders.

Office of Neighborhood Involvement. 2016. Origins and Early Years. https://www.portlandoregon.gov/oni/article/492415. Accessed June 2016.

Okagaki, Alan. 2008. *Federation of Appalachian Enterprises: A Case Study*. Berea, KY, 2–8, 19.

O'Shea, Bridget, and John O'Shea. 2011. Biggest Stock of Foreclosed Homes: Right Here. *Chicago News Cooperative*, July 7.

PDX.history.com. 2013. Historic Portland. http://www.pdxhistory.com/.

Perlman, Alan. 2015. Interviewed by Bob Zdenek, 22 September 2015.

Peters, Kathy. 2015. Interviewed by Bob Zdenek, 3 September 2015.

Randolph, Eric. 2016. Interviewed by Bob Zdenek, 22 January 2016.

REACH Community Development Annual Reports. 2009–2012.

REACH Community Development. Mission and History. http://reachcdc.org/about-us/mission-and-history/. Accessed June 2016.

RGV Texas.com.

Simon, Josh. 2015. Interviewed by Bob Zdenek, 17 November 2015.

Snyder, Howard. 2015. Interviewed by Bob Zdenek, 7 June 2015.

Snyder, Howard. 2015. Interviewed by Bob Zdenek, 14 May 2015.

Snyder, Howard, and Tina Daniell. 2011. *The Northwest Side Community Development Corporation: Transforming the Approach to Creating Positive Economic Impact in Distressed Communities*, 2–6. Chicago, IL: ProfitWise, Federal Reserve Bank of Chicago.

Snyderman, Robin, and Beth Dever. 2013. *Building Capacity Through Collaboration in Chicago's Suburbs. Confronting Suburban Poverty in America*. Brookings Metropolitan Policy Program.

Summers, Evan. 2015. Interviewed by Dee Walsh, 30 July 2015.

Tam, Tse-Ming. 2016. Interviewed by Bob Zdenek, 16 January 2016.

TD Bank Project Summary. Foundation Center. 2011.

U.S. Census Bureau. http://www.census.gov/topics/income-poverty/poverty.

US Census Bureau. June 2016. https://www.census.gov/quickfacts/table/ PST045215/4159000.

Vigness, David M., and Mark Odintz. 2016. Rio Grande Valley. *Handbook of Texas*. https://tshaonline.org/handbook/online/articles/rnr05. Accessed 2016.

Walsh, Dee, and Robert Zdenek. 2011. *The New Way Forward: Using Collaborations and Partnerships for Greater Efficiency and Impact*, 9–10. San Francisco, CA: Community Development Investment Center, Federal Reserve Bank of San Francisco.

West Cook County Housing Collaborative. 2014. WCCHC Strategic Planning. Powerpoint, February 24.

West Cook County Housing Collaborative. 2015. WCCHC Presentation to Maywood Finance Committee. Powerpoint, March 11.

Woodstock Institute Staff. 2016. *Regional Housing Partnership: A Housing Blueprint for the Chicago Region*. Woodstock Institute.

http://www.pewtrusts.org/~/media/assets/2013/11/11/portland_profile.pdf? la=en.

http://www.mbta.com/about_the_mbta/history/?id=970.

CHAPTER 8

Lessons from the Case Studies

In this chapter, we will examine the lessons learned from the case studies and take a look at both the successes and challenges that the participating organizations faced. The seven case studies described how core competencies were used as comparative advantages to advance strategic partnerships in community development. In selecting case studies for the book, we sought compelling examples of community development organizations that are able to choose the right partners to obtain the requisite competencies and capacities to achieve significant outcomes for the community. Case studies were selected that represent both urban and rural settings throughout the USA with participating partners from diverse sectors. We sought collaborations that could be durable over time and financially viable and that represented unique funding models and new approaches. We also looked for high-performing organizations.

Common themes and patterns emerge from the case studies, and this chapter will compare and contrast the themes and lessons. In each case study, we'll explore whether or not the organizations understood their *core competencies* and leveraged them as their *comparative advantage*. We'll also examine the collaborations that were undertaken and whether or not they reflect the *characteristics of successful collaborations*. Finally, we'll discuss whether or not the collaborations were *financially viable*.

© The Author(s) 2017
R.O. Zdenek and D. Walsh, *Navigating Community Development*,
DOI 10.1057/978-1-137-47701-9_8

Understanding and Utilizing Core Competencies

Looking at the lead organizations that were featured in each case study, the organizations have ambitious missions with one or more lines of business and numerous proficiencies. Several of the organizations are hybrids, meaning they are a combination of a CDC, RHDO, or CDFI, and thus have a diverse set of competencies. Yet when going after large and complex problems, they chose to collaborate and partner with others who had the capabilities that they were missing.

NWSCDC is an example of an organization that developed competencies to address a strong, singular focus. They transitioned from being a major project developer and real estate owner to a catalyst convener role. While they are a CDC first, they also are a CDFI, which they use to aggregate and deliver their financial resources. Their focus is to revitalize a community through the creation of opportunities, primarily employment, for residents living in northwest Milwaukee. As their role changed over the years, they have modified their board and staff to reflect the skills and competencies that they need to do this work. They recognized which resources and capabilities they needed to be successful and have carefully selected partners that can deliver the things they cannot deliver alone. Through their partnership with Wisconsin Energy Research Consortium (WERC), a consortium of three engineering schools in the Milwaukee area, and eight firms representing businesses in energy, power, and control, they have worked to create an industrial technology base that will employ local residents with good wages.

The partners in the Fairmount Indigo Line collaborative spent long hours building a working relationship and pulling in other organizations that had skills and relationships that they lacked. Sharing of philosophy of community empowerment, the collaborative was keen to involve local residents and stakeholders in their process. This competency was essential for gaining community support and developing a meaningful plan.

In addition to working with prominent employers and research institutions, NWSCDC also worked with grassroots organizations, whose competencies include community organizing, advocacy, and knowledge of local residents. The community, with support from NWSCDC's organizer/planner, helped start neighborhood block watch clubs in 2003 and 2004, and then organized the block clubs into the Century City Triangle Neighborhood Association. The initial goal of the association was safety and community improvements to retain and attract businesses that provide living wages. Previously, the community had several auto manufacturing businesses that contributed to a sizeable black middle class and there was a desire to attract companies back to the community to provide good living wage jobs to local residents. The Association provides grassroots support and leadership to NWSCDC so that local people can benefit from the economic opportunities (Snyder and Daniell 2011).

The CDC of Brownsville is an excellent example of an organization with multiple related lines of business. They are a lender, a developer, and also provide housing counseling. When they embarked on a mission to combat payday lending, they branched out into related territory—financial literacy. They understood that if families in the Rio Grande Valley were going to be able to purchase homes and be successful homeowners, they couldn't get caught in the web of high-interest payday finance. To tackle this issue, they leveraged their innovation, entrepreneurship, and facilitation competencies to find partners who could deliver the software and services to their target clientele. The CDC of Brownsville (CDCB) understood the problem and recognized the need to bring in specific expertise to solve the problem at hand.

IFF on the other hand had many of the competencies needed to address the foreclosure crisis in West Cook County suburbs. They had been working in these communities on housing policy and affordable development projects and they understood the local market and political dynamics. By working with the local governments of five suburban communities, they were able to access resources and political will to address the foreclosure problem regionally. This was important because the foreclosure crisis did not confine itself to specific jurisdictions. While IFF had the skill set to do much of the work itself, they recognized the importance of collaborating with local partners and contracted out some of the housing work to smaller, community-based organizations that had local presence and support.

Fahe is indeed a hybrid. It is a membership organization but it is also a CDFI. When it took on the challenge of tackling affordable housing issues in Appalachia, Fahe knew that they could not do it alone, and they needed to grow the capacity of their local members. They needed to organize and facilitate a group effort that maximized the skills of their various partners. Fahe's core competencies are finance and collaboration, and they used these skills to engage a range of partners to play various roles needed to positively impact affordable housing production. By proposing a bold performance challenge and then coordinating its implementation, Fahe leveraged its skills to provide a scaled solution for the region.

In the case study about the REACH–ACE merger, the organizations understood both their competencies and their weaknesses. ACE needed to find a strong financial partner to survive and thrive, and the Executive Director had the foresight to be proactive in acting before they were in a crisis situation. REACH had strong capabilities and an interest in expanding into a new community and state, but understood that their chance of success would increase greatly if they had a local partner with local connections and credibility.

CHARACTERISTICS OF SUCCESSFUL COLLABORATIONS

There are several common characteristics of successful community development collaborations. While each organization must understand their competencies and know how best to leverage them with others, they also need to understand the fundamentals of what makes strategic partnerships successful. Following are six essential characteristics and a description of how the organizations in the cases studies reflected them:

- There is a leader, quarterback, or backbone organization that marshals the effort.
- The organizations are ready and well positioned to proceed.
- There is strong public sector support.
- The challenge that the collaboration is trying to tackle is strategic and of a meaningful size, but not so large that progress can't be made.
- The time is right for action.
- There are quick wins that help coalesce support and propel the collaboration forward.

LEAD ORGANIZATIONS

In each of our case studies, there is either an individual or an organization that leads the collaborative work. Community development organizations will need to partner with other nonprofit organizations, public institutions, and private entities in order to tackle complex problems. In each case, these organizations became skillful facilitators to pull together coalitions of groups to address issues. The leaders have been likened to quarterbacks, but in reality they function more like symphony conductors. They are not the star player acting on their own, but the person responsible for bringing out the best of everyone involved and ensuring their coordinated effort results in a great outcome. The term quarterback is more widely used term for describing the individual or organization that leads a collaborative effort, and that is how we will refer to this role throughout the book.

NWSCDC frequently took on the quarterback. By leveraging their strategic planning, facilitation, and community organizing competencies, they were able to recruit major corporations to see the advantage of locating or remaining in their community.

As the convener of a strong network of local organizations, it was natural for Fahe to play the leading role. When Fahe launched the Berea Compact, they helped build the capacity of their members to operate at scale in through strategic partnerships. The Berea Compact consisted of five initiatives described in the previous chapter. Fahe's strategy was to pick one member with a particular core competency to be the primary aggregator or distributor of the services for other members. They did a pilot project to test concepts and attempt to standardize what worked and then rolled out the model for larger scale and impact. As a result of Fahe's leadership, the Berea Compact partners significantly ramped up the production of affordable housing in Central Appalachia.

EBALDC serves as the backbone organization for their healthy neighborhood collaborative. The collaborative incorporated the core values of EBALDC including collaboration, respect for diversity, skillful listening, shared leadership, accountability, and commitment to their mission. They accomplish more by engaging others and encouraging people to be leaders and problem solvers in their community. To do this work, EBALDC draws from more than 30 years of experience creating successful partnerships in diverse initiatives.

In the West Cook County Housing Collaborative, IFF played the role of the quarterback by functioning as the central administrator and facilitator for the collaborative's work. IFF was selected through a public request for proposal process to manage the collaboration. Once the WCCHC was up and running, IFF became the key player for organizing meetings, developing a common strategy, seeking, administering, and lending funds and implementing specific programmatic components. Given their financing and real estate development competencies, they could also be directly involved with a real estate project.

In the Fairmount Indigo Line effort, four CDCs were actively involved in the planning and implementation of the revitalization work along the rail line. The Dorchester Bay EDC, and its then Executive Director Jeanne

Dubois, were a primary force behind the collaboration, working in close partnership with the other CDCs. Ms. Dubois' strong commitment to community engagement and tireless dedication to the cause of improving the corridor were essential factors to the collaboration's success.

The CDC of Brownsville has been a community development leader in the Rio Grande Valley for many years. Because of its commitment to its mission, stepping up to lead an effort to address the payday lending problem was not a stretch. They were already serving many of the people who were impacted by this issue and they had a broad network of relationships that they could tap to tackle the issue. By giving people an alternative mechanism to access short-term debt, they were helping potential home buying customers from ruining their credit, while strengthening the financial viability of the entire region by stemming the drain of cash in the form of exorbitant loan fees.

The Executive Directors of both REACH and ACE took leadership roles to make their collaboration happen. Working closely together, they mapped out a strategy that would result in a win–win for both organizations. They recognized that to get what they needed, they both needed to compromise. And while they both understood this, they had to manage the expectations of both boards that had their own views on how the partnership should be structured.

ORGANIZATIONAL READINESS

With each of our case studies, the lead organizations either had experience with and knowledge of the issue they chose to address, or they were willing to make significant organizational changes to educate and prepare themselves.

Organizational readiness for NWSCDC required divesting of 250,000 square feet of commercial and industrial property, including their office in a historic fire station. It took five years to complete this work. Next, NWSCDC demonstrated the ability to forge a partnership with the Wisconsin Energy Research Consortium (WERC), now called the Midwest Energy Research Consortium (MERC). MERC acts as a mentor to technology-based businesses that NWSCDC recruits, finances, and assists. NWSCDC and MERC have also formed a workforce development program in the power controls and energy fields that draws upon NWSCDC's expertise in workforce development. NWSCDC quickly succeeded with their new strategic direction and have had additional successes with the partnership model.

Fahe took a 2-pronged approach of quality control and technical expertise to build their organizational capacity and readiness. The first prong was to emphasis quality control to meet and exceed industry standards for mortgage origination. They hired staff and created systems to meet these standards. This enabled them to raise significant pools of capital in a capital-starved region. Secondly, Fahe spent extensive time with its 50 plus members to provide support and direction as needed. Fahe staff and members have created a learning environment based on open communication and trust. The ability to ask and answer tough questions is critical to the learning and success of the collaboration, and the open questioning of strategies and issues is a hallmark of an effective collaboration according to the Nonprofit Finance Fund Catalyst project.

Fahe meets twice a year with all of their members in the spring and fall, and have quarterly caucus meetings in four states (Kentucky, Tennessee, Virginia, and West Virginia) that comprise their primary membership. These meetings emphasize training and technical assistance. They also create an environment for sharing information and build knowledge among the members toward a goal of having Fahe members ready to benefit from Fahe's housing financing products.

EBALDC has spent considerable time over several decades building organizational leadership and readiness to lead collaborative efforts. The Healthy Neighborhood initiative is grounded in the concept of collective impact, which prescribes developing a common agenda and shared measurement system, focusing on mutually reinforcing activities of participating organizations and partaking in continuous communication with all participants. EBALDC provided "backbone" support by dedicating staff and leadership to this effort.

Collective Impact efforts tend to be led by major institutions, and what is unique about the San Pablo Avenue Revitalization Coalition (SPARC) initiative, is that a grassroots community development organization, EBLADC, is leading the effort. They are respected by both community leaders and powerful institutions. EBALDC brings a deep understanding of the roles of relationships before engaging in partnerships.

In the West Cook County Housing Collaborative, IFF prepared prior to formally joining the collaborative by participating in housing policy forums and developing affordable housing in the impacted areas. In responding to the request for proposal to lead the effort, IFF had to think through its approach and identify its human and other resources that it could dedicate to the work.

The four CDCs who comprised the Fairmount Indigo Corridor Collaborative had worked in the communities affected by the lack of transit for decades. They were ready to proceed in that they understood both the challenges and opportunities. They were able to build upon the work already underway by the Greater Four Corners Action Coalition, and they were careful to lay out a plan with clear goals and actions. They developed an MOU that defined the goals, principals, a decision-making process, and the responsibilities of the participating groups.

CDC of Brownsville readied itself by learning about the issue through the discussion of the members of the "kaffeklatsch" that Nick Bennett Mitchell participated in. The availability of grant funds for a public education campaign on the topic prompted the group to develop a better solution—one that did more than educate and actually provided people with a good alternative. The group did significant research about the problem before arriving at a solution.

Both REACH and ACE were very ready to proceed. One organization was poised for growth and the other poised for a partner. The only drawback to the process was that the REACH Executive Director left just prior to the finishing the transaction and was not there to facilitate the integration of staff and activities. While it still happened, it did slow down the process and created a lack of continuity in leading the transition.

Strong Local Public Sector Support

Community development organizations have had a long history of support from local and state governments, in part because of the availability of federal block grants (CDBG, CSBG and HOME), and the Low-Income Housing Tax Credit program. Relationships across the USA between community development organizations and governmental units were for many years a traditional funding relationship with a grantor and a grantee. Over the years, as public funds have dried up, some local and state governments have turned to nonprofit community development organizations to help implement their policies and programs. The case studies in this book suggest that the evolving relationship between community development organizations and local and state government is dynamic, with local and state governments viewing community development organizations as genuine partners.

IFF had tremendous public sector support in the West Cook County Housing Collaborative. They were viewed by the participating local suburban governments as the trusted facilitator of a multi-year strategy to combat the foreclosure crisis. Based on their success with WCCHC, they were subsequently asked by the public sector to lead a similar effort for suburbs south of Chicago.

In the case of the Fairmount Indigo Corridor Collaborative, much of the early work was aimed at getting local governmental bodies to respond to a problem that they had ignored for years. The lack of viable transportation for residents in the impacted neighborhoods had contributed to disinvestment in the areas along the rail line. Once the Collaborative achieved some success, many of the local governments stepped up and fully supported the goals of the group.

The CDC of Brownsville Community Lending Center was created in part because public policies allowed payday lenders to charge huge fees to borrowers, so an alternative lower-cost small-loan system was needed. Now that their good payday lending system is operational, local governments are some of their customers, offering the services of CLC to their employees.

NWSCDC has forged strong relationships with local elected officials including aldermen. Additionally, the CDC has in-depth knowledge of federal government policies and funding sources have made them a valued partner. The technology organizations consider NWSCDC to be an ideal partner, because they help provide financial support and technical assistance to small businesses through their CDFI, as well as assistance with political support. NWSCDC has been able to secure major federal grants from the Office of Community Services (OCS) for facility improvements and specialized equipment important for the growth of the industrial firms.

Fahe and their members serve hundreds of small rural communities where there is limited capacity and activity. Fahe has built strong relationships with state housing finance agencies in the states where they and their members work. Fahe is pursuing work with energy efficiency, healthy homes, and aging in community initiatives. They will be able to utilize state government resources to help achieve those results.

EBALDC has a strong partnership with the Alameda County Public Health Department located in Oakland. The Public Health Department informed EBALDC staff and stakeholders on the importance of addressing the social determinants of health. The Health Department study, Life and Death Through Unnatural Causes, showed the enormous difference in health and education outcomes based on where one lives. The Public Health Department has been an invaluable partner and has brought other major stakeholders to work with EBALDC including St. Mary's Hospital and Life-Long Federal Qualified Health Center.

In the REACH-ACE collaboration, the public sector partners in Washington State had to be convinced that the partnership would be a positive. While they respected REACH and appreciated the organization's strengths, they openly stated that they would have much preferred it if ACE partnered with another organization from the same community. Once they understood that that option wasn't available to ACE, they got on board and supported the merger.

THE CHALLENGE IS STRATEGIC AND BIG ENOUGH TO BE A PRIORITY

The lead organizations in each of the case studies faced a substantial challenge or opportunity where the traditional status quo was not sufficient given the scale of the issue and the communities' needs. They recognized that addressing the issue was aligned with their organizational goals and strategically important to their missions.

As noted in the case study, the foreclosure crisis had a huge negative impact on Chicago's suburban communities. On their own, these local governmental bodies did not have the staff or tools in place to adequately respond. By pulling together with neighboring communities and engaging a partner like IFF that had the knowledge and skills to obtain and deploy resources, they were able to strategically respond to the problem. Now that much of the problem has been addressed and with some government institutions shifting priorities to new issues, the collaboration may wind down.

Texas has one of the biggest payday lending problems in the USA, with payday and title loan lenders doing nearly $6 billion of total business done in 2013. This challenge was so big that it couldn't be ignored, and strategically fit the mission of CDCB.

For those living along the Fairmount Indigo Line, quick, inexpensive transportation to the jobs and services of the central city had evaded them for decades. The challenge was big and the solutions to it were expensive, but by rising up and demanding improvements the communities along the line the Fairmount Indigo Corridor Collaborative were able to strategically channel new resources to the community and revive not only a transit line but four communities that surround it.

The neighborhoods on the northwest side of Milwaukee had suffered from disinvestment and unemployment for decades. The challenge is to bring and retain companies with good paying jobs to the community. As noted in the case study, historically, Northwest Side CDC had pursued a commercial/industrial development agenda that was typical for CDCs focused on commercial revitalization activities. After considerable strategic analysis the board and executive staff shifted the direction of the organization to focus on strategic partnerships where it could add value.

The value add was that NWCDC was skilled at accessing federal grants for major economic development and business financing. They had a long history of solving economic development problems in the neighborhood and they had strong relationships with the business community. NWSCDC has focused on providing financing, real estate support, and political support to industrial firms that have national and global markets.

Fahe's big challenge was different than NWSCDC. Their organizational future was not in jeopardy, but the ability of Fahe and its members to continue to produce new units of affordable housing and continue their effectiveness and impact was questionable. The production trajectory of Fahe and its members was flat and their self-sufficiency rate was low. As noted in the case study, Fahe and its network members which have grown from 30 to over 55 organizations launched in the Berea Performance Compact. Over the period of a decade, they were able to quadruple the annual housing production of the Fahe network to well over 8000 units and grow their self-sufficiency ratio. Fahe has used this big challenge to position itself to strategically pursue new opportunities in the future.

EBALDC is a well-operated diversified CDC and has developed over 2000 units of housing, commercial development, and asset-building programs. However, the organization's leadership realized that while the CDC had engaged in significant physical revitalization of core neighborhoods in Oakland and surrounding communities in Alameda County, the health and social outcomes of the community were low by comparison to surrounding communities.

The study by Alameda County Public Health Department and additional analysis spurred EBALDC into focusing on healthy neighborhoods as their core priority moving forward. The challenge was large and timely. EBALDC's strategic response was to focus on healthy neighborhoods. EBALDC has not reduced their real estate development activity; rather, it has targeted the real estate development to neighborhoods that are in their core target areas. EBALDC leads a collaboration of 13 organizations of the SPARC Coalition to tackle and improve health outcomes for local residents at all ages.

THE TIME IS RIGHT FOR ACTION

In all of the case studies, the ability of those involved to proceed in a timely fashion was critical. Organizations must identify the right partners and begin the work of aligning systems and resources. Being ready to proceed does not imply that all the capacity and competencies are in place, but it does suggest that organizations have adequate collaborative leadership and capacity in place to launch their new initiative. Strategic partnerships and multi-sector collaborations are a different way of doing business, and the lead community development organizations have to create the learning environment and capacity to succeed. The collaboration leadership needs to acknowledge inherent risks and uncertainties. It is hard to know the outcome of the collaborative as the partnership is being launched. It is important that the value added by working together is genuine and that the criteria for working together are clear.

The trigger that prompted action in each of the case studies varied. Two groups were prompted by financial need (NWSCDC and ACE). The West Cook County Housing Collaborative was prompted by a major crisis pertaining to home foreclosures. New information about health outcomes prompted EBALDC to take action. Fahe and the partners of the Fairmount Indigo Line were responding to community issues that had been building over years. No matter what the trigger for action, the community development organizations needed to be willing to act and be open to new ways of doing their work. They also had to get outside of their comfort zone of business as usual and develop new partners. Both attitude and aptitude play a role in their success.

QUICK WINS AND INITIAL SUCCESS

Collaborations that involve big challenges and new directions can take many years. It can be difficult to engage and retain stakeholders and funding over the long haul. Organizational change practitioners and experts strongly encourage organizations to secure quick wins (Kotter 1994). The notion is simple: having clear tangible successes early on that vest the members, and that help the collaborative stay engaged and achieve its long-term goals.

For the partners of the Fairmount Indigo Line, first success was the completion of the Indigo Line plan and the MOU that identified goals and desired outcomes for the community and laid out the roles and responsibilities of the collaborative members. Major physical improvements to stations that resulted as part of a legally mandated program to mitigate increased pollution caused by the "Big Dig" brought visible improvements to the community.

For IFF and West Cook County Housing Collaborative, the award of a large federal grant (Neighborhood Stabilization Funds) allowed work to get underway fairly quickly.

NWSCDC had the dual challenges of selling commercial real estate that was draining the organization and forming new strategic partnerships. NWSCDC "quick win" was to secure a large grant from the Office of Community Services to finance facility renovation, which created an initial success and momentum.

To quadruple their housing production impact, Fahe pursued several critical initiatives early on. Their first win was the creation and adoption of the Berea Performance Compact, which laid out a plan for how Fahe members would scale up. Secondly, Fahe became a broker and was able to originate market rate housing loans with 5th Third Bank and Kentucky Housing Corporation. The broker role enabled them to expand their products, while not being constrained by their balance sheet.

EBALDC started with a Healthy Neighborhoods Strategic Plan that assesses each project, program, and partnership for its potential to create resources and opportunities to achieve healthy outcomes and vibrant lives. To build momentum, they focused on reducing emergency room and hospital visits due to high blood pressure. EBALDC and their partners emphasized preventive treatment at health clinics and by providing access to healthy foods. EBALDC also promoted exercise and health education (San Pablo Area Revitalization Collaborative plan 2015). SPARC brought health technicians from Life-Long Medical, a Federally Qualified Health Center and St. Mary's Hospital to provide blood pressure screening for 10 weeks for adults living in the SPARC target area.

EBALDC and their partners worked to improve area safety by reducing blight and improving streets, parks, and abandoned land. Improving the physical environment can improve the perception that neighborhood is safer. They focused on five "hot spots" in the neighborhood that needed improvement through activities such as mural wall paintings, cleaning up trash and making the streetscape more attractive and active.

ADAPTING ORGANIZATIONAL STRUCTURES TO ADVANCE COMPETENCIES AND STRATEGIC PARTNERSHIPS

Community development organizations operate in an ever-changing environment. As such, the challenges that they are facing today may morph and change into something else in the future. To be effective at responding to these shifts, the organizations will need to develop new competencies to respond to the challenges and create collaborative structures that are resilient and flexible and able to pivot and adapt.

In *Toward a New Business Model*, Laura Choi and David Erickson of the Federal Reserve Bank of San Francisco underscore the importance of understanding complex adaptive systems. They note "that everything is connected to everything and interacts in ways that we cannot predict or control." Adaptive challenges present problems that are not understood and that are messy. They require innovation, learning, and evolving strategies. The ability for a collaboration to adapt is a critical element of the community development ecosystem because of the constant change that occurs with leadership, resources, and communities. Adaption works best when multiple stakeholders are engaged and part of the process, leading to changes in numerous ways across organizational and stakeholder boundaries (Choi and Erickson 2015).

Another challenge is to do the work that is necessary to build or acquire the needed competencies and develop the relationships in new strategic partnerships. Community development organizations must weigh the cost/benefit of investing in these structures, taking into consideration what can be gained by working with others, rather than proceeding alone.

In moving toward a strategic partnership model, NWSCDC revised its governance structure and procedures of the organization. They decided to expand the board of directors reflecting the new competencies and strengths needed for the organization. NWSCDC enlisted board members who were recruited with specialized expertise in marketing, law, and human resources to assess potential economic partners. At the staff level, the CDC made some strategic staff realignments to reflect the new competencies needed for the new direction of the organization. A position was created for an organizer/strategic planner to engage the community in a neighborhood strategic planning process. The net result of these changes was to make the organization able to develop a comparative advantage that made them an attractive partner to others. They adapted to the changing environment and created new strategic partnerships.

For Codman Square CDC, a member of the Fairmount Indigo Corridor Collaborative, the experience gave the organization a better understanding of their core competencies and the confidence to take on bigger issues. Going forward they looked for the right partners with complementary competencies to address specific issues. They learned that collaborations take time and that the relationship building work that is necessary for working well with others is necessary and ultimately pays off. Collaborative member Dorchester Bay EDC related the importance of creating alliances with others to build political power and obtain additional resources. While these alliances take time and patience, they are necessary to bring a voice to communities.

Fahe leadership realized that simply adapting the Berea Performance Compact was not enough. They needed to develop a stronger competency for operating a first-rate mortgage platform. Among their first hires was a former Fannie Mae senior lender to develop the systems and quality control necessary to succeed. The organization invested in mortgage origination software. Fahe became a leader in loan servicing in their region and by 2015 had attracted 33 investors including state housing mortgage finance agencies and Habitat for Humanity.

EBALDC made major changes to embrace a "Healthy Neighborhoods" framework. EBALDC's healthy neighborhood lens helped them identify the neighborhood assets and stressors, and determine which stressors they could address with a collaborative strategy that built on their strengths. EBALDC began adapting to a new set of issues and strategies that will undergird their future work.

CDC of Brownsville created a new entity, the Community Lending Center, to provide their alternative to predatory payday lending. They used their experience and competency to develop the collaborative effort to build the program and engaged other individuals and organizations with complementary competencies to provide technical skills for the company's software and legal expertise, and provide customers access to it.

REACH changed its by-laws and board makeup to require the inclusion of members of the Vancouver and SW Washington community. This was necessary to show that they were committed to having the involvement of local residents and stakeholders in guiding the future work in that community.

The Fairmount Indigo Line CDC collaborative spent countless hours developing an MOU to clearly define roles and responsibilities that built on the various organizations' competencies and comparative advantages. This document guided their collaboration for many years.

Financial Viability

Community development organizations operate in challenging environments and serve people with limited resources. Often, the mission-driven work that is done does not produce adequate revenue to support the cost of the work. Frequently organizations need to seek resources to subsidize this work. Financial viability is critical for organizations and collaborations to operate and succeed. These initiatives have to cobble together diverse streams of funding. Multi-sector partnerships that focus on long-term outcomes and impact will likely need to access many different sources of funding over the life of the partnership.

Historically, funding for community development work came from four primary sources: the public sector, earned revenue, private capital, and philanthropy, including individual, corporate, and foundation gifts.

The most common public sector sources included CDBG, HOME, LIHTC, Tax Increment Financing, New Market Tax Credits, the CDFI and Capital Magnet Funds and HHS Office of Community Services Urban and Rural Economic Development Program. These are important sources for financing affordable housing and for community development lending. One of the challenges facing the field in the last decade is that some of the traditional public funding sources have declined—notably Community Development Block Grants (CDBG) and HOME Partnership dollars.

Earned revenue for community development organizations comes from fees and revenue for the services they provide, which may include rental income, loan fees, and program fees. For CDFIs and RHDOs, earned income can comprise a significant portion of their budget. Community development organizations also rely on private capital to finance much of their community development and real estate development work, and to invest in their loan funds. Private donations from philanthropic sources support the services and non-cash generating activities of community development organizations. In recent years, new sources of funding have surfaced, such as impact investments, social impact bonds and funds from other sectors, such as the health-care sector via the Affordable Care Act.

Funding for collaborative efforts is less well defined. It may come from public or private sources, but can be short lived and unreliable. Frequently, organizations must rely on their own balance sheets to engage in these efforts. As community development work is a long-term process that requires long-term capital, finding adequate support can be challenging. While funding can be episodic, organizations need to be able to have enough support to build momentum that will last the duration.

These financial constraints can make it difficult for smaller community development organizations to take on significant roles in starting collaborations. However, once established it is very possible, as in the Fairmount Indigo Line, that new resources can be accessed that grow the work of the collaborative and also benefit the individual organizations.

Effective community development organizations, especially those who play the quarterback role, have to consciously plan for and allocate resources to form collaborations. However, as our case studies show, there can be very significant payoffs in terms of improved outcomes for residents and communities.

NWSCDC has had considerable success securing large community economic development grants from the Office of Community Services (OCS) for their collaborative work on industrial and technology projects. These sources coupled with the federal and state support including tax credits that the manufacturing firms have accessed, has the net effect of leveraging significant new dollars into the low-income neighborhoods of Northwest Milwaukee and attracting and retaining large employers.

Fahe deploys both an internal and external strategy for raising significant new source of capital. Their internal strategy has been to grow their membership and housing production capacity to generate additional money. As of 2014, Fahe and their 55 members have increased the annual level of capital deployed from $7 million in 2003 to over $80 million in 2014. Fahe has been very creative in terms of deepening existing funding and accessing new funding sources. They became a correspondent lender for JP Morgan Chase & Co. and Flag Star Bank, enabling them to originate, underwrite, and sell loans to both of these financial institutions. They also have established a broker network allowing local organizations, Fahe members, and partners, to originate USDA guarantee loans and they earn a fee for loans closed.

EBALDC has a strong history of launching comprehensive community development initiatives with an array of different funding sources. They have raised over $200 million in their first 40 years of existence.

The WCCHC relied on public sector funding to do its initial work. As the foreclosure crisis subsides and communities develop new priorities, the collaborative's role, and possibly its existence, is likely to change in the coming years.

CDCB has developed a franchise model that relies on little subsidy and many partners. By designing an income-producing program that is more beneficial for borrowers but still produces revenue, the Community Lending Centers should be able to proliferate and flourish.

REACH and ACE sought philanthropic sources to support their initial collaborative and due diligence work. Now that the partnership is formed and functioning, no further subsidy is needed.

CONCLUSION

The seven case studies featured in this book describe a wide variety of community development challenges, organization types, and solutions. The organizations featured all share certain commonalities, including: a strong understanding of their goals and purpose, an understanding of their competencies, and an ability to select appropriate partners. In some cases, organizations need to pursue a tactical strategy that is not comprehensive initially, in order to obtain the visibility, wins, and resources needed to employ a more holistic approach. While there are no absolute right and wrong ways to pursue collaborative solutions, success is enhanced when organizations know their competencies and understand how to leverage them in a particular situation.

REFERENCES

Choi, Laura, and David Erickson. 2015. Towards a New Business Model: Strengthening Families Helps To Strengthen Communities and the Nation. What It's Worth. San Francisco. CA: Federal Reserve Bank of San Francisco and CFED, 373.

Kotter, John P. 1996. *Leading change*. Boston, MA: Harvard Business School Press.

Snyder, Howard, and Tina Daniell. 2011. *The Northwest Side Community Development Corporation: Transforming the Approach to Creating Positive Economic Impact in Distressed Communities*, 2–7. Chicago: Federal Reserve Bank of Chicago.

CHAPTER 9

The Community Development Ecosystem: The Next Generation

In this chapter, we look at how the economic, social, political, and technological forces will impact the community development ecosystem of the future. We share findings from recent studies that examine the characteristics and competencies that will be needed by community development organizations to succeed. We also review some of the trends in strategy, organization, and leadership that we anticipate will occur based on a survey of community development leaders.

THE RAPID PACE OF CHANGE

According to the *New York Times* columnist Thomas Friedman, "Average is over for everyone." Friedman believes that we are entering a period of unprecedented change that will require better-than-average performance by individuals and organizations. This change is the result of the growth and pace of globalization, the exponential quickening of computing power, and climate change. Friedman believes that community resiliency will be achieved only by working horizontally, utilizing diversity and finding solutions in small-scale networks rather than traditional hierarchies. This networked approach builds strong communities, which are the foundation of a stable world (Friedman 2015, 2016).

Applying Friedman's advice to the next generation of community development is not a far reach. As we saw in the case studies in this book, working horizontally with a diverse network of other organizations is already an approach embraced by many community development groups.

© The Author(s) 2017
R.O. Zdenek and D. Walsh, *Navigating Community Development*,
DOI 10.1057/978-1-137-47701-9_9

The challenge moving forward will be to become better and more effective at operating this way, and to expand these networks to have a broader reach. As change accelerates, community development organizations will need to invest in their infrastructure and people to keep up with changing technologies and demands.

The efficacious organizations in the community development ecosystem of tomorrow will be sophisticated, impactful nonprofit developers and lenders of all sizes, who are focused on the neighborhood, city, regional, and/or national level. These groups will be part of a highly networked system, closely connected to the public sector, private sector, and community institutions and civic leaders. They will have developed sound approaches and highly effective financial and communication skills, knowledge of how to manage and utilize data, while retaining their mission focus, commitment, and entrepreneurial approach to solving the problems of poverty.

FUTURE TRENDS

Recent research and literature about the future of the community development field, whether it is the community development quarterback role described in What Works in America's Communities or the "collective impact" approach to problem solving advanced by the Stanford Social Innovation Review, all speak to a need for a more comprehensive, networked, and orchestrated approach.

To understand more about how community development organizations are thinking about the future, a survey was conducted of 98 nonprofit regional housing development organizations and community development financial institutions in the spring of 2014 (Walsh and Davidson-Sawyer 2014). While the organizations were of diverse size, focus, and location, at the time all were members of the Housing Partnership Network (HPN) and as members met certain minimum standards with regard to size, impact, and financial strength. HPN membership criteria specifies that organizations be a market leader in their primary geography and have a strong, collaborative CEO, good governance, and financial strength. CEOs of these organizations were asked to identify their current and future strategy and business practices with regard to governance, management, growth, and mission. The survey was modeled on a longitudinal study recently undertaken by the Australia Housing and Urban Research Institute (AHURI) of social housing organizations in Australia.

In total, 49 CEOs, half of those surveyed, responded. When asked to name the three most significant areas of change their organization experienced during the period 2010–2012, CEOs identified the availability of capital for projects, the competitive environment with both nonprofits and for-profits, and changes in board priorities. These responses reflect the economic conditions during this period as organizations were very much impacted by the tightening credit after 2008. Obtaining capital for real estate projects and lending programs became more challenging and underwriting processes became lengthier and more comprehensive. Competition increased for both the usual sources of funding, such as HOME dollars and Low Income Housing Tax Credits (LIHTC), as well as the new sources of project funding, such as American Recovery and Reinvestment Act (ARRA). Organizations and their boards had to take a hard look at the risk profile of their development and/or lending portfolios and pipelines and adjust future plans accordingly to adapt to an era of greatly reduced resources and greatly increased need.

In the 2014 CEO survey, organizations predicted the most change over the coming three years would occur in four areas: collaboration, customer focus, business line diversification, and geographic reach. According to the survey responses, CEOs anticipated that going forward they would be collaborating more frequently to accomplish their missions. They expected that to fulfill their missions they would need to develop new business lines. CEOs also planned on growing their customer focus to include a broader range of incomes, serving more people in the communities where they work. And, they expected to expand their work to additional communities. These changes reflect a recognition that to stay relevant and respond to community needs, organizations must do more work, with more partners, impacting more people. These results are reflected in the case studies in this book. For example, CDC of Brownsville expanded into a new business line of "good payday lending" in order to respond to an urgent need being faced in Texas. The four CDCs in Boston became experts at transit-oriented development so that they could effectively address issues along the Fairmount Indigo Line. IFF moved into the suburbs to address the devastation that the foreclosure crisis caused in these communities. Fahe took collaboration of its members to a new level with the Berea Compact.

The CEO survey also shed light on where organizations will need to gain additional competencies if they are to succeed at collaboration and business diversification. Becoming a leader that is an astute collaborator may require a shift in style that is more facilitative and less "command and control."

SUCCEEDING IN THE ECOSYSTEM OF TOMORROW

To succeed in the future and to achieve maximum impact in a limited-resource environment, community development organizations need to learn how to tackle big, multi-sector challenges efficiently and effectively using a collaborative, facilitative approach. This will require being impactful at a larger scale; taking a leadership role in cross sector collaborations; learning how to compete well; developing both people-focused and place-based strategies; reaching a broader scope of customers; developing new skills; and finding new sources of capital.

SCALE

In the community development sector, going to scale typically means producing more affordable housing units or making more loans in a larger geographic area. The goal of working at scale is to achieve greater operational efficiencies and become more financially self-sufficient while reducing poverty and improving livability. This is achieved by helping more people, businesses, and community institutions. In the past, the assumption has been that by getting larger and working at scale, community development groups will be able to be more impactful.

However, in a limited-resource environment, it can be more efficient to reach scale by specializing and partnering with others, rather than scaling up on your own. The four CDCs who came together to form the Fairmount Indigo Line CDC Collaborative are an excellent example of how to scale up efforts by leveraging each other's strengths and competencies to have a regional impact. For the CDC of Brownsville, collaborating with organizations that could act as franchisees of the Community Lending Center was critical to scaling the good payday lending program.

Organizations that maximize their competencies and comparative advantages and leverage these skills and resources with others, can oftentimes achieve more than those who attempt to do it alone. Getting to scale is not just about being bigger; it is about being impactful and relevant to the communities being served. This often involves looking beyond the immediate projects and programs to larger, fundamental changes that result in systems change. Systems change is an alteration in the way in which a community makes decisions, allocates resources, and delivers services with the goal of being more effective. It requires a collaborative approach among multiple interested parties—public agencies, residents, and institutions that lead to service coordination and integration (cciTools 2016).

While both social change and systems change have been important concepts in community development circles since the civil rights movement, systems change has gained momentum in recent years because of the reduction in public sector support for the work. This austere "new normal" world means that the old systems and ways of doing business must transform to make the most of those resources that are available today. Business as usual is not a path to economic sustainability or success. Community development practitioners must rethink their assumptions of how they do their work and what tools they use. They also need to determine which partners they will engage with to accomplish their mission. The NWSCDC understood this when they moved from a property developer/owner to a coordinator and strategic leader that brought together the right partners to meet the economic needs of NW Milwaukee.

Both large and small organizations can increase their impact by working with others. For small community-based groups, this may mean collaborating with several other small organizations or with one or more larger groups that have specialized skills and more human and financial resources. Large organizations can find advantages to partnering with small organizations that have local insight and strong connections and ties critical to a successful strategy that benefits existing low-income residents. The REACH–ACE merger is a good example of how a larger organization leveraged its balance sheet and financial acumen with a smaller organization with deep ties to the community.

While getting to scale requires careful planning and steady, oftentimes aggressive, growth, operating at scale is the real challenge and requires a keen business sense and the ability to balance the needs and interests of multiple parties with the community development goals. Keeping collaborations working for a long period of time is an incredible amount of work, needing frequent communication and attention. Multi-sector collaborations may also require significant changes for organizations such as an expansion of their target customer/client base; extension of their geographic footprint; the development of new skills, expertise, and products and business lines; and the pursuit of new sources of capital. EBALDC's work with the health sector is a good illustration of how cross-sector partnerships can fill community needs, with each organization utilizing their comparative advantage.

QUARTERBACK ROLE

In addition to working at scale, organizations that succeed in the new community development ecosystem will need to consider a comprehensive approach to their work. According to David Erickson, Ian Galloway, and Naomi Cytron in *Routinizing the Ordinary*, to create a community development system that works in the future, three things will be necessary. The effort must be entrepreneurial and cross-sectoral to address a range of needs; the strategy must be data driven and flexible so that it is capable of adjustments; and it should be composed of both people and place-based interventions (Erickson et al. 2012).

In *Investing in What Works in America's Communities*, a facilitative leader or organization that can promote a compelling, comprehensive vision of success and gather the necessary resources to implement integrated strategies with specific, measurable outcomes has grown in importance.

In the West Cook County Housing Collaborative, IFF took the facilitative leadership role to coordinate the efforts of public and private entities to address the huge problems caused by the foreclosure crisis. Because of their expertise in finance and development, as well as strategy and resource development, IFF proved to be an invaluable partner and quarterback for the effort.

COLLABORATION

Collaboration is a key characteristic for community development strategy in the future, because community development organizations are finding it necessary to connect to other sectors and/or reach new partners in order to make meaningful change in communities. As noted throughout the book, complex, entrenched problems cannot be solved with a single solution by a single organization. Community development and housing organizations are finding the need to align themselves with the health, education, and employment sectors.

According to the 2014 CEO Future Strategy survey, 77% of CEO respondents anticipate that they will engage in very frequent collaboration in the future as compared to 32% who collaborated very frequently in the past (prior to 2014). Undertaking collaborations takes time and resources, and fortunately the philanthropic community had stepped up to support some of this work, including the Catalyst Fund and the Sea Change

Lodestar Fund for Nonprofit Collaboration, among others. An assessment of a five-year initiative by the Catalyst Fund found that mergers and collaborations were important strategic tools that shouldn't be considered last resorts. Organizations motivated by a shared vision and dedicated leadership resulted in powerful instruments to increased impact (Kramer 2016).

Collaboration can also be an important strategy for spreading risk among organizations. Collaborative efforts can improve the odds for success by increasing the technical and financial resources available to implement the effort.

All of the organizations featured in the case studies are collaborating with multiple partners. As mentioned in an earlier chapter, collaborations can be structured in a variety of ways with the most common being Hub and Spoke, Cross Sector, and Service Specialization. Regardless of how they are organized, collaborations need to share a common vision, provide mutual benefit, and require mutual responsibility, with one of more partners leading the effort.

COMPETITION

While collaboration in today's world is viewed as an essential core competency of nonprofits, the reality is that organizations must compete with others all of the time. Author and consultant David LaPiana in *Play to Win: The Nonprofit Guide to Competitive Strategy* asserts that organizations should develop winning competitive strategies to advance their mission and learn to achieve the optimal balance of collaborative and competitive relationships. In an article for the *Stanford Social Innovation Review*, Spencer Critchely notes the reality that many nonprofits survive not by collaborating, but by competing for resources and opportunities.

According to Critchely, asking nonprofits to collaborate more often does not always make sense, as each partner must divert scarce resources to a goal that may only partially relate to its core mission, while receiving little or no additional compensation for the effort (Critchley 2015).

For organizations to be successful they need to be strategic about when they compete versus collaborate. In the case of REACH and ACE, REACH could have made a decision to move into ACE's territory and directly compete for resources, but it knew that they would have to overcome the perception by local community members and leaders that they were outsiders. By choosing to collaborate, they were able to maximize the competencies of both organizations and be more effective more quickly. This partnership enabled them to better compete for resources.

According to the 2014 CEO Future Strategy Survey, most organizations expect moderate changes to the competitive environment with both their peer organizations and for-profits in the near future, with a quarter of the respondents expecting fairly big changes in the competitive environment. An increase in competition with both peer nonprofit and for-profit entities reflects the reduction of resources in an environment of increasing demand for product. There are more nonprofits competing for existing resources, plus for-profit developers and service providers are also competing for public dollars to launch initiatives. Given this environment, collaboration can offer opportunities for groups to jointly access funds that they could not access alone, as exemplified in the Fairmount Indigo Corridor Collaboration case study.

Interplay of Place-Based and People-Based Approaches

The goal of community development is to create vibrant and sustainable communities that benefit local residents, organizations, and businesses. To be successful in the future, community development organizations need to develop competencies or partnerships that address the human, physical, and social capital and assets of the community. While physical improvements are important to community revitalizations, equally important are human service programs that address employment, education, and health. The traditional funding and programmatic barriers that direct funding for either people or placed-based work need to be changed so that the various sectors can work more easily with each other. For example, linking health-care service funding to residents of affordable housing in low-income communities can have extremely beneficial impacts. The services can improve health outcomes and property stability while reducing overall system costs, such as emergency room usage for routine health care needs.

It has long been debated which approach, people- or place-based, is preferable and which one garners the most results. Numerous studies over the past two decades have tried to compare the effectiveness of each approach, and while some argued in favor of one over the other, the practical intelligence on this is that both are needed. Community development is by definition about both people and place. One approach cannot substitute for the other. People-based community development tools, such as job training, skills building, mental health counseling are all important to help individuals succeed. Yet, the environment in which they live and work is equally important, and thus approaches that look to revitalize and sustain livable communities are equally important.

Recently, the importance of place has gained attention with regard to how it can impact a person's health. The conditions in the environments where people live and work can impact a variety of health and quality-of-life outcomes and risks according to the Office of Disease Prevention and Health Promotion. These factors are referred to as the "social determinants of health" and can greatly influence individual and household outcomes (US Dept. of Health and Human Services 2016). Data about the increased number of high poverty census tracts and the increased number of low-income people living in these tracts, speak to the need for giving people the tools and resources they need to lift out of poverty (Cortright and Mahmoudi 2014). A safe and healthy community is an essential component of making individual change possible.

All of the case studies show the importance of a people and place approach, as the organizations are keenly aware of the social, political and economic conditions of their communities while embarking on strategies that help the people who live and work in these communities.

Going forward, community development organizations will need to collaborate with service organizations to ensure that their work has the dual benefits of improving communities and quality of life for individuals.

Expanding the Target Customer/Client Base and Geographic Footprint

Organizations are finding that to both cope with the reduction of government financial supports and to respond to community needs, they need to develop programs and initiatives that serve a broader range of incomes to cross-subsidize their operations, to meet a broader range of community needs, and/or to gain broader public support. For example, in high-cost communities that have a shortage of moderately priced housing, community development organizations may find it necessary to serve households with higher incomes than they have in the past to meet the housing needs of working families. In addition, some organizations are also expanding their service areas to capture new markets and resources in adjacent jurisdictions.

According to the 2014 CEO Future Strategy survey, there was a clear trend for organizations to shift their customer focus from predominately low-income groups to customers with a broader range of incomes. There was also a trend to expand their footprints to serve more geographic areas than in the past. While geographic growth is a common strategy for larger regional organizations, some smaller CDCs are also considering boundary expansions or moving into adjacent territory through mergers or collaborations. This is necessary to grow the number of opportunities available to them to sustain their work.

These changes will necessitate some shifts in core competencies and both of these changes result in a shift in scale. For example, if housing development organizations are going to start building and leasing units to renters and purchasers who have more options in the market, the community development organization is going to have to become adept at market research and customer service to attract and serve these new customers.

Likewise, expanding to a broad geography and working in multiple markets requires a new level of sophistication and understanding of various political and market conditions. In the West Cook County Housing Collaborative, IFF had to learn the political and economic dynamics of five suburban communities. As the quarterback for the collaborative, understanding and balancing the interests of all of the partners was essential.

While operating on a larger scale can bring efficiencies, it also brings complexity. Complex organizations demand a high level of skill to manage and a more complex infrastructure system to handle the accounting, compliance, technology, and other systems (Walsh and Zdenek 2007). Selective partnering with local organizations in new markets can help community development organizations gain political acceptance and market knowledge more quickly and leverage their competencies with those groups already on the ground. The CDC of Brownsville understood the need to partner with organizations in other geographies to expand their reach, and they also learned of the importance of picking stable employers to reach more people who were good candidates for the payday loans.

LEADERSHIP

Heading today's community development organizations takes high-performing leadership. As noted earlier, to excel at collaboration, leaders must have excellent communication and facilitation skills. According to a recent study of critical leadership attributes conducted by McKinsey and Company, of the nearly 200 social-sector CEOs and top management surveyed, leaders are not up to the challenge. Key leadership attributes identified by those surveyed included the ability to innovate and implement, the capability to surround themselves with talented teams, competent collaboration skills and capacity to work with multiple stakeholders, and the skill to manage to outcomes.

Faulting a chronic underinvestment in leadership development within the social sector, none of those surveyed thought that they or their colleagues' skills were sufficient. While the report cited that there wasn't a lack of talented individuals in the social sector, it recognized that there was a lack of training, support, and opportunities for growth. When comparing private sector and social sector approaches to leadership development, McKinsey found that the social sector spends annually $29 per employee versus $120 in the private sector (McKinsey 2014).

The McKinsey study also found that CEOs believe that there is a gap in talent and capability between the CEO and other managers. This gap not only compromises performance, it complicates succession planning when there are no viable internal managers ready to advance. Given the huge number of boomer CEOs facing retirement age, finding the next generation of leaders is critical. Young people and college students need to be exposed to professional opportunities in the community development sector to bring more people into the human resources pipeline. Funding is needed for new and/or larger internship programs that would provide young people with real working experience and provide additional personnel to organizations needing extra staff capacity.

Over the past three decades, there have been several significant efforts aimed at training new leadership for the field. One of the biggest leadership training programs for the sector was the Development Training Institute (DTI), which started in the 1980s and had an annual residential training program for community development practitioners for over twenty years. It focused on building solid technical real estate skills as well as softer leadership skills.

In the 1990s, NCCED developed the Emerging Leaders program, which was aimed at helping staff who were in the mid-ranks of an organization, hone leadership and technical skills to strengthen organizations, and provide a pipeline of future leaders.

One of the most dynamic leadership training programs in the community development sector is the Achieving Excellence (AE) program launched in 2003 by NeighborWorks America in partnership with Harvard University's Kennedy School of Government and the lead program architect Douglas K. Smith. Serving about 40 practitioners a year, the AE program is an intensive 18-month program that combines classroom experience, peer group support, and individual coaching with on-the-job work on a key organizational performance challenge. The program is targeted to CEOs and other top leadership staff and is currently recruiting its 8th class.

A few years ago, OFN developed an 11-month leadership program for CDFIs with Citi and the Wharton School of the University of Pennsylvania, to help emerging leaders, mid-career and executive leaders develop stronger leadership and managerial skills.

While all of these programs were beneficial, many struggled with maintaining financial support over the long run. The AE and OFN/Citi programs are helpful to the industry, but they need to be expanded and/or replicated to have a larger-scale impact on the sector. Also, what is missing from these excellent leadership programs are programs focused on fostering cross-sector collaboration. To help train the leaders of tomorrow, leadership programs should reach across programmatic boundaries to include many sectors that work together to solve performance challenges. This approach will help build the professional competencies needed to work across sectors in the future.

The organizations featured in our case studies reflect a variety of leadership models. Most of the CEOs had been with their organizations for many years; however, the work described in the cases was implemented by a number of people within each organization. Having a broad and deep bench of informed and committed staff can provide a cushion for leadership when transitions do occur. In the REACH-ACE merger, the departure of the REACH Executive Director near the end of the process did slow the process for completing the deal, but enough staff were involved that the merger did happen a few months later. When the Executive Director of Dorchester Bay EDC left the organization, plans were in place and many projects of the Fairmount Indigo Line had been implemented. To help with the transition, the Executive Director was retained as a consultant to assist with some of the key initiatives. This helped ease the transition of duties to new staff.

New Skills and Expertise

As organizations grow, it will become necessary to adjust their leadership and management approach. Larger organizations with multiple business lines require more formal structures for communicating with each other and for carrying out the work. Both automated systems and general processes need to be developed to keep the organization efficient and effective.

Staff and board members who perform well at small and mid-sized organizations may not meet the demands of a large, complex organization. The requisite skill set for employees will change with growth, and some employees may not be able to meet the challenge. In a study conducted in 2006 of nine high-performing RHDOs, CEOs related two approaches to getting top-level staff: "growing your own" or "buying the talent" (Walsh 2006). Each approach has its advantages and disadvantages.

Many CEOs try to work with the staff they have and provide training and mentoring to help the staff perform at a more demanding level. This "grow your own" approach is used for several reasons. There is usually a sense of loyalty to current staff and a desire to provide staff with opportunities to grow and advance. For some organizations, a number of staff may live in the community or be current or past program participants or residents of the agency's housing. It may be an important part of the organization's mission to provide growth opportunities for these individuals. By working with existing staff, training can be tailored to augment the skills of the staff person that is interested in advancement. Also, organizations that use the "grow your own" approach may do so because they cannot afford to hire the high-skilled, high-cost people that they need, so working with the existing employee pool is the best option.

For organizations that have had rapid or extreme growth, hiring outside talent may become a necessity due to the new scale of operation. Hiring new staff with more professional or technical experience usually requires paying a higher salary, which may trigger salary adjustments throughout the management team and possibly the entire organization, resulting in large financial impacts. Also, it can sometimes be difficult to meld new employees with technical or corporate backgrounds with long-time employees who have a service or mission approach to their job. Leaders need to be aware of the potential culture clash among new and current employees and openly discuss issues as they arise. Cultural shifts can be sudden or gradual and recognizing that they are happening is an important first step to creating constructive dialogue among staff.

Hiring new talent is as much an art as a skill that may take some time to get the right talent in place. Good employee orientations and mentoring can help offset some of the cultural challenges. When launching new initiatives and hiring staff, community development organizations should be aware of how their organizational culture impacts their ability to act.

Organizations pursuing an aggressive growth strategy will need to advance the work of the staff in ways that may be more rapid and/or complex than in the past. If the organization's culture needs to change to achieve this, leadership will need to work closely with staff to articulate expectations and help each person understand their role in achieving the organization's goals.

As an organization grows, it is important that the bar of accountability go beyond the CEO, and that the senior management team has the ability to not only do the job, but also exercise leadership and contribute to strategic planning for the organization.

In the 2006 study, CEOs identified several infrastructure and human resource investments as being key to successful growth and operations. CEOs recognized the need to invest in their current staff and to build systems that would enable all of their staff to work more efficiently and effectively. The top investments needed for organizations cited by CEOs in the survey included several items including: strong financial management systems, networked computer systems with powerful servers and ample capacity for tracking data, dedicated information technology and human resources staff, a strong executive team with a chief operating officer and a chief financial officer, and strong asset management teams. The CEOs interviewed found that investing in these systems and their personnel were key to running the corporation smoothly at a large scale.

The composition and skill set of Board of Directors will also need to change as an organization scales up and expands its work. According to the 2014 CEO Future Strategies Survey, approximately 30% of respondents anticipated significant change in their board composition and skill set over the next three years, which was about double the prior period. As organizations begin working in other sectors (such as health and education) and in new geographies, it is important to bring new people on to the board who are knowledgeable of these new areas. And, as the organization becomes more sophisticated and complex, the makeup of the board needs to reflect people with the right skills to help guide the organization's work.

The board is responsible for the strategic direction of the organization along with staff leadership. Boards need to adapt to change and change the course of the organization if needed. This requires a board that is seasoned, thoughtful, and representative of key stakeholders in the community.

For the NWSCDC to work effectively with the large industrial and technology companies in Milwaukee, they had to develop stronger financial skills and organizational infrastructure to position themselves as a legitimate, capable resource for these huge corporations. They also added a staff person with community organizing and strategic planning skills and broadened their board of directors. REACH changed its board structure to include representatives of SW Washington to ensure that the needs of this community had a voice in strategic decisions of the organization.

The late George Knight, long-time executive director of Neighborhood Reinvestment (now called NeighborWorks America) was fond of saying that "Lots of organizations die from making poor strategic decisions. Private companies fail from taking the wrong strategic path, too. Maybe even nations! That is why strategic decisions should be the top concern of a CDC board." This also applies to multi-sector collaborations and partnerships (Zdenek and Steinbach 2002).

Advancing Business Practices and Learning

When asked what type of training had been important to the organization's growth in the 2006 study, the most common response was training that was experiential and involved instruction, coaching, and peer exchange. Some CEOs have instituted their own in-house training programs while others turned to national training organizations and trade associations. Individual consultants and coaches were also brought in for specific training functions.

Looking to the future, peer-to-peer sharing appears to be one of the better means of learning what is needed for an organization to grow and thrive. While there are several associations and networks that help make this possible, meeting a couple times a year isn't really adequate to meet the need for this type of information sharing. The sector could benefit from financial support for the facilitation of peer-to-peer learning at a local, regional, or national level, online forums, or organizational mentoring, where a more advanced organization would be paid to offer direct technical assistance and coaching to an organization in a growth mode.

Documenting effective practices on internal operating systems and processes is needed to help our field grow. Knowing what has worked for others would assist those trying to select the best systems and structure for their own organization. However, just documenting best practices isn't enough to have a wide-scale impact on the field.

In the article *New Pathways to Scale for Community Development Finance*, by Kristen Moy and Gregory Ratliff (2004), the authors give a compelling argument for the need to not only document best practices but to also promote standardization, infrastructure building, and wide-scale rollout of these new standardized business practices. While their work focuses on the CDFI industry, there are a number of parallels for CDCs and RHDOs pursuing real estate development, economic development initiatives, and healthy community initiatives. Research can be conducted to help identify and document those systems that can be standardized and rolled out on a large scale, or that would allow groups who have particular expertise with certain systems to provide services to others, rather than every organization investing in the same infrastructure. HPN Select, a procurement program developed by the Housing Partnership Network, is a good example of this approach. The goal of this program is to centralize and standardize procurement systems, and leverage purchasing power by utilizing complex software and highly trained experts to provide improved procurement services for its members.

Taking this concept one step further, the community development field could benefit from taking a more franchise-like approach to facilitate expansion. Historically, the community development sector has had a very individualistic approach where by each organization operates in a unique and not easily replicable way. The rationale for this has been in part that each community has its own special set of needs and therefore each community development organization must have a unique response. While this theory may hold true when tailoring goals and strategies, it isn't the most efficient approach when developing programs and systems. Oftentimes, organizations spend time and money reinventing the wheel rather than replicating and adapting a proven process or program. Developing standardized systems and processes that could be used by a large number of organizations would lead to increased efficiency and ultimately greater impact on the part of the organization as well as the whole field.

One organization that has embraced the franchise approach to expanding its impact is the CDC of Brownsville, and their effort to take their good payday lending program throughout Texas nationwide. It relies on a franchise approach and to date has been quite successful.

New Sources of Capital

Community development organizations need to cultivate new sources of capital for operations and programs and projects. As public resources for affordable housing and community development have shrunk, community development organizations are finding that they need to look to non-traditional sources to finance their work and to consider raising funds and investments from individuals. Historically, community development organizations have not had large individual fundraising efforts because they were able to count on local and federal grants or large intermediaries to support their operations. That situation has changed, and now more community development organizations are leveraging their extensive community relationships to cultivate individual and local corporate donors to provide donations for programs and operations. This work requires a new competency that organizations must either learn, or hire the talent, to be effective.

Strategies that build upon strategic partnerships with non-traditional partners can also open up new streams of funding. The CDCs working on the Fairmount Indigo Line were able to access new resources for their community by partnering with environmental organizations and leveraging the resources available for the transit station redevelopment. Organizations need to be both strategic and creative in seeking out new partners that add value and help expand resource opportunities.

Another approach to increasing cash flow is to implement operational efficiency measures that save the organization money by streamlining processes, partnering with others, and/or improving efficiencies. Fahe's approach that each member would specialize in a particular programmatic competency and then deliver that service to all of the others, was key to leveraging their impact. Rather than everyone doing a little of everything, they each did a lot of fewer things.

Removing the regulatory barriers to organizational financial self-sufficiency can be just as important as finding new sources of capital. For example, affordable housing projects funded by the US Department of Housing and Urban Development typically require that each property be structured as a single asset entity and that each entity have an annual audit. The ability to conduct a single audit on a portfolio of five properties rather than five separate audits can generate substantial savings to the owner. Similarly, as affordable housing projects are financed with multiple sources of funding, and each funding source has its own specific compliance and inspection requirements, the asset management and compliance burden for the owners can be significant. By working with funders to coordinate compliance requirements and inspections, owners and funders can save significant time and money, and lessen the impact on the residents who may have multiple inspectors entering their home in any given year.

Additionally, with millions of dollars locked in mandated property reserves, many community development organizations are sitting on money that they cannot access due to funder restrictions. While it is prudent to have adequate operating and maintenance reserves, excess reserve funds should be available to other properties within the organization's portfolio or to support other aspects of the organization's mission.

Community development organizations often find that there are federal, state, and local regulations that make it impossible for groups to benefit financially from their own success. Furthermore, some funders restrict the amount of money an organization can be awarded, regardless of its effectiveness, in order to respond to policies or pressure to spread the money out to a broad number of recipients, without regard to impact. The other issue is that there is a lack of flexible working capital to be deployed effectively to the project.

Changing these policies is a complex undertaking because the regulations come from both private and public sector funding sources. Documenting best practices and success stories on regulatory and policy changes is helpful in generating support from public sector partners to provide increased flexibility for community development work. Practitioners and trade associations need to actively promote new policies and legislation that will benefit the organizations working to achieve a greater degree of financial independence.

In recent years, there has been a growing interest in attracting money from socially motivated investors, known as "impact investors." Impact investing is defined as an investment from someone who intends to create positive impact alongside various levels of financial return, both managing and measuring the blended value they create (Bugg-Levine and Emerson 2011). The goal of impact investors is to pursue a financial return while also addressing social and environmental issues.

By 2012, there were roughly 200 registered impact investment funds, and numerous foundations and mainstream financial institutions that were active in this area (Mair and Milligan 2012). But, this is not a homogeneous group of investors with a common set of goals and expectations and to date. Often, the financial goals of these investors do not align with those seeking the investment. Housing has not yet received a lot of attention from the investors.

One of the big challenges to making impact investing successful is to figure out how to manage expectations and match investor goals with the investee's needs. While community development organizations want investments with low interest rates and longer terms, the impact investors are seeking short-term, fairly liquid investments with a market return. Affordable housing also is seen by some investors as high risk, even though the track record of affordable projects funded through the LIHTC program is very strong. Impact investing is about balancing risk and reward.

To make impact investing a meaningful source of funding for community development, a number of changes will need to occur to encourage impact investing at a significant scale. First, impact investors will need to become comfortable with taking greater risk, or at least perceived greater risk, and be more flexible in the financing terms and instruments that they use. There will also need to be an increase in the amount of philanthropic capital and soft capital that facilitates impact investments. Finally, borrowers are going to need to become adept at documenting and communicating their impact, to both attract funds and to keep the investments flowing.

While the future is challenging to predict, the recent presidential election, as noted in Chap. 3, will likely result in big changes and/or cuts to programs that have been widely used by community development practitioners for the past 40 years. The Trump Administration will likely question the role of the federal government in supporting community development. This makes cross-sector work even more important, but with the likelihood of fewer resources. More focus will need to be given to generating resources at the local and state levels during this period to counter losses at the federal level.

However, we can take heart in knowing that community development practitioners have a strong ability to adapt, as has been demonstrated in the first half-century of community development (1966–2016). The community development sector grew significantly during the Reagan years in spite of major funding cuts to federal housing programs. While we do not know the shape of the strategies that will emerge in the next 10, 20, and 50 years, we do know they will continue to evolve. This is the DNA of community development.

Community development is much more than the sum of its parts. The vision of community development is to enable individuals and communities to take control of their future by taking control of the process, systems, and resources. The critical goal is to have a healthy and resilient community development ecosystem at the local, regional, national, and arguably the global levels. Core competencies that lead to strategic partnerships and outcomes are the critical components of the ecosystem. This leads us to the big question for the future: How will we use comparative advantages to best position organizations and communities to succeed and respond to the challenges and opportunities of the next 50 years?

REFERENCES

Bugg-Levine, Antony, and Jed Emerson. 2011. *Impact Investing: Transforming How We Make Money While Making a Difference*, 9. San Francisco, CA: Wiley.

Callanan, Laura, Nora Gardner, Lenny Mendonca, and Doug Scott. 2014. *What Social Leaders Need to Succeed*. McKinsey and Company.

cciTools for Federal Staff. 2016. A Toolkit for Comprehensive Initiatives. http://www.ccitoolsforfeds.org/systems_change.asp.

Cortright, Joe and Dillon Mahmoudi. 2014. *Lost in Place: Why the persistence and spread of concentrated poverty—not gentrification—is our biggest urban challenge. Portland.* OR: City Observatory.

Critchley, Spencer. 2015. Does your Backbone Organization have a Backbone? *Stanford Social Innovation Review.*

Erickson, David, Ian Galloway and Naomi Cytron. 2012. Routinizing the Extraordinary. *Investing in.*

Friedman, Thomas. 2015. *The World's Most Disruptive Forces.* Atlantic-Community.org.

Friedman, Thomas. 2016. *World Affairs Council lecture.* Portland, Oregon.

Kramer, Peter. 2016. Advice to Strengthen Strategic Mergers and Collaborations. A Catalyst Fund Report, 1–3.

Mair, Johanna and Kate Milligan. 2012. Roundtable on Impact Investing. *Stanford Social Innovation Review.*

Moy, Kristen and Gregor Ratliff. 2004. New Pathways to Scale for Community Development Finance. *Profitwise.*

Steinbach, Carol F. and Robert Zdenek Robert. 2002. *Managing Your CDC: Leadership Strategies for Changing Times.* Washington D.C.: National Congress for Community Economic Development, 15.

US Department of Health and Human Services. Social Determinants of Health. 2016. https://www.healthypeople.gov/2020/topics-objectives/topic/social-determinants-of-health.

Walsh, Dee. *Joining the Big League.* 2006.

Walsh, Dee and Robert Zdenek Robert. 2007. Balancing Act. Montclair. New Jersey: *Shelterforce.* Winter 2007, 14–19.

Walsh, Dee and Jessica Davidson-Sawyer. 2014. Housing Partnership Network CEO Future Strategy Survey.

CHAPTER 10

Implications for Community Development Practice

In the short period of time since the working paper on "Comparative Advantages" was published by the Federal Reserve Bank of San Francisco in September 2013, there has been a significant advancement of strategic partnerships as the primary strategy for comprehensive community development initiatives. The concepts of collective impact and the community development quarterback have become wide spread, and are now part of the community development vernacular. The extensive research on competencies and case studies in this book clearly suggest that community development has an important strategic role to play in improving economic and social issues, from addressing inequality to creating healthy communities to ensuring less toxic environments. Community development has always been dynamic and adaptable, traits that position the field to take advantage of new directions and opportunities in partnering with other organizations and sectors.

The next portion of this chapter will answer the questions that were posed in Chap. 2, and offer our thoughts on what this implies for the future of the community development field.

© The Author(s) 2017   223
R.O. Zdenek and D. Walsh, *Navigating Community Development*,
DOI 10.1057/978-1-137-47701-9_10

QUESTION 1. DOES THE COMMUNITY DEVELOPMENT ENVIRONMENT REQUIRE INCREASED SPECIALIZATION AND COLLABORATION TO EFFECTIVELY ADDRESS TODAY'S CHALLENGES?

Today's environment requires more specialization and collaboration because the problems our nation faces are multi-faceted, entrenched, and complicated. Each of the seven case studies showed the lead organization and partners leveraging their specialized competencies via a comparative advantages framework. There are several forces at play that are influencing community development organizational behavior and practice to operate in this manner. These forces are described below.

Devolution and the Transfer of Power to Localities: During the 1980s, President Ronald Reagan championed the "devolution revolution," a shift of power from the federal government to the states. This trend continued over the next three decades as federal funding for housing and community development programs diminished, leaving states and localities with the responsibility of solving problems. In recent years, the dysfunctional state of national politics has led to legislative gridlock further reducing the relevance of the federal government in addressing today's pressing issues. According to Bruce Katz of the Brookings Institute, "Centralized, hyper-specialized, one-size-fits-all approaches are fundamentally ill-suited for today's challenges. Twenty-first century problems demand rapid, locally-tailored solutions that take a holistic approach to problem solving—approaches that deploy the expertise, capacity and resources of the public, private and civic sectors in collaboration" (Katz 2016).

The Emergence of Networked Organizations: Networked organizations are those that connect together based on the demands of the task rather than a formal structure (Global Integration 2016). Networked organizations form clusters as a means to leverage information and increase competitive advantage, as well as build social capital and knowledge. To assemble the competencies needed for solving complex problems, it is necessary to move from one organization attempting to do everything, to a broad network of organizations that are highly specialized and together deliver a comprehensive solution. Diverse organizations and innovative community development networks are both emerging and expanding, like Fahe and their 50 plus local community development partners. Networks made up of organizations from several sectors are able to bring additional skills and insights to community development. To effectively network, organizations need competencies in community engagement, specifically with stakeholder development and the ability to access new types of resources.

An Increase in the Number of Actors: Professional fields of practice that have not previously been involved in community development work are now becoming active. The last decade has seen the involvement of hospitals, schools, federally qualified health centers, child care centers, and environmental justice organizations in community development efforts. Many of these types of organizations were part of the EBALDC SPARC collaboration. These other sectors offer different strategies, funding resources, technical knowledge, as well as new data and evaluation capacities. The challenge is to coordinate and mesh these skills and resources into a comprehensive community development strategy. This speaks to the need for organizations that can operate effectively as quarterbacks. To work effectively with a broad range of actors, organizations need competency in designing and managing collaborations, ability to communicate with diverse stakeholders from community residents to civic leaders, and the ability to guide and sustain diverse viewpoints.

New Measurements of Success: Community development has traditionally been defined through outputs such as number of housing units, jobs created, and people receiving services. Public and private funders of community development are placing more emphasis on achieving both people and place interventions that result in positive outcomes. For example, an affordable green housing development is not only more energy efficient, but also creates a healthier living environment that reduces the likelihood of elevated lead blood levels (EBL) for children or asthma triggers that can lead to missed school days. Organizations today must have skills in performance measurement including data collection and analysis and know how to design and implement outcome measurement strategies.

New Financing Strategies and Resources: Community development organizations that are partnering with new sectors, such as transit agencies in the case of the Fairmount Indigo CDC Collaborative. Some, as in the case of EBALDC, are working with healthcare entities. Hospitals are now required to meet the community health assessment needs of residents living in their service area in order to maintain their nonprofit tax-exempt status (Zuckerman 2013). This change has caused some hospitals to direct resources to community development supports that improve health outcomes, such as affordable housing.

Another example of a new resource for community development is impact investors. The growth in the last decade of impact investors who want to achieve social financial objectives (affordable housing, health, education, and environment) has begun to provide new opportunities for community development organizations to obtain funds from investors who are interested in supporting work in these areas. Organizations that are seeking to diversify their funding base with these new resources must be competent in resource development, capital aggregation, and fundraising.

Long-Term Nature of Problems: Communities aren't easily improved with a quick fix. Community development is a long-term strategy for revitalizing low-income communities and improving the economic, social, and physical outcomes of local residents. Low-income communities have been negatively impacted by macro-economic factors from the Great Recession to loss of industry and low-skill jobs over a 40-year period. Due to globalization and the rapid pace of economic change, organizations need to wisely select where they focus their energy.

Community development organizations must have specialized technical and process skills and competencies to create effective revitalization initiatives and mobilize resources and partners. To succeed in this environment, organizations need to understand the larger economic factors at play in their community and how their strategies leverage these dynamics. They also need to be competent at both strategic and project planning leading to the successful execution of an initiative over a long period of time.

QUESTION 2. ARE THERE CORE COMPETENCIES SPECIFIC TO EACH TYPE OF COMMUNITY DEVELOPMENT ORGANIZATION?

Most successful community development organizations have a broad array of competencies, and thus it is not possible to attribute one competency as specific and unique to a particular type of organization.

Fundamental to all types of organizations are the competencies that fall under organizational leadership, capacity, systems, and management, for without them, organizations will suffer and never reach their full potential. Also, research has shown that organizations that are weak in these areas have less chance of successfully implementing collaborative efforts (Greco et al. 2015). Good governance, the right human capital, including solid leadership that values diverse perspectives, functional infrastructure, and financial management, and the ability to learn and adapt, are all essential for high performing organizations, be they CDCs, RHDOs, or CDFIs.

There are certain competencies that are more commonly found in some types of community development organizations than others. For example, most CDCs are built on the foundation of strong community engagement, while RHDOs might be less closely involved in some or all of the communities in which they work. RHDOs typically have highly skilled real estate development staff. Successful CDFIs have sophisticated financial systems and the ability to aggregate and deploy capital. The chart in Chap. 6 attempts to show where each type of organization typically has strengths. Utilizing a comparative advantage approach allows organizations to leverage each other's competencies which leads to success such as we saw with the Fairmount Indigo Line collaboration where CDCs worked with organizations focused on the environment to plan greenway and park improvements, or in the West Cook County collaborative where a CDFI partnered with local CDCs to improve foreclosed properties and provide homeownership opportunities to residents.

Inherently, some activities are best done by larger organizations with strong internal infrastructure and the ability to have a broad reach, while other activities need to be carried out in a decentralized fashion on a "retail" level with individuals. A good example of this is the case study where the CDC of Brownsville is developing a franchise with organizations located around the state to deliver the Community Loan Center good payday lending program. Picking the right partners to fill these roles can maximize energy, effectiveness, efficiency, and outcomes.

Question 3. How Do Organizations Best Maximize Their Roles and Strengths Pertaining to Their Comparative Advantages?

Organizations can best maximize their comparative advantages by understanding their competencies and how they add value to specific types of collaborations. This is only achieved by thoroughly understanding your organization's strengths and deficits, as well as knowing the goals and objectives for the collaboration, and the attributes and abilities of the other partners. Shared understanding can lead to a shared vision when managed in an open and transparent process.

Doing a skills and assets inventory of your organization is one way to better understand your abilities. The competency chart in Chap. 6 could be a useful reference to compare community development competencies with skills that need to be acquired by the organization or through partnerships. A third-party review can also be useful for getting an honest assessment of your core competencies. Once this is understood, organizations need to invest in their strengths and consistently improve their competencies to hone their comparative advantages. This is not a one-time activity, but an ongoing journey to continue to learn and improve. Community development organizations need to embrace performance measurements as a core part of their organization's business strategy. One approach to getting performance measurement done is to partner with organizations with expertise in data management and analysis. Groups with these competencies can help design information systems that assess and measure performance.

As organizations become confident about their abilities, they need to develop a track record of accomplishments and then market their accomplishments and their competencies to create a brand identity. Northwest Side CDC has been able to brand and blend their skill in attracting financial resources with the technology and market expertise of their industrial partners.

Branding can be a valuable tool for marketing your comparative advantages to other organizations. The creation of the Berea Performance Compact was a powerful way to communicate that the entire Fahe network had a major role in increasing affordable housing production. To successfully brand your organization, you need to differentiate yourself in the marketplace. As the missions of many community development organizations are similar, what makes an organization stand out? Well-understood and communicated competencies help organizations stand out and become the "go to" partner for particular types of collaborations.

QUESTION 4. DOES THE COMMUNITY DEVELOPMENT SUPPORT SYSTEM (GOVERNMENT, PHILANTHROPY, INTERMEDIARIES, AND PRIVATE CAPITAL) ENCOURAGE OR DISCOURAGE COMPARATIVE ADVANTAGES AND MULTI-SECTOR COLLABORATIONS?

The answer to this question is mixed, as some actors in the support system support competency-building efforts and collaborations, while others do not. Just as our political and economic culture emphasizes individualism, entrepreneurship and competition, early government and philanthropic support for community development has focused on funding individual community development organizations whether they are CDCs, RHDOs, or CDFIs. The first wave of CDCs in the late 1960s and 1970s were comprehensive in nature and combined real estate, business development, and social services (Parachini 1980). Furthermore, most government community development funding sources are targeted to projects rather than to support the organizations. For example, the HOME program has dollars targeted to housing projects. During this period, funding from national and local intermediaries for organizational "capacity building" and operating support was common, and this funding allowed groups to build their competencies and thus their comparative advantages.

Capacity building and operational funding shrunk in the 2000s as the major foundation support for these activities from national entities such as Living Cities and Fannie Mae ended. In today's community development ecosystem, foundations may fund research and development activities that lead to new programs or products, or they may fund specific initiatives that build an organization's abilities in one area, but there are no longer broadly available national programs to support operations and capacity building.

As collaborative efforts can be an uncompensated investment of time and money at the onset, (and perhaps throughout the life of the effort), the lack of operational support can limit the amount of time organizations can devote to collaborative activities. For example, the CDC of Brownsville spent many hours developing the Community Lending Center model without receiving direct compensation for their efforts. They were able to get their software developed for no cost up front in exchange for a fee on the back-end once the system was up and running. This creative approach allowed them to get work done without significant up-front costs.

The lack of flexible and patient capital is also a barrier to multi-sectoral work since funding perimeters are often narrowly defined and can't be used for broader purposes.

As noted in Chap. 2, in the last decade, there has been a noticeable shift where some funders are encouraging and funding collaborative and integrative initiatives. This support represents a change in the funding culture and practice as they are emphasizing community development partnerships as opposed to individual organizations. According to Diana Scearce in *Catalyzing Networks for Social Change*, "funders know that they need big platforms with diverse players to tackle the complexity of 21st century problems." To accomplish this, funders will need to learn how to become facilitators and connectors, helping various groups with similar agendas come together. According to the Catalyst Fund evaluation of 20 collaborations, these efforts need dedicated human, financial, and technical resources to be successful. Too often, organizations must cover these costs themselves. Under-resourced collaborations have less chance of success, especially over time.

Traditional funders can find it challenging to fund multi-sector, complex collaborations as it can take longer for collaborative projects to gain traction and show results. Without a track record it can be harder to attract funders initially, and long-term collaborations may lose appeal over time.

The successful Comprehensive Community Revitalization Project (CCRP) led by the Surdna Foundation is a good example of a collaboration that worked. Community building emerged as a strategy in the 1990s and it was supported both by funding individual organizations and collaborations. The Surdna Foundation was able to attract financial and technical support from over a dozen national and local private and public funders to support six CDCs to develop comprehensive initiatives. Those CDCs partnered with organizations that had the additional expertise they needed whether it was workforce development, health care, child care, or economic development (Miller and Burns 2006). Community building initiatives had a mixed track record and some funders lost interest over time including the Ford Foundation, which closed its Neighborhood Transformation Initiative (Kubisch 1996). Both of these examples illustrate how significant financial support can help launch collaborative efforts, and when the funding fades, the level of activity often subsides.

QUESTION 5. WHAT NEW STRATEGIES AND SUPPORT SYSTEMS ARE NEEDED?

If collaborative undertakings are the best way to go forward, the community development ecosystem will need to respond to support this work.

Patient and long-term funding: As collaborative endeavors are attempting to solve long term, complex issues, they will need patient, long-term funding. The funding will support the planning and implementation of the effort, as well as the cost of managing and staffing the collaboration. This approach represents a shift from how many philanthropic giving that is aimed at giving money to one strong organization that can deliver a quick fix. The Catalyst Fund found that the lack of available funding was a major barrier to implementing collaborations. Key to obtaining this capital, as well as new investments from those interested in a social impact, will be the ability of the collaborative to document results and prove impact.

Supportive policies that better enable different sectors to work together: Much public funding, whether it be at the national, state or local level, is distributed through silos that don't communicate with each other, and that sometimes restrict the ability of organizations from different sectors to work together on the same goal. Successful pilots that demonstrate the benefits of overcoming these divides are needed to move policies and regulations.

The creation of networks and sector connecting coalitions: The traditional approaches and boundaries that used to reinforce the siloed approach to problem solving are falling away as social media and technology have torn down walls and opened up new information, and as our society has become more global and interconnected. For example, new electronic platforms, such as Cap Nexus, list opportunities for organizations to participate in specific lending opportunities. Another example, MemberExchange, a site sponsored for members of the Housing Partnership Network and International Housing Partnership, has a "yellow page" feature, which is a sophisticated search function that allows people to search for individuals or organizations with specific skills. Member Exchange also has a "marketplace" where people can buy or sell services, products or collaborative business opportunities.

The documentation and sharing of best practices: Case studies that document how organizations can best succeed, as well as the availability of funding for consultants and training are necessary to help support collaborative efforts. The case studies in this book provides several examples that are aimed at helping others learn what works when attempting complex partnerships.

Collaborations don't come together without forethought and the ability to adjust. EBALDC senior staff and board leadership spent several years discussing, planning, and researching collaborative efforts before launching SPARC. It takes someone or several people to navigate complex relationships and build connections and trust between several parties who may have diverse perspectives. Guides such as "Catalyzing Networks for Social Change" by Diana Scarce, provide a framework to help funders develop a network mindset, cultivate and support networks and learn from their impact. More of this type of analysis and guidance is needed to help build support for the kind of collaborations that are needed to address the major problems of today's world. The public sector can also be helpful by embracing this approach and providing support and authority to collaborative, cross-sectoral community development work. Community Development organizations can amplify their results by tapping the new ideas and resources that result for a networked approach.

Develop local coordinators and build a guiding coalition around them: Community development organizations play an important role in multi-sector partnerships that include public sector entities. However, not every community development related issue needs a sector-based organization to lead it. Sometimes the work begins with a school or health clinic. The community development organization of the future will need to become adept at recognizing these opportunities and depending on the situation, either lead the initiative or participate as a partner that supports the school or health clinic that is acting as the quarterback. This type of expertise requires competencies in leadership development, governance, organizational systems, data analysis, and an ability to engage and communicate widely with diverse representatives.

In forming a collaboration, special attention should be given to who takes the coordinating or facilitation role, sometimes referred to as the quarterback role. For example, community development organizations can be better suited than the public sector to lead collaborative projects over an extended period of time since local government is more susceptible to change due to the election cycles and changing priorities. Some collaborations require more grassroots organizing and political action, and in these cases it isn't always best to have the organization who is leading the high profile activist work be seen externally as the leader of the collaborative. Another party that is seen as more neutral who can come in and negotiate could be more helpful to get the political wins needed.

No matter who fills the role, the party must be transparent and trusted, and able to communicate well with all of the partners. Long term support for this role is needed if collaborative approaches to problem solving are to thrive. For example, in the NWSCDC case study, the leadership of NWSCDC is the trusted party to both the technology and industrial firms as well as local community organizations including Century City Triangle Neighborhood Association. Their priorities aligned to improve the economic and job climate in the neighborhood to benefit local residents and improve the economic environment.

QUESTION 6. WHAT CAN WE LEARN FROM THE EXPERIENCE OF COMMUNITY DEVELOPMENT ORGANIZATIONS TO MORE FULLY UTILIZE AND DEVELOP A COMPARATIVE ADVANTAGE FRAMEWORK?

As is evident throughout this book, community development organizations are creative, resilient organizations that are adept at reading their environment and pivoting and/or adjusting their business model to best respond to new forces and opportunities. In doing this, community development organizations leverage their competencies and comparative advantages to respond to new circumstances.

As community development organizations become involved with more collaborative partnerships, they have learned how their comparative advantages can be used successfully in a collaborative venture. While collaboration is difficult and cross-sectoral collaboration, more so, successful community development organizations understand that good partners and shared goals are key to achieving significant results. It is essential to have a long-term commitment and be more concerned with outcome than recognition. This type of collaboration is built upon the competencies of planning and communication.

Even community development organizations focused solely on affordable housing production understand the importance of partners. Every project involves a plethora of partners, including financers, lawyers, accountants, construction management and architects, etc. Finding the right partners is critical, and building solid relationships is important before any action happens. Community Development organizations understand this. Project development is a core competency in community development, and it is essential to have at least one partner with strong management skills whether they are a CDC, RHDO or CDFI. Fahe plays the role of orchestrator in bringing together the expertise of the 55 local members, and Fahe also helps assemble the resources to dramatically increase housing production in Central Appalachia.

One of the advantages to collaboration is that it can reduce overall risk to a single partner. When entering a collaborative endeavor, organizations need to do a thorough risk analysis both for themselves and the group as a whole, and then develop a plan to mitigate any excessive risk. This speaks to strong organizational management and system skills. There are a number of CDCs that took too great a risk on a major project or two, and are no longer in existence.

Some collaborations will have a shelf life. The initial goals will be met, and the funding or key partners may decide it is time to move on. For example, in the West Cook County Collaborative case study, after the problems associated with the foreclosure crisis waned in some of the communities, priorities changed and some of the jurisdictions became less involved. Even if a collaborative venture is not over, we have to accept that not all partners will want to stay in long term. Change is the only constant. Organizations need to plan an exit strategy for themselves and others at the beginning of the project, so that the transition can happen smoothly. When partners drop out, organizations need to be able to pivot and adapt.

Collaboration is not for every community development organization. Some may be very under-resourced and/or have a very focused mission. It is difficult for these organizations to be comprehensive as it takes time and resources to enter into these activities.

Question 7. What Does the Next Generation of Community Development System Look Like?

Community development is a dynamic field and process that is always evolving. The community development support system is constantly adapting to meet new challenges and opportunities. In *Toward a New Business Model*, Laura Choi and David Erickson of the Federal Reserve Bank of San Francisco, underscore the importance of understanding complex adaptive systems. They go on to say "that everything is connected to everything and interacts in ways that we cannot predict or control." Adaptive challenges present problems that are not understood and are messy, and require innovation, learning, and evolving strategies. The ability to adapt is a critical element of the community development ecosystem, and works best when multiple stakeholders are engaged in the process, leading to changes across organizational and stakeholder boundaries (Choi and Erickson 2015).

Some of the major issues and trends are:

New views of leadership: The growing influence of cross-sector collaborations is leading to new leadership strategies and approaches that are more networked, horizontal and dispersed. Community development leadership in its early years was more entrepreneurial and participatory, often characterized by strong leaders who built organizations, and made the bulk of the decisions. Community development organizations that embrace the quarterback model have to be adept at guiding diverse coalitions and sectors and keeping key organizations at the table. The dispersion of leadership, which is a sub-competency of organizational development and management, suggests that individuals interacting with diverse organizations must be empowered to make decisions and provide leadership within their organizations.

As the leadership torch moves from the boomers to the millennials, organizations will need to plan for these transitions and expect some disruptive change. New, younger leaders will likely bring new approaches including more technology, more flexibility and more transparency (Larson Marketing and Communications 2015). Community development organizations that will perform well in the future will have thoughtful succession plans in place and an open, communicative culture where issues about corporate culture can be engaged and changed when necessary.

Fragmentation of community development organizations: With the demise of the broad-based national CDC trade association, the National Congress for Community Economic Development (NCCED) in 2006, the CDC field has become increasingly fragmented at the national level. A number of specialized "trade" organizations have emerged including the National Association of Community Economic Development Associations (NACEDA), National Coalition for Asian Pacific American Community Development (NCAPCD), National Association for Latino Community Asset Builders (NALCAB). They have started meeting together periodically to share info and identify common ground and have sponsored two conferences under the theme of People and Place. There is growing concern that the CDCs need a more unified voice and that comes from CDCs, RHDOs, and CDFIs given the importance knowledge, promotion, advocacy, and policy roles that associations perform for their constituency. Both the RHDOS and CDFIs have strong member associations (Opportunity Finance Network (OFN) and the Housing Partnership Network (HPN)). Specialized associations and networks respond to the needs of their members but not necessarily the interests and opportunities from other sectors. Community development networks that are able to connect different sectors will advance and build the evolving community development ecosystem. This is easier to do at the local level and several of the case study profiles represent organizations that connect across sectors, demonstrating effective communication and collaboration.

More voices and more views: One of the strengths of community development is that it is grounded in the aspirations of diverse low and moderate income communities throughout the US Community development has taken root in communities that serve a wide range of racial and cultural diversity, including African-American, Latino, Asian, Native American, and Caucasian communities. As community development organizations expand their geographic area, notably RHDOs and CDFIs, or as CDCs experience a change in the ethnicity of an area they serve, organizations will need to become very adept at working in multi-racial communities and serving multiple racial constituencies.

More voices can reach out to new sectors (health, education, and environment) introducing a wide range of new actors. The net result is that with more voices and views, the community development support system needs to be more adept in developing strategies that draw upon the comparative advantages and strengths of diverse leaders. Community engagement, advocacy, and policy analysis skills are just as important as the hard development skills and competencies in community development, and are starting to receive more serious attention as the field pursues more cross cutting initiatives.

Working with diverse organizational cultures: Organizations reflect the culture of their leaders, communities, and sectors. Multi-sector collaborations require the ability of organizations to adapt and focus on common objectives. Community development organizations need to be sensitized to how organizations in different sectors such as education or health care communicate and operate. It is important to appreciate and integrate the strengths of different organizational cultures that contribute to the success and outcomes from the initiative. Learning and being aware of the respective organizational cultures of diverse organizations is critical toward the success of partnerships. For example, public health organizations who partner with community development organizations can have a more preventative focus through healthy housing, elimination of blight and hazards, and wealth-building resources.

Social equity and income equality as operational priorities: Recent studies and political commentary have pointed to the growing inequality in America between the haves and have-nots, and the educated and employed and the uneducated and un- or under-employed. In a 2007 survey conducted by the Pew Research Center, 48% of those surveyed believed that America was divided into two classes. This perception reflects the statistics that document the rise of the top 1% of Americans as compared to the other 99% (Cortright and Mahmoudi 2014, Pew Research Center 2007). As a result, community development organizations will need to work hard to ensure that their strategies are inclusive and work to achieve greater income equality. Some funders are putting a premium on these issues and are encouraging grantees to develop hiring and engagement practices that work toward greater staff and board diversity and broader community engagement (Meyer Memorial Trust 2016). The successful organizations of tomorrow will have these principles fully integrated into their business practices.

Technology: The rapid changes in technology will change the way community development work is done, both in how complex tasks are executed and how people communicate with their constituents. Big data, financial software systems known as Fintech, sophisticated analytic and process software, and social media tools, will all be factors in how community development is done in the future. The pace of change in technology is constantly speeding up and while the work will still need a human touch, the way that "touch" is felt may be very different than how it happens today.

Integrative or blended approaches: The community development support system will need to orchestrate and lead blended approaches to community development, such as partnering with education, employment, health care, and environmental justice advocacy groups. A number of the original CDCs that formed in the 1960s had a very comprehensive focus and worked in several sectors. They could do this because they were able to attract large grants from the Office of Economic Opportunity and—for a few organizations—the Ford Foundation. Comprehensive federal funding only lasted the decade of the 1970s, and the early comprehensive CDCs had a mixed track record. An integrative comprehensive approach in the second decade of the twenty-first century requires specialization, coordination, capacity, and resources that are beyond the reach of the vast majority of individual community development organizations. Networks and collaborations are the best ways to achieve multi-sector integrative outcomes. There are creative collaborations involving community development organizations and anchor institutions such as hospitals. The Greater University Circle Initiative in Cleveland, which is a partnership with the Cleveland Clinic—one of the largest hospitals in the USA—local universities, community-based organizations, and The Democracy Collaborative has spawned The Evergreen Cooperatives, a number of worker-owned businesses, including The Evergreen Cooperative Laundry, Evergreen Energy Solutions, and Green City Growers. This is an exciting comprehensive community development and wealth building initiative (Howard 2012).

Leveraging Strength; Thriving in the Future

Since community development has always been grounded in the needs of places and people, it has always been a dynamic and evolving field. The ecosystem and infrastructure that support community development have changed dramatically in the past half century. It has gone from a formal system of operating and capacity-building grants mostly supporting affordable housing development, to a more entrepreneurial approach that rewards organizations that hone and leverage their strengths. Many community development organizations have thrived in the changing environment, but some have struggled, especially small, under-capitalized CDCs. It is clear from the research and practice that community development organizations that use core competencies to forge comparative advantages that lead to strategic partnerships can expand the impact and reach of their organizations. To thrive in the future, these organizations will need a community development ecosystem that supports a collaborative approach. Doing so will allow community development groups to work with existing and new stakeholders, which will lead to new approaches and impact for building healthy and sustainable communities.

Chapter 11, which is the final chapter in the book, will offer a series of practical and tactical recommendations.

References

Choi, Laura, and David Erickson. 2015. Towards a New Business Model: Strengthening Families Helps to Strengthen Communities and the Nation. *What It's Worth.* San Francisco, CA: Federal Reserve Bank of San Francisco and CFED, 373.

Cortright, Joe and Dillon Mahmoudi. 2014. Lost in Place: Why the persistence and Spread of Concentrated Poverty—Not Gentrification—Is our Biggest Urban Challenge. Portland, OR: City Observatory.

Diana Scearce in *Catalyzing Networks for Social Change.*

Global Integration. 2016. What is a Networked Organization? http://www.global-integration.com/matrix-management/networked-organization/networked-organization/. Accessed 27 Mar 2016.

Greco, Lois, Maggie Grieve, and Ira Goldstein. 2015. Investing in Community Change: An Evaluation of a Decade of Data-Driven Grantmaking. *The Foundation Review* 7 (3): 69.

Howard, Ted. 2012. Owning Your Own Job is a Beautiful Thing: Community Wealth Building in Cleveland, Ohio. In *Investing in What Works For America's*

Communities. San Francisco, CA: Federal Reserve Bank of San Francisco and Low Income Investment Fund, 204–214.

Katz, Bruce. 2016. *Devolution for an Urban Age: City Power and Problem-Solving*. Bookings: Metropolitan Revolution Blog.

Kubisch, Anne C. 1996. Comprehensive Community Initiatives: Lessons in Neighborhood Transformation. *Shelterforce*, 8–10.

Larson Marketing and Communications. 2015. A Boomer to Millennials: Lessons I've Learned and Lessons I'd Offer. http://www.larsonmarcom.com/blog/what-boomers-and-millennials-can-learn-from-each-other/. Accessed 18 July 2015.

Meyer Memorial Trust. 2016. Equity Statement. http://mmt.org/about-meyer/equity-statement/. https://www.fordfoundation.org/work/challenging-inequality/our-approach/. Accessed 1 May 2016.

Miller, Anita and Tom Burns. 2006. Going Comprehensive: Anatomy of an Initiative that Worked: CCRP in the South Bronx. Philadelphia, PA: OMG Center for Collaborative Learning, 7–15.

Parachini, Lawrence F. 1980. *A Political History of the Special Impact Program*. Cambridge, MA: Center For Community Economic Development, 13–27.

Pew Research Center. 2007. A Nation of "Haves" and "HaveNots?" http://www.pewresearch.org/2007/09/13/a-nation-of-haves-and-havenots/. Accessed 13 Sept 2007.

Zuckerman, David. 2013a. Contributions from Holly Jo Sparks, Steve Dubb and Ted Howard.

Zuckerman, David. 2013b. Hospitals Building Healthier Communities: Embracing The Anchor Mission. 2013. Washington DC: The Democracy Collaborative, 25–40.

Recommendations and Guide Posts for Navigating Community Development

One of our primary goals in researching and writing this book was to draw from the collective experience and wisdom of community development organizations that are leveraging their core competencies for comparative advantage. We reviewed current research and best practices from academics and practitioners, and reported on a series of case studies that demonstrate both the benefits and challenges in multi-sector collaboration. This chapter presents a number of specific recommendations; they should be viewed as guide points, not binding pronouncements. The recommendations can be applied and adjusted according to the circumstances. We have combined practical advice with a number of analogies and a small dose of humor, for good measure.

Be Really Good at a Few Things

It is hard for community development organizations to be successful in multiple lines of business or project initiatives. In Chap. 5 of this book, we identified over 50 community development competencies and sub-competencies, and while this is not an exhaustive list, it does cover most of the skill areas needed to execute various types of community development business lines. As noted earlier, it is challenging to master all these competencies. Community development organizations should sharpen their areas of expertise and strategically select a few key strategic

© The Author(s) 2017
R.O. Zdenek and D. Walsh, *Navigating Community Development*,
DOI 10.1057/978-1-137-47701-9_11

business lines and project areas that become their comparative advantages. This will help set them apart from others, potentially leading to new relationships, resources, and impact.

Engage with Other Sectors; Expand Your Circle

Community development organizations should become active in at least one multi-sector collaboration that is relevant to fulfilling their mission. This will give them a chance to broaden their resources and potentially deepen their impact. Organizations can also learn in a new field from a new set of partners, while not having to take all the risk. Organizations new to collaboration should start small so that they can determine if a collaborative structure and initiative is right for them. As participating in collaborations is time-consuming and requires some different skill sets, organizations need to be selective in participating in them.

Be Flexible and Adapt

Charles Darwin was right: The survival and evolution of humans is based on adapting to the environment. Adaptability is a core competency as noted in Chap. 5. Organizations should reassess their environment and their strategy at least every two years. Adaptive practices require reflection, learning, and creativity. As David Erickson and Laura Choi point out: No single expert holds a solution, multiple stakeholders must be part of the discovery process, and change must occur in numerous places and across organizational boundaries (Erickson and Choi 2015). Adapting strategy can require an organization-wide or department-wide effort with significant engagement of internal and external leaders and staff.

Alignments are not just for automobiles; they are also vital for organizational effectiveness. Community development experience suggests that as organizations adapt their strategy, they need to check to see that the leadership, management, systems, infrastructure, and initiatives are all aligned with these new strategies. For example, there are different skill sets for organizations that focus on a single business line versus those organizations that are participating in multi-sector collaborations.

BUILD A STRONG BENCH WITH FACILITATIVE LEADERSHIP SKILLS

Most successful collaborations have a person or an organization that helps lead and facilitate the effort. In this book, we refer to these actors as the quarterback or backbone organization. In order for an organization to engage in multi-sector collaboration and allocate the staff time that it takes to participate in these processes, it is essential that (1) the management bench of the organization is strong and deep, and (2) the staff active in collaborative engagements have an aptitude and ability to lead differently. Collaborations do not work with a command and control model. Leaders must know how to listen, facilitate, and build consensus. They need to shine a light rather than cast a shadow.

EMBRACE TECHNOLOGY

To stay relevant, community development organizations need to use technology to carry out their mission. Even in a resource-constrained environment, a priority must be put on utilizing technology for enhancing operations and impact. Organizations should look to other sectors and figure out how they can adapt approaches and systems to help them do more.

For example, should we look at the new business growing out of the "shared economy" and see if they can be adapted to community development work? Could we offer our transit-deficient residents ride share to get to jobs? Could elderly empty nesters better make ends meet if they rented out empty rooms? How can we use social media, fintech, and sophisticated software platforms for customer relationship management to do more. All of these tools and more need to be part of the community development organization's tool chest. Technological change is continuing to accelerate, so organizations need to adapt and stay ahead of the curve in terms of staff, board, systems, and technology.

PROFIT IS NOT A BAD WORD

In a restrained resource environment, organizations need to be creative about generating income to support their mission-driven work. Creating related revenue-generating businesses or services can be a helpful way for organizations to diversify their funding streams and reach financial self-sufficiency. Before jumping into new ventures, organizations must be smart about selecting and assessing business opportunities. Starting new ventures on a small scale initially to test the concept can help prevent a massive loss. New business ventures should also be measured against the time and energy it will take leadership to do this work versus the mission-driven work. Partnerships with experienced entities can help reduce risk and boost the odds of success.

THE WORLD IS DIVERSE; MAKE THE MOST OF IT

Our world is becoming more and more culturally diverse. To be effective, organizations that embrace and adapt to this diversity will get ahead. To be relevant, we must understand the needs of community members. To do that, we need staff and board that understand and relate to the community. Actively working toward greater cultural competence is essential for the successful community development organization of the future.

DATA IS KEY

Research and data for community development are increasingly important for many reasons. Data tell a powerful story on the impact of community development. To obtain and maintain the financial and political support needed to be successful, organizations need to be able to accurately describe the need in the community and the impact of their work. For example, Isles Inc., headquartered in Trenton, recently used data on lead poisoning to establish a $10 million healthy homes fund in New Jersey. Research and data can help elevate important issues for community development organizations and drive impact investments, policy, and practice.

YOUTH ARE OUR FUTURE; EMBRACE MENTORING AND TRAINING

Community development leaders are aging and retiring in large numbers. It is essential that we do more to bring young practitioners along so that they are prepared to take over the reins. Work should be done to create internships and learning and leadership opportunities deeper in organizations. Universities need to step up and provide relevant training by working closely with community development groups in their communities. Seasoned professionals need to mentor and be open to new ideas and new approaches to our work. Boards need to do a better job of planning for executive transitions, and for ensuring that their current leaders have adequate resources to retire.

Look Beyond the City

Poverty is not limited to urban neighborhoods or isolated rural communities. Community development organizations should pay more attention to suburbs and regional development opportunities. Suburbs have experienced the fast population growth, as well as representing the largest percentage growth of poverty in the past few decades due to population expansion and other demographic forces. Community development organizations and infrastructure have concentrated mostly in urban neighborhoods and a few rural areas. Community development organizations can expand their initiatives into suburb areas leading to new opportunities and resources.

Peer Learning is Where it's at

Encourage and develop small-scale networks where you can learn, innovate, improve public policies, and access new sources of funding. The growth of community development especially in the past 40 years is attributable to associations, networks, and coalitions that have helped organize, improved practice, designed policy, and advocated and created resources that enable organizations to become more effective. There are national, regional, state, and local networks that cover the spectrum of community development organizations and strategies. The world is becoming more networked. Electronic platforms are another emerging way to network including electronic "yellow pages."

If You Can't Beat Them, Join Them

It can be hard for one organization to beat the competition. However, if organizations can team up to form a strong partnership based on their respective strengths, there is a better chance of being able to participate in large and/or complex initiatives. Rather than viewing other organizations as threats, look to how you can leverage your competencies with theirs to do more. This can be especially helpful in responding to requests for proposals that have complex scoring criteria that requires mastery of many areas.

Look for Money in New Places

Collaboration allows creative ways to identify new funding and look to identify new funding sources and funding streams. The passage of the Affordable Care Act (ACA), which requires that nonprofit hospitals develop a community needs assessment every three years, has provided a unique opportunity for health-care institutions and financial institutions to partner with community development organizations. Traditional federal and other public sector community developments are declining and short of fee generation, acquisition and mergers, and joint ventures; community development organizations can use new funding sources from multi-sector sources to pursue a more diversified and sustainable base.

Community Development is Political; Policy Matters

Community development work has been grossly under-funded for years. While most community development groups do not have the budget to hire full-time policy staff, it is essential that members of the staff and/or board participate in key policy-making bodies that impact resources. The current housing crisis in many of our nation's cities and rural areas has finally elevated this issue to the top of local and state political agendas, but it shouldn't take a crisis for policy makers to respond. We need to make sure that the needs of the poor and disenfranchised are heard, and that solutions and resources are allocated to address their needs.

Be Smart About Risk

Risk is inherent in most community development work, since community development organizations work in distressed markets and often lead new economic activity. Community development organizations should assess organizational and project risk on a regular basis by asking several key questions. How much of my balance sheet can I afford to risk? What will this effort cost and can I absorb the expense if it is not successful? How much staff and board time will the project or initiative realistically require? How will projects or initiatives affect other work and priorities within the organization? Is there a more efficient way of getting accomplished by partnering with other organizations? These questions lead to a better ability to assess, measure, and spread organizational risk. Risk is reduced in complex undertakings if it is shared. Success and failure are shared among the partners, which reduces the likelihood of a possible failure crippling an organization. The failure of a major initiative can doom a community development organization, if the risk is too high leaving the organization with inadequate time to recover.

GET THE WORD OUT. BEING A BEST-KEPT SECRET IS NOT ADVANTAGEOUS

Community development is one of the best-kept secrets. Communication skills should be a core competency of every community development organization. Awareness and knowledge is generated in part through communication strategies, which can be targeted to different sectors and markets of the community. Communication is more than just an annual report. Messaging and storytelling allows an organization to tell its story in improving lives and outcomes through the vision and accomplishments of the organization.

Health-care institutions, educational institutions, cultural institutions, and other anchor institutions are not familiar with most community development organizations. When these anchor institutions learn more about community development, these institutions are often eager to engage community development organizations and practitioners. You need to get familiar with who is in your community and develop alliances that will reinforce your work.

IN CLOSING

Both authors, Bob and Dee, are still very active in community development work at the local and national levels. Please share your feedback to the recommendations, concepts, and research in the book. Community development is one giant learning community, and we all benefit from each other's collective experience and diverse backgrounds; that is the glue of community development. Finally, we are quite encouraged and thankful for the devotion to the field we see so often demonstrated by a new generation of practitioners who bring fresh thinking and enthusiasm to the important work of community development. That makes our work and the publication of *Navigating Community Development* all the more satisfying.

Reference

Choi, Laura and D. Erickson. (2015). Towards a New Business Model: Strengthening Families Helps To Strengthen Communities and the Nation, in What It's Worth. San Francisco, CA: Federal Reserve Bank of San Francisco and CFED.

Appendix I. Community Development Organization Profiles

CDC Profiles

Following are profiles of CDCs featured in the case studies.

Dorchester Bay Economic Development Corp

Type of Organization: CDC

Date of Incorporation: 1979

Operating Area: The Dorchester neighborhoods of Boston, MA.

Corporate Headquarters: Boston, MA.

Consolidated Operating Budget: $3.8 million (2014)

Number of FTE: 28

Certifications and membership: NeighborWorks America chartered member.

General Description: Dorchester Bay EDC works with residents, businesses, and community partners to build strong, thriving communities in Boston's Dorchester neighborhoods (Dorchester Bay Economic Development Corporation website).

Business Lines and Programs with Accomplishments: Dorchester Bay EDC's primary lines of business are to preserve and develop home ownership and rental housing, to create and sustain economic development opportunities for businesses and individuals, and to build community through organizing, civic engagement, and leadership development. As of 2012, they had developed 774 units of rental housing and 169 home ownership units and rehabbed 297 units of owner-occupied housing. They also completed 156,260 ft^2 of commercial space. In addition, they played a leadership role in the Fairmount Indigo CDC Collaborative and helped make substantial improvements to mass transit service to the area and improvements to the

© The Editor(s) (if applicable) and The Author(s) 2017
R.O. Zdenek and D. Walsh, *Navigating Community Development*,
DOI 10.1057/978-1-137-47701-9

surrounding area. Resident initiatives include youth camps, after-school sports, computer training, and leadership programs. They have placed over 620 adults and youths in jobs and launched a re-entry program for ex-offenders returning to the community (Dorchester Bay EDC Annual Report 2011–2012).

Codman Square CDC

Type of Organization: CDC
Date of Incorporation: 1982
Operating Area: Codman Square and South Dorchester area of Boston
Corporate Headquarters: Boston, MA
Consolidated Operating Budget: $3.8 million (2014)
Number of FTE: 21
Certifications and membership: NeighborWorks America Chartered Member, United Way of Massachusetts Bay.

General Description: Codman Square Neighborhood Development Corporation's mission is to build a better, stronger community in Codman Square and South Dorchester by creating housing and commercial spaces that are safe, sustainable, and affordable. They also promote financial and economic stability and opportunities and skills for residents and for the neighborhood, and provide residents of all ages.

Business Lines and Programs with Accomplishments: Codman Square has three primary business lines: real estate development, economic development, and community building. Codman Square is also involved in four initiatives: Millennium 10 (a comprehensive community planning process for Codman Square and Four Corners), Eco-Innovation District (a neighborhood sustainability effort that involves transit-oriented development, renewable energy, sustainable food systems, and waste reduction for a 13 block section of Codman Square, using LEED-ND rating system), Fairmount Initiative, and the Men of Color Men of Action (Codman Square Website 2016).

Northwest Side CDC Profile

Type of Organization: CDC
Date of Incorporation: 1983
Operating Area: Several neighborhoods in the Northwest Section of Milwaukee
Corporate Headquarters: Century City Towers, Milwaukee, Wisconsin
Consolidated Operating Budget: $1.2 million 2015

Number of FTE: 8

Certifications and membership: CDFI Certification, Eagles, Greater Wisconsin Opportunity Fund, Employ Milwaukee.

General Description: Northwest Side Community Development Corporation (NWSCDC) was founded in 1983 to reverse the decline of the 30th Street industrial corridor in Milwaukee, the home of several major factories that provided well-paying jobs to thousands of individuals in Milwaukee. During its first decade, NWSCDC owned and managed 250,000 ft² of commercial and industrial property. NWSCDC did not have the financial or management capacity to improve the properties, and by 1994 found themselves in a severe cash flow problem with their businesses and real estate ventures, including a budget deficit of $200,000 (Snyder and Daniell 2011).

The NWSCDC board and staff made a major decision in 1994 to shift the priority of the organization from owning and managing large real estate projects, to partnering with leading technology and industrial firms in Milwaukee. NWSCDC strategic advantage in these partnerships would include financing, technical support of small businesses, community engagement, and helping these firms have a strong relationship with local community and political leaders.

Business Lines and Programs with Accomplishments: Northwest Side CDC, working with a local neighborhood association, has built 47 units of low-income rental housing above the Villard Library for grandparents and grandchildren housing, and they have renovated seven homes, and are in the process of rehabbing an additional ten owner-occupied homes.

To keep and strengthen technology and industrial firms in the community, NWSCDC formed a partnership with Midwest Energy Research Consortium (MERC). NWSCDC and MERC formed a partnership to create the Energy Innovation Center and accelerator, which helps local firms develop their commercialization capacity to pursue contracts with defense and other government contractors (Snyder and Daniell 2011).

NWSCDC provides financing to technology-based businesses through the NWSCDC Community Development Financial Institution (CDFI). NWSCDC has also launched a workforce development program in the power controls and energy; identifying real estate space; and helping emerging technology businesses access and navigate government support (Howard Snyder interview 2015).

NWSCDC is forging community development networks that help employers train and hire workers for their industrial and technology positions. Successful community development efforts understand, utilize, and build community networks such as the Historic Garden Homes neighborhood association. Community networks connect the fabric of a community, and local community development organizations are best positioned to play a leadership role in local community networks. Comprehensive development initiatives are a good way to connect various networks in a neighborhood toward building a common agenda.

CDC of Brownsville Profile

Name of Organization: CDC of Brownsville (CDCB)
Type of Organization: CDC and CDFI
Date of Incorporation: 1974
Operating Area: Texas
Corporate Headquarters: Brownsville, Texas
Consolidated Operating Budget: $6,337,060 (2014)
Number of FTE: 35
Certifications: CHDO, CDFI, FHLB Member, HUD Approved Counseling Agency, NeighborWorks Member.

General Description: The CDC of Brownsville creates housing opportunities for low-income families in the southernmost tip of Texas through below-market financing, quality construction, and efficient home designs. The CDC has earned national recognition for its work in the Colonias along the border with Mexico and for its innovative bank consortiums for homeownership lending and production. CDCB has been providing safe, sanitary affordable housing to the citizens of Brownsville, Texas, since 1974. CDCB is the largest nonprofit producer of single-family affordable housing for homeownership in the State of Texas.

Business Lines and Accomplishments: CDCB is an active single-family for-sale developer. To date, they have produced over 2700 units of affordable housing. They have recently begun to develop multi-family rental properties and have one property with 56 units. They are an active consumer mortgage lender and have closed over 6200 loans since inception. As indicated in the case study, they conceived and incubated the Community Loan Center that provides "good pay day" loans. They also provide housing counseling and have helped over 6500 households learn how to save for and purchase a home.

RHDO Profiles

Following are profiles of two RHDOs featured in the case studies.

REACH Community Development, Inc. Profile

Name of Organization: REACH Community Development, Inc.

Type of Organization: RHDO (formerly a CDC)

Date of Incorporation: 1982

Operating Area: Portland-Vancouver Metropolitan Statistical Area

Corporate Headquarters: Portland, Oregon

Consolidated Operating Budget: $15 million

Number of FTE: 120

Certifications and membership: NeighborWorks America, Housing Partnership Network, CHDO

General Description: REACH was created in 1982 by community activists concerned about housing deterioration and neighborhood livability in southeast Portland. REACH began as a neighborhood-based CDC serving six neighborhoods. Its primary focus initially was the acquisition and renovation of single-family homes for affordable rental housing. REACH's mission is to create quality, affordable housing for individuals, families, and communities to thrive.

REACH expanded both its geography and business lines over its 34-year history and currently works throughout the Portland-Vancouver metropolitan area. In 2013, it completed a collaboration with Affordable Community Environments (ACE), a small nonprofit CDC based in Vancouver, Washington. ACE is now a subsidiary of REACH.

REACH is governed by a volunteer Board of Directors comprised of people representing the various communities it serves as well as the professional skills needed to guide the business.

Business Lines and Programs with Accomplishments: REACH currently has four main lines of business: affordable housing development, property and asset management, resident services (primarily financial literacy), and home repair. In addition, REACH has an active fundraising and public relations department, as well as administrative and finance staff. REACH is a leader in sustainability and developed one of the first, and the largest, affordable housing apartments built to Passive House standards in the USA. REACH is ranked among one of the Best Green Companies to work for by Oregon Business Magazine.

Housing Development: REACH has developed or preserved nearly 1900 units of affordable housing and 60,000 ft^2 of commercial space.

Home Repair: In 1995, REACH created the Community Builders program to provide free home repairs to senior and disabled home owners. REACH repairs approximately 200 homes per year. Many of the repairs are done by volunteers and through partnerships with local contractors and related companies.

Services: REACH provides an array of services to help residents maintain success in their housing and build financial independence. Services include eviction prevention, information and referral, and financial education.

East Bay Asian Local Development Corporation Profile
Name of Organization: East Bay Asian Local Development Corporation
Type of Organization: CDC that has grown into a RHDO
Date of Incorporation: 1975
Operating Area: City of Oakland, Alameda County, portions of Contra Costa County
Corporate Headquarters: Oakland, CA
Consolidated Operating Budget: $13 million
Number of FTE: 105
Certifications and membership: NeighborWorks America, CAPACD

General Description: The East Bay Asian Local Development Corporation (EBALDC) was established in 1975 by local Asian American activists who wanted to convert a warehouse in Downtown Oakland into a mixed-use multi-purpose center. This center became the Asian Resource Center, for retail businesses, medical facilities, and nonprofit organizations, and opened in 1980. EBALDC has emerged as one of the most comprehensive CDCs in the USA in combining physical revitalization with economic development and asset-building programs, social services, and more recently to address health disparities through a healthy neighborhoods framework. EBALDC has invested over $200 million in the past 40 years in seven targeted neighborhoods in Oakland and Alameda County to improve the physical, social, and economic well-being of low-income residents (Building Healthy Neighborhoods Annual Report 2014–2015). EBALDC launched the San Pablo Area Revitalization Corridor (SPARC) initiative in 2013 as a comprehensive multi-sectoral initiative to improve health, economic, and social outcomes in the SPARC corridor, which serves a predominately low-income community in a section of Oakland and a portion of Emeryville.

Business Lines and Programs with Accomplishments:
EBALDC has had the following program accomplishments:

- Affordable Housing Development—as of 2015, EBALDC has developed 2053 townhouse and apartment units of affordable housing. The organization has also built 158 units of owner-occupied housing, and manages an additional 1126 units of townhouses and apartments (Building Healthy Neighborhoods Annual Report 2014–2015).

- Commercial revitalization—EBALDC has developed over 300,000 ft^2 of commercial space throughout Oakland that brings street-level vitality with critical services including pharmacies and optometrists, childcare and health centers, and food purveyors.

- Asset building and wealth creation—EBALDC was one of the original pilot sites for Individual Development Accounts (IDAs) as part of the American Dream Demonstration led by CFED in the late 1990s. They have continued to have a significant IDA program and expanded their financial stability and asset-building work through sponsoring free operating VITA (Volunteer Income Tax Assistance) sites that enable low-income residents to have free tax preparation, Earned Income Tax Credit (EITC) refunds, and asset-building products and services (Building Healthy Neighborhoods Annual Report 2014–2015).

- EBALDC was one of the first CDCs to adopt Age-Friendly Community practices and received funding from The Atlantic Philanthropies to develop what became the Age-Friendly San Pablo Corridor Initiative, one of the first of its kind in 2011. EBALDC has organized a number of older adults who live in the San Pablo Avenue Corridor to establish neighborhood priorities. The priorities that they established include public safety, transit improvements, wellness, and access to fresh, nutritious food. EBALDC has awarded small grants to local residents to work on health, wellness, and community engagement activities. The residents determine the usage and recipient of the funding between $100 and $1000. The total funding available was $7000. A number of the older adults live in EBALDC-owned and EBALDC-managed housing, and the organization will continue to develop additional housing and commercial facilities to serve the older adults and residents.

- In 2013, EBALDC launched a new strategic direction focusing on a comprehensive "Healthy Neighborhoods" approach that connects social, environmental, and economic factors that determine the length and quality of an individual's life. EBALDC's healthy neighborhood lens will help identify the neighborhood assets and stressors, and determine which stressors (lack of jobs and affordable housing, violence, public safety, and pollution) can be mitigated in a collaborative strategy that builds upon EBALDC's strengths. EBALDC launched its Healthy Neighborhood Strategic Plan in 2013 as a four-year plan through 2016. The Healthy Neighborhoods Strategic Plan assessed each project, program, and partnership for its potential to create resources and opportunities that enable local residents to have healthy outcomes and vibrant lives. The organization will integrate its core work in housing options, social supports, and income and wealth with other factors and priorities identified by local residents including community gardens, green building design, environmental remediation, transit development, access to health, and school partnerships (Building Healthy Neighborhoods Annual Report 2014–2015).

CDFI Profiles
Following are profiles of two CDFIs featured in the case studies.

IFF Profile
Name of organization: IFF
Type of Organization: CDFI
Date of Incorporation: 1988
Operating Area: Nine states: Iowa, Illinois, Indiana, Kansas, Kentucky, Michigan, Minnesota, Missouri, Ohio, and Wisconsin
Corporate headquarters: Chicago, Illinois
Consolidated Operating Budget: $30,277,049 (2016)
Number of FTE: 92
Certifications: CDFI, AERIS rated, FHLB member

General Description: IFF is a CDFI that provides flexible, affordable financing and real estate development and consulting services to nonprofits in several Midwest states. IFF has expertise in feasibility analysis, complex transaction structuring, and construction management. IFF's breadth of development services supports nonprofits as they implement important housing, nonprofit facilities and other critical community development projects.

Business Lines and Accomplishments: IFF's primary business is that of a lender for nonprofit facilities, charter schools, health centers, healthy food stores, and affordable housing. To date, IFF has made over $620 million in loans, leveraged $2.1 billion in community investment, and has total assets of $528 million. IFF provides flexible, affordable financing to service agencies, health centers, schools, housing developers, and grocery stores. They have closed 44 New Market Tax Credit transactions and financed the creations of more than 9100 child care slots, over 56,000 charter school seats, and 8100 housing units.

IFF is also active as a consultant and technical assistance provider for single-family for-sale housing and is a direct developer of multi-family and special needs housing. IFF has staff that provide real estate consulting services to its customers to help them plan and construct their real estate projects. They also have research staff that can help inform government policy and spending decisions (Cerda 2016).

Fahe Profile

Name of Organization: Fahe
Type of Organization: CDFI and membership organization
Date of Incorporation:
Operating Area: Eleven States: Alabama, Florida, Kentucky, Michigan, Mississippi, Ohio, Tennessee, Virginia and West Virginia.
Corporate Headquarters: Berea, Kentucky
Consolidated Operating Budget: $7,374,360 (2014)
Number of FTE: 37
Certifications: CDFI, Aeris rated, FHLB member, NeighborWorks member

General Description: Fahe is a nonprofit organization that provides support to 50+ member housing development organizations. Founded in 1980, Fahe's vision is a Central Appalachia "proud of sustaining its culture and environment and where growth, opportunity, and hope are balanced so that all people fulfill their potential with regard to housing, employment, educational opportunity and quality of life." Fahe's primary service territory includes all of Central Appalachia, a region that encompasses the mountainous areas of northern Alabama, eastern Kentucky, western Maryland, eastern Tennessee, southwestern Virginia, and the entire state of West Virginia. Fahe also serves the entirety of the states listed previously as well as Florida, Indiana, Michigan, Mississippi, and Ohio. Historically, Fahe is best known for servicing loans, for providing financing and support services for the construction of affordable housing, and for the purchase of homes by low-, moderate-, and middle-income families. Fahe is certified by the US Department of the Treasury as a community development financial institution (CDFI) and is a member of the NeighborWorks America network.

Business Lines and Programs with Accomplishments: Fahe provides financing for affordable housing, childcare facilities, community facilities, energy/retrofit, health centers, and small business. Since inception, they have closed $137,345,057 and financed over 92,000 housing units. They also provide consumer mortgage lending and have closed more than 3000 loans to date. Fahe created an equity fund and has invested over $41 million in affordable housing projects (HPN 2015). Fahe has over 55 member community-based development organizations throughout Central Appalachia, and they provide financial and technical support to their member organizations.

Appendix II. Major National Organizations

There are numerous local, state, and national organizations, public sector bodies, universities, and foundations that are active in the community development ecosystem. While the entire list is too lengthy to include here, we have noted a few of the major national organizations that provide resources, technical assistance, and/or research to support the sector.

Corporation for Enterprise Development
https://cfed.org/
Enterprise Community Partners
http://www.enterprisecommunity.org/
Federal Home Loan Banks
http://www.fhlbanks.com/
Housing Assistance Council
http://www.ruralhome.org/
Housing Partnership Network
http://www.housingpartnership.net/
Living Cities
https://www.livingcities.org/
Local Initiative Support Corporation
http://www.lisc.org/
National Alliance of Community Economic Development Associations
http://www.naceda.org/
National Association of Affordable Housing Lenders
http://naahl.org/
National Association of Latino Community Asset Builders
http://www.nalcab.org/

© The Editor(s) (if applicable) and The Author(s) 2017   259
R.O. Zdenek and D. Walsh, *Navigating Community Development*,
DOI 10.1057/978-1-137-47701-9

National Coalition Asian Pacific American Community Development
http://www.nationalcapacd.org/
National Community Reinvestment Coalition
http://www.ncrc.org/
National Council of La Raza
http://www.nclr.org/
National Housing Conference
http://www.nhc.org/
National Housing Institute
http://www.nhi.org/
National Low Income Housing Coalition
http://nlihc.org/
NeighborWorks America
http://www.neighborworks.org/
Opportunity Finance Network
http://ofn.org/

Appendix III. Blank Competency Chart

Understand your strengths. Organizations can use the following chart to conduct an inventory of their competencies (Chart A.1).

Chart A.1   Blank Competency Chart

Plot your Organization's Competencies by ranking the following competencies as primary, secondary or optional for your organization	
Organizational Development and Management	
Governance	
Human Capital	
Learning organization	
Assessing core competencies	
Adaptability	
Capable leadership	
Internal infrastructure	
Financial management	
Organizational risk management	
Compliance and reporting	
Community Engagement and Public Policy	
Local knowledge and expertise	
Political relationships and support	
Advocacy and public policy	
Resident, business, and institution engagement	
Community network	
Stakeholder development	
Planning	
Strategic planning	
Community planning	
Project planning	

(continued)

© The Editor(s) (if applicable) and The Author(s) 2017
R.O. Zdenek and D. Walsh, *Navigating Community Development*,
DOI 10.1057/978-1-137-47701-9

Chart A.1 (continued)

Communications	
Internal communications	
External communications	
Storytelling	
Communicating impact	
Robust Web site with interactive links	
Social media	
Marketing	
Project Development (Real Estate)	
Real estate development team	
Project management	
Needs and market analysis	
Feasibility analysis	
Land assemblage and site control	
Project financing	
Lending	
Deal structuring	
Underwriting	
Capital aggregation	
Work outs	
Loan administration and servicing	
Asset management of loan portfolios	
Property and Asset Management	
Property management and maintenance	
Tenant selection	
Asset management and preservation	
Asset disposition	
Resident services	
Program/Business Line Development and Management	
Idea generation	
Program development	
Program launch	
Program execution	
Program close and evaluation	
Resource Development, Capital Aggregation, and Fundraising	
Federal, state, and local	
Foundations and corporations	
Financial institutions	
Intermediaries	
CDFIs	
Individuals	

(continued)

Chart A.1 (continued)

Collaboration and Partnerships	
Shared vision	
Shared leadership and decision making	
Shared participation	
Innovation	
Accountability	
Performance goals/measurements	
Constant communication	
Everyone benefits	
Performance Measurement and Evaluation	
Data collection and analysis	
Performance measurement	

REFERENCES

CDFI Coalition. 2015. What are CDFIs? http://www.cdfi.org/about-cdfis/what-are-cdfis/.

CDFI Coalition. 2015. CDFI Types. http://www.cdfi.org/about-cdfis/cdfi-types/.

CDFI Coalition. 2015. What are CDFIs? http://www.cdfi.org/about-cdfis/what-are-cdfis/.

CDFI Fund. 2015. CDFI Certification Factsheet. https://www.cdfifund.gov/Documents/CDFI_CERTIFICATION.

CDFI Fund. 2016. Snap Stat. https://www.cdfifund.gov/Documents/Snap%20Stat%20June%201.%202016.pdf.

Cerda, Jose. 2016. Vice President of Corporate Communications and Public Affairs at IFF. Email Communication, December 15.

Christman, Raymond, Gaynor Asquith, and David Smith. 2009. *Mission Entrepreneurial Entities: Essential Actors in Affordable Housing Delivery*, 10. Affordable Housing Institute.

Codman Square Website. 2016. Who We Are. http://www.csndc.com/about.php, October 16.

Dorchester Bay Economic Development Corporation. 2016. http://www.dbedc.org/about-us/mission/, October 16.

Dorchester Bay EDC Annual Report 2011–2012. http://www.dbedc.org/Annual%20Report%202011-2012.pdf.

East Bay Asian Local Development Corporation. 2014. *Building Healthy Neighborhoods*, 3–8. 2014 Annual Report, Oakland, CA.

Housing Partnership Network. Member Profile. HPN. 2015.

IFF. 2016. History and Mission. http://www.iff.org/history, June 2016.

National Alliance of Community Economic Development Associations. 2010. *Rising Above: Community Economic Development in a Changing Landscape.* Washington DC: NACEDA.

Opportunity Finance Network. 2014. Inside the Membership: Fiscal Year 2014 Statistical Highlights. OFN.

BIBLIOGRAPHY

Abele, John. 2013. *Bringing Minds Together in on Collaboration.* Cambridge, MA: Harvard Business Review.

Adler, Neil. 2007. Fannie Mae Foundation to Close. New Charitable Office to Be Created. *Washington Business Journal.*

Amadei, Bernard. 2015. A Systems Approach to Modeling Community Development Projects. New York, NY: Momentum Press.

American Communities Survey. 2012.

Andrews, Nancy O., and Nicolas P. Retsinas. 2012. *Inflection Point: New Vision. New Strategy. New Organization. Investing in What Works in America's Communities.* San Francisco, CA: Federal Reserve Bank of San Francisco and Low Income Investment Fund.

Anglin, Roland V. (ed.). 2004. *Building the Organizations that Build Communities: Strengthening the Capacity of Faith- and Community-Based Development Organizations.* Washington DC: US Department of Housing and Urban Development, Office of Policy Development and Research.

Ansorage, Kate, and Dana Bell. 2015. Interviewed by Dee Walsh, 10 July 2015.

Baer, Kathryn. 2015. Nonprofit Housing and Service Providers Face Funding Crisis. Poverty and Policy Blog, July 6.

Beleche, Marcos. 2016. Interviewed by Dee Walsh, 19 February 2016.

Bhatt, Keane, and Steve Dubb. 2015. *Educate and Empower: Tools for Building Community Wealth.* Washington DC: The Democracy Collaborative.

Blaustein, Arthur F., and Geoffrey Faux. 1973. *The Star Spangled Hustle: The Nixon Administration and Community Development.* Garden City, NY: Anchor Press/Doubleday.

Boshara, Ray. 2015. *The Future of Building Wealth: Can Financial Capability Overcome DemographicDestiny? What It's Worth.* San Francisco, CA: Federal Reserve Bank of San Francisco and CFED.

© The Editor(s) (if applicable) and The Author(s) 2017
R.O. Zdenek and D. Walsh, *Navigating Community Development,*
DOI 10.1057/978-1-137-47701-9

Bratt, Rachel G., Langley C. Keyes, Alex Schwartz, and Avis Vidal. 1994. *Confronting the Management Challenge: Affordable Housing in the Nonprofit Sector*. New York, NY: New School University Community Development Research Center.

Bratt, Rachel G. 2012. *Social Housing in the United States: Overview*. Medford, MA: Tufts University.

Bratt, Rachel G. The Quadruple Bottom Line and Nonprofit Housing Organizations in the United States. *Housing Studies* 27 (4): 438–456. doi:10.1080/0267037.2012.677016.

Breaking Ground. https://breakingground.net/. Accessed June 2015.

Bruyn, Severyn, and James Meehan (eds.). 1987. *Beyond the Marketplace: New Directions in Community Development*. Philadelphia, PA: Temple University Press.

Buckman Community Association. 2007. The History of Buckman. http://www.neighborhoodlink.com/Buckman/pages/38240.

Bugg-Levine, Antony, and Jed Emerson. 2011. *Impact Investing: Transforming How We Make Money While Making a Difference*. San Francisco, CA: Wiley.

Callanan, Laura, Nora Gardner, Lenny Mendonca, and Doug Scott. 2014. What Social Leaders Need to Succeed. McKinsey & Company, November 2014.

cciTools for Federal Staff. 2016. A Toolkit for Comprehensive Initiatives. http://www.ccitoolsforfeds.org/systems_change.asp, May 30.

CDC of Brownsville. 2015. Community Loan Center: Affordable Small Dollar Loans. PowerPoint presentation, March 2015.

CDFI Coalition. 2015. CDFI Types. http://www.cdfi.org/about-cdfis/cdfi-types/.

CDFI Fund. 2015. CDFI Certification Factsheet. https://www.cdfifund.gov/Documents/CDFI_CERTIFICATION.

CDFI Fund. 2016. Snap Stat. https://www.cdfifund.gov/Documents/Snap%20Stat%20June%201.%202016.pdf.

CDFI Coalition. 2015. What are CDFIs? http://www.cdfi.org/about-cdfis/what-are-cdfis/.

Center on Budget and Policy Priorities. 2016. Chart Book: Cuts in Federal Assistance Have Exacerbated Families' Struggle to Afford Housing. http://www.cbpp.org/research/housing/chart-book-cuts-in-federal-assistance-have-exacerbated-families-struggles-to-afford, April 12.

Cerda, Jose. 2016. Vice President of Corporate Communications and Public Affairs at IFF. Email Communication, December 15.

Choi, Laura, and David Erickson. 2015. *Towards a New Business Model: Strengthening Families Helps to Strengthen Communities and the Nation, in What It's Worth*. San Francisco, CA: Federal Reserve Bank of San Francisco and CFED.

Christman, Raymond, Gaynor Asquith, and David Smith. 2009. *Mission Entrepreneurial Entities: Essential Actors in Affordable Housing Delivery.* Affordable Housing Institute.

Clark, Steve. 2013. Local Loan Program Takes Issue with 'payday' Label. MGN Online. The Brownsville Herald, April 11.

Clements, Allison Milld. 2015. Interviewed by Dee Walsh, 18 August 2015.

Consumer Financial Protection Bureau. What is a Payday Loan. http://www.consumerfinance.gov/askcfpb/1567/what-payday-loan.html.

Cook, James. 1994. *Community Development Theory.* Columbia, MO: Extension Division, University of Missouri.

Cortright, Joe, and Dillon Mahmoudi. 2014. *Lost in Place: Why the Persistence and Spread of Concentrated Poverty—Not Gentrification—Is Our Biggest Urban Challenge.* Portland, OR: City Observatory.

Cramer, David, and Zdenek, Robert O. 2006. A Merger of Equals, Montclair, New Jersey. *Shelterforce Journal of Affordable Housing and Community Building* (Winter).

Critchley, Spencer. 2015. Does your Backbone Organization Have a Backbone? Stanford Social Innovation Review, December 10.

Cytron, Naomi. 2012. Doing the Math: The Challenges and Opportunities of Measuring in Community Development. *Community Investments* 24 (1). Federal Reserve Bank of San Francisco.

Dubb, Steve. 2013. Hospitals Building Healthier Communities. National Housing Institute. Rooflines: The Shelterforce Blog. Montclair, NJ, March 5.

Dubois, Jeanne. 2016. Interviewed by Dee Walsh, 3 February 2016.

Duffrin, Elizabeth. 2015. Thwarting Payday Lenders at the Texas Border. NACEDA. http://www.naceda.org/index.php?option=com_dailyplanetblog&view=entry&category=people-places&id=6:thwarting-payday-lenders-at-the-texas-border, April 27.

East Bay Asian Local Development Corporation. 2014. Building Healthy Neighborhoods. Annual Report, Oakland, CA.

EBALDC Fact Sheet 2015.

EcoDistrict website. 2015. Target Cities Programs. http://ecodistricts.org/get-started/technical-and-advisory-services/target-cities-program/. Accessed 26 Dec 2015.

Enterprise. 2013. Adapting to a Changing Environment: Organizational Sustainability in the Pacific Northwest's Affordable Housing Development Community. http://www.enterprisecommunity.com/where-we-work/pacific-northwest/see-the-work/ace-reach-partnership.

Erickson, David, Ian Galloway, and Naomi Cytron. 2012. *Routinizing the Extraordinary, in Investing in What Works for Americas Communities.* San Francisco, CA: Federal Reserve Bank of San Francisco and Low-Income Investment Fund.

Erickson, David J. 2009. *The Housing Policy Revolution: Networks and Neighborhoods*. Washington DC: Urban Institute Press.

Fairmount Collaborative. 2015. http://fairmountcollaborative.org/, March 20.

Fairmount Indigo CDC Collaborative Website. http://fairmountcollaborative. org/. Accessed 20 March 2015.

FEDPAYDAY.com. 2014. Payday loans in Texas. FAQ. http://www. fedpayday.com/.

Federal Reserve Bank of San Francisco & Low Income Investment Fund. 2012. *What Works for America's Communities: Essay on People, Place, and Purpose*. San Francisco, CA: Federal Reserve Bank of San Francisco.

Federal Reserve Bank of San Francisco & Corporation for Enterprise Development. 2015. *What It's Worth: Strengthening the Financial Future of Families, Communities, and the Nation*. San Francisco, CA: Federal Reserve Bank of San Francisco.

Forbes. 2015. The Best Places for Business and Careers. Boston, MA. At a Glance. http://www.forbes.com/places/ma/boston/.

Friedman, Thomas. 2016. World Affairs Council Lecture, Portland, Oregon, February 29.

Friedman, Thomas. 2015. The World's Most Disruptive Forces. Atlantic-Community.org, May 26.

Gallun, Alby, and Micah Maidenberg. 2013. Will the Foreclosure Crisis Kill CHICAGO? *Crain's Chicago Business*, November 9.

Garrison, Trey. 2015. Supreme Court: Fair Housing Act Claims Can Use "Disparate Impact". Housingwire, June 25.

Glickman, Norman J., and Lisa J. Servon. 1998. More Than Bricks and Sticks: Five Components of CDC Capacity. Housing Policy Debate. Fannie Mae Foundation. Volume 9. Issue 3.

Glickman, Norman J., and Lisa J. Servon. 1997. *More Than Bricks and Sticks: What is Community Development Capacity*. New Brunswick, NJ: Rutgers Center for Urban Policy Research.

Global Integration. 2016. What is a Networked Organization? http://www.global-integration.com/matrix-management/networked-organization/networked-organization/. Accessed 27 March 2016.

Goodling, Erin, Jamaal Green, and Nathan McClintock. 2015. *Uneven Development of the Sustainable City: Shifting Capital in Portland, Oregon*.

Greco, Lois, Maggie Grieve, and Ira Goldstein. 2015. Investing in Community Change: An Evaluation of a Decade of Data-Driven Grantmaking. *The Foundation Review* 7 (3).

Grogan, Paul S., and Tony Proscio. 2000. *Comeback Cities: A Blueprint for Urban Neighborhood Revival*. Boulder, CO: Westview Press.

Grossman, Tammy. 2015. Interviewed by Dee Walsh, 27 August 2015.

Halpern, Robert. 1995. *Rebuilding the Inner City a History of Initiatives to Address Poverty in the US.* New York, NY: Columbia University Press.

Harrington, Michael. 1962. *The Other America: Poverty in the United States.* Baltimore, MD: Penguin Press.

Harrison, Bennett, Marcus Weiss, and Jon Gant. 1993. *Building Bridges with the World of Employment.* New York, NY: Ford Foundation.

Harvard Business Review 10 Must Reads. 2013. *On Collaboration.* Boston, MA: Harvard Business Review Press.

Harvey, Frederick B. (Bart). 2016. Email Message to Authors, August 11.

Hewings, Geoffrey J.D. The Hidden Cost of Foreclosures in Chicago Neighborhoods; Study Finds Distressed Properties Impact Home Prices. Illinois Realtors. http://www.illinoisrealtor.org/foreclosureimpact.

Holt, Jeff. 2009. A Summary of Primary Causes of the Housing Bubble and the Resulting Credit Crisis—A Non Technical Paper. *The Journal of Business Inquiry* 8: 1.

Hickman, Gill Robinson. 2010. *Leading Change in Multipl e Contexts.* Thousand Oaks, CA: Sage Publications.

Holmstrom, Chris. 2016. Will Portland's housing crisis become a housing bubble? http://koin.com/2016/04/28/will-portlands-housing-crisis-become-a-housing-bubble/, April 28.

Homewise. 2016. About Us: How We Do What We Do. www.homewise.org/about-us/, May 14.

Howard, Ted. 2012. Owning Your Own Job Is a Beautiful Thing: Community Wealth Building in Cleveland, Ohio. In Investing in What Works for America's Communities. San Francisco, CA: Federal Reserve Bank of San Francisco and Low Income Investment Fund.

HUD Exchange. HOME CHDO. https://www.hudexchange.info/home/topics/chdo.

Ibarra, Hermina, and E. Hansen Morton. *Are You A Collaborative Leader, in on Collaboration.* Cambridge, MA: Harvard Business Review.

IFF Website. 2015. http://www.iff.org/, July 30.

Isles Inc. 2014. Annual Report, Trenton, NJ.

Johnson, Marty. 2016. Power Point Presentation on Health Disparities, NCRC 2016 Annual Conference, March 18.

Jones, Katie. 2014. An Overview of the HOME Investment Partnerships Program. Congressional Research Service, September 11.

JPMorgan Chase & Co. Introducing PRO Neighborhoods. https://www.jpmorganchase.com/corporate/news/stories/pro-neighborhoods-main.htm, May 2016.

Kali, Karen, and Robert Zdenek. 2016. *Staying At Home: The Role of Financial Services in Promoting Aging in Community.* San Francisco, CA: Federal Reserve Bank of San Francisco.

Katz, Bruce. 2016. Devolution for an Urban Age: City Power and Problem-Solving. Bookings: Metropolitan Revolution Blog, March 25.

Keating, W.Dennis, Norman Krumholz, and Phillip Star (eds.). 1996. *Revitalizing Urban Neighborhoods*. Lawrence, KS: University of Kansas Press.

Kelly, Kevin S. 1997. *State Association Models for CDCs*. Washington DC: National Congress for Community Economic Development.

Kelly, Marjorie, Steve Dubb, and Violetta Duncan. 2016. *Broad Based Ownership Models: As Tools for Job Creation and Community Development*. Washington DC: The Democracy Collaborative.

Kramer, Peter. 2016. Advice to Strengthen Strategic Mergers and Collaborations. A Catalyst Fund Report, April 2016.

Kretzmann, John P., and John I. McKnight. 1993. *Building Communities from the Inside Out: A Path Toward Finding and Mobilizing Community Assets*. Evanston, IL: Northwestern University, Center for Urban Affairs and Policy Research.

Kubisch, Anne C. 1996. Comprehensive Community Initiatives: Lessons in Neighborhood Transformation. *Shelterforce: Journal of Affordable Housing* 8–12.

LaPiana, David. 2000. *The Nonprofit Mergers Workbook: The Leader's Guide to Considering, Negotiating, and Executing a Merger*. St. Paul, MN: W. Amherst H. Wilder Foundation.

Larson Marketing and Communications. 2015. A Boomer to Millennials: Lessons I've Learned and Lessons I'd Offer. http://www.larsonmarcom.com/blog/what-boomers-and-millennials-can-learn-from-each-other/, July 18.

Leonard, M.A. 2013. Leah Greenwood, Brett Sheehan, Susan Duren and Ben Nichols. Almost a Merger: The ACE-REACH Journey to Successful Collaboration. Housing Washington Presentation. http://www.wshfc.org/conf2013/presentations/T8.pdf.

LISC Philadelphia. 2016. Helping Neighbors Build Communities: Sustainable Communities Initiative. http://programs.lisc.org/philly/what_we_do/sustainable_communities_initiative.php, May 2016.

Living Cities. 2016. The Integration Initiative. https://www.livingcities.org/work/the-integration-initiative, May 2016.

Longworth, Susan. 2011. *Suburban Housing Collaborative: A Case for Interjurisdictional Collaboration*. Community Development and Policy Studies Division of the Federal Reserve Bank of Chicago.

Maciag, Mike. 2015. Gentrification in America Report. Governing The States and Localities: Governing Data, February 2015.

Mair, Johanna, and Kate Milligan. 2012. Roundtable on Impact Investing. Stanford Social Innovation Review, Winter 2012.

Massachusetts Association of Community Development Organizations. 2015. How it Works. https://macdc.org/how-it-works.

Massachusetts Bay Transportation Authority. http://www.mbta.com/about_the_mbta/history/?id=970.

Mayer, Neil S. 1984. *Neighborhood Organizations and Community Development: Making Revitalization Work.* Washington DC: Urban Institute Press.

McDermott, Richard, and Douglas Archibald. 2013. *Harnessing Your Staff's Informal Networks, in on Collaboration.* Cambridge, MA: Harvard Business Review.

McKibben, Bill. 2007. *Deep Economy: The Wealth of Communities and the Durable Future.* New York, NY: Henry Holt and Company.

Meyer Memorial Trust. 2016. Equity Statement. http://mmt.org/about-meyer/equity-statement/. https://www.fordfoundation.org/work/challenging-inequality/our-approach/, May 1.

Miller, Anita, and Tom Burns. 2006. *Going Comprehensive: Anatomy of an Initiative that Worked: CCRP in the South Bronx.* Philadelphia, PA: OMG Center for Collaborative Learning.

Miller, Michael Victor, and Robert Lee Maril. 1979. Poverty in the Lower Rio Grande Valley of Texas: Historical and Contemporary Dimensions. Texas Agricultural Experiment Station, Texas A&M University.

Mt. Auburn Associates and Nancy Nye. 1993. *An Evaluation of the Public Policy Initiatives of the National Congress for Community Economic Development.* Somerville, MA: Mt. Auburn Associates.

Moy, Kristen, and Gregor Ratliff. 2004. New Pathways to Scale for Community Development Finance. Profitwise, December 2004.

Nanus, Burt, and Steven M. Dobbs. 1999. *Leaders Who Make A Difference: Essential Strategies for Meeting the Nonprofit Challenges.* San Francisco, CA: Jossey-Bass Publishers.

National Alliance of Community Economic Development Associations (NACEDA). 2010. *Rising Above Community Economic Development in a Changing Landscape.* Washington DC: NACEDA.

National Commission on Neighborhoods. 1979. People Building Neighborhoods, Final Report to the President and the Congress of the United States, Washington DC, Government Printing Office.

National Congress for Community Economic Development. 1988. Against All Odds: The Achievements of Community-Based Development Organizations, Washington DC.

National Congress for Community Economic Development. 1991. Changing the Odds: The Achievements Community Development Organizations, Washington DC.

National Congress for Community Economic Development. 1995. Tying It All Together: The Comprehensive Achievements of Community-Based Development Organizations, Washington DC.

National Congress for Community Economic Development. 1998. Coming of Age: Trends of Achievements of Community-Based Development, Washington DC.

National Congress for Community Economic Development. 2005. Reaching New Heights: The Achievements of Community-Based Development, Washington DC.

Neri, Joe. 2015. Interviewed by Dee Walsh, 30 July 2015.

North West Housing Partnership. http://www.nwhp.net/. Accessed June 2015.

Office of Consumer Credit. https://www.consumeraffairs.com/payday-loans-and-lenders.

Office of Neighborhood Involvement. Origins and Early Years. https://www.portlandoregon.gov/oni/article/492415. Accessed June 2016.

OFN. 2014. Inside the Membership. http://ofn.org/sites/default/files/InsideMembership_FY2014_103015.pdf.

Okagaki, Alan. 2008. *Federation of Appalachian Enterprises: A Case Study.* Berea, KY.

Opportunity Finance Network. 2014. CDFIs Provide Opportunity for All. Infographic. Opportunity Finance Network.

Osborne, David. 1988. *Laboratories of Democracy: A New Breed of Governors Creates Models for National Growth.* Boston, MA: Harvard University Press.

O'Shea, Bridget, and John O'Shea. 2011. Biggest Stock of Foreclosed Homes: Right Here. Chicago News Cooperative, July 7.

Parachini, Lawrence F. 1980. *A Political History of the Special Impact Program.* Cambridge, MA: Center For Community Economic Development.

Perry, Stewart E. 1987. *Communities on the Way: Rebuilding Local Economies in the United States and Canada.* Albany, NY: State University of NY Press.

Pew Research Center. 2007. A Nation of "Haves" and "HaveNots?" http://www.pewresearch.org/2007/09/13/a-nation-of-haves-and-havenots/, September 13.

Pew Charitable Trusts. http://www.pewtrusts.org/~/media/assets/2013/11/11/portland_profile.pdf?la=en.

Pierce, Neil R., and Carol F. Steinbach. 1987. *Corrective Capitalism: The Rise of America's CDCs.* New York, NY: The Ford Foundation.

Pietila, Antero. 2010. Not in My Neighborhood: How Bigotry Shaped a Great American City. Baltimore, MD: Ivan R. Dee Publisher.

Porter, Michael E. 1996. *New Strategies for Inner-City Economic Development.* Boston, MA: InitiativeFor a Competitive Inner City.

Price, David. 2014. 7 Policies That Could Prevent Gentrification. Rooflines: The Shelterforce Blog, May 23. http://www.rooflines.org/3731/7_policies_that_could_prevent_gentrification/.

REACH Community Development Annual Reports. 2009–2012.

REACH Community Development. 2016. Mission and History. http://reachcdc.org/about-us/mission-and-history/. Accessed June 2016.

Rienzi, Greg. 2013. The changing face of East Baltimore. Gazette. Johns Hopkins Magazine, January 2013.

Rohe, William M., Rachel G. Bratt, and Protap Biswas. 2003. *Evolving Challenges for Community Development Corporations: The Causes and Impacts of Failures, Downsizing, and Mergers.* Chapel Hill, NC: University of North Carolina Center for Urban and Regional Studies.

Rubin, Herbert J. 2000. *Renewing Hope Within Neighborhoods of Despair: The Community-based Development Model.* Albany, NY: State University of New York Press.

Scearce, Diana. Catalyzing Networks for Social Change.

Senge, Peter M. 1990. *The Fifth Discipline: The Art and Practice of the Learning Organization.* New York, NY: Doubleday-Currency.

Sherman, Natalie. 2013. East Baltimore Development Moves to Next Phase. The Baltimore Sun, December 14.

Sherraden, Michael. 1991. *Assets and the Poor: A New American Welfare Policy,.* Armonk, NY: M.E. Sharpe, Inc.

Shiffman, Ronald and Susan Motley. 1990. *Comprehensive and Integrative Planning for Community Development.* New York, NY, New School University Community Development Research Center.

Smith Hopkins, Jamie. 2012. Huge Drop' in Funding for Community Development. The Baltimore Sun, September 20.

Snyder, Howard, and Tina Daniell. 2011. *The Northwest Side Community Development Corporation: Transforming the Approach to Creating Positive Economic Impact in Distressed Communities.* Chicago, IL: ProfitWise, Federal Reserve Bank of Chicago.

Snyderman, Robin, and Beth Dever. 2013. *Building Capacity Through Collaboration in Chicago's Suburbs. Confronting Suburban Poverty in America.* Brookings Metropolitan Policy Program.

Stannard-Stockton, Sean. 2010. Getting Results: Outputs, Outcomes & Impact. Tactical Philanthropy. http://www.tacticalphilanthropy.com/2010/06/outputs-outcomes-impact-oh-my/, June 29.

Steinbach, Carol F., and Robert O. Zdenek. 1999. Lessons From a Fall: What Went Wrong at ECI? Washington, DC. *The Neighbor Works Journal* (Fall).

Steinbach, Carol F., and Robert Zdenek. 2002. *Managing Your CDC: Leadership Strategies for Changing Times.* National Congress for Community Economic Development: Washington DC.

Stoecker, Randy. 1997. The CDC Model of Urban Redevelopment: A Critique and an Alternative. *Journal Of Urban Affairs* 19 (1): 1–22.

Stoutland, Sara E. 1999. Levels of The Community Development System: A Framework For Research and Practice. Urban Anthropology and Studies of Cultural Systems and World Economic Development 28. no. 2.

Sullivan, Patricia. 2011. Freddie Mac. Fannie Mae donations disappearing study predicts. Washington Post, October 2.

Summers, Evan. 2015. Interviewed by Dee Walsh, 30 July 2015.

TD Bank Project Summary. Foundation Center. 2011.

Temail, Mihalio. 2002. *The Community Economic Development Handbook: Strategies and Tools to Revitalize Your Neighborhood*. Minneapolis, MN: Amherst Wilder Foundation.

The Democracy Collaborative at the University of Maryland. 2005. *Building Wealth: The New Asset-Based Approach to Solving Social and Economic Problems*. Washington DC: The Aspen Institute.

US Census Bureau. http://www.census.gov/topics/income-poverty/poverty.

US Census Bureau. June 2016. https://www.census.gov/quickfacts/table/PST045215/4159000.

US Department of Health and Human Services. 2016. Social Determinants of Health. https://www.healthypeople.gov/2020/topics-objectives/topic/social-determinants-of-health, March 20.

US Department of Housing and Urban Development. 2016. HUD History. http://portal.hud.gov/hudportal/HUD?src=/about/hud_history, May 15.

Urban Institute and Weinheimer Associates. 1996. The Performance of Community Development Systems: A Report on the National Community Development Initiative, Washington DC.

Vidal, Avis C. 1992. *Rebuilding Communities: A National Study of Urban Community Development Corporations*. New York, NY: New School University Community Development Research Center.

Vigness, David M., and Mark Odintz. 2016. Rio Grande Valley. Handbook of Texas. https://tshaonline.org/handbook/online/articles/rnr05. Accessed 2016.

Walker, Christopher. 2002. *Community Development Corporations and Their Changing Support Systems*. Washington DC: The Urban Institute.

Walker, Christopher, and Mark Weinheimer. 1998. *Community Development in the 1990s*. Washington DC: The Urban Institute.

Walsh, Dee. 2006. Joining the Big League, December 2006.

Walsh, Dee and Jessica Davidson-Sawyer. 2014. Housing Partnership Network CEO Future Strategy Survey, April 2014.

Walsh, Dee, and Robert Zdenek. 2007. Balancing Act, Montclair, New Jersey. *Shelterforce Journal of Affordable Housing and Community Building* (Winter).

Walsh, Dee, and Robert Zdenek. 2011. *The New Way Forward: Using Collaborations and Partnerships for Greater Efficiency and Impact*. San Francisco, CA: Community Development Investment Center, Federal Reserve Bank of San Francisco.

West Cook County Housing Collaborative. 2014. WCCHC Strategic Planning. Powerpoint, February 24.

West Cook County Housing Collaborative. 2015. WCCHC Presentation to Maywood Finance Committee. Powerpoint, March 11.

Woodstock Institute Staff. 2016. Regional Housing Partnership: A Housing Blueprint for the Chicago Region. Woodstock Institute.

Zdenek, Bob, and Dee Walsh. 2009. Coming Together: The Need for a Unified Voice in Community Development, Montclair, New Jersey. *Shelterforce The Journal of Housing and Community Development* (Fall).

Zdenek, Robert O. 1987. Community Development Corporations. In *Beyond the Market and the State: New Directions in Community Development*, ed. Severyn T. Bruyn and James Meehan, 112–127. Philadelphia, PA: Temple University Press.

Zdenek, Robert O. 2013. *Comparative Advantages: Creating Synergy in Community Development*. San Francisco, CA: Community Development Investment Center, Federal Reserve Bank of San Francisco.

Zdenek, Robert O., and Robinson, Carla J. 2010. CDC Management Lessons: Insights From the Demise of Eastside Community Investments Inc. In *Mistakes to Success: Learning and Adapting When Things Go Wrong*, ed. Robert Giloth and Colin Austin, 222–240. Bloomington, IN: Universe Press.

Zdenek, Robert O. 1993. *Investing in Distressed Communities: The Role and Potential of CDCs in Economic Development*. Washington DC: Economic Development Commentary, Winter 1993, National Council for Urban Economic Development.

Zdenek, Robert O. 1990. *Taking Hold: The Growth and Support of Community Development Corporations*. National Congress for Community Economic Development: Washington DC.

Zuckerman, David, with Contributions from Holly Jo Sparks, Steve Dubb, and Ted Howard. 2013. *Hospitals Building Healthier Communities: Embracing the Anchor Mission*. Washington DC: The Democracy Collaborative.

INDEX

© The Editor(s) (if applicable) and The Author(s) 2017
R.O. Zdenek and D. Walsh, *Navigating Community Development*,
DOI 10.1057/978-1-137-47701-9